BEYOND

BEYOND EDUCATION

RADICAL STUDYING FOR ANOTHER WORLD

Eli Meyerhoff

UNIVERSITY OF MINNESOTA PRESS

Minneapolis · London

An earlier version of chapter 5 was originally published as Erin Dyke and Eli Meyerhoff, "Toward an Anti- and Alter-University: Thriving in the Mess of Studying, Organizing, and Relating with ExCo of the Twin Cities," in *Out of the Ruins: The Emergence of Radical Informal Learning Spaces,* ed. Robert H. Haworth and John M. Elmore, 174–94 (Oakland, Calif.: PM Press, 2017).

Published by the University of Minnesota Press
111 Third Avenue South, Suite 290
Minneapolis, MN 55401-2520
http://www.upress.umn.edu

Printed in the United States of America on acid-free paper

The University of Minnesota is an equal-opportunity educator and employer.

25 24 23 22 21 20 19   10 9 8 7 6 5 4 3 2 1

Library of Congress Cataloging-in-Publication Data
Names: Meyerhoff, Eli, author.
Title: Beyond education : radical studying for another world / Eli Meyerhoff.
Description: Minneapolis : University of Minnesota Press, [2019] | Includes
  bibliographical references and index. |
Identifiers: LCCN 2018055523 (print) | ISBN 978-1-5179-0202-5 (hc) |
  ISBN 978-1-5179-0203-2 (pb)
Subjects: LCSH: Education, Higher—Aims and objectives—United States. |
  Education, Higher—Economic aspects—United States. | Education, Higher—
  Political aspects—United States. | Capitalism and education—United States. |
  Alternative education—United States.
Classification: LCC LA227.4 .M48 2019 (print) | DDC 378.00973—dc23
LC record available at https://lccn.loc.gov/2018055523

Contents

Against the Romance of Education

SNAPPING IN AND AT THE UNIVERSITY

> If our happiness depends on turning away from violence, our
> happiness is violence.
> —Sara Ahmed, "Resignation Is a Feminist Issue"

Feminist scholar Sara Ahmed snapped at her university. After building up
frustration over years, in 2016 she publicly called out academia's sexism,
especially the sexual harassment of students by professors, portending
the explosion of the #MeToo movement in 2017. Then she resigned.
After years of trying to address these problems through the "proper"
institutional channels, she concluded that the issue was not merely a few
individuals acting badly but rather "an issue of institutional culture, which
had become built around (or to enable) abuse and harassment."[1] Despite
some small victories, she became exhausted with the lack of progress:
"so much work not to get very far." In a blog post titled "Resignation Is a
Feminist Act," she described the moment she snapped:

> Watching histories be reproduced despite all our efforts was one of the
> hardest experiences of my academic career—well one of the hardest
> experiences of my life. I just found it shocking. And to complete the
> story: I originally asked for unpaid leave because doing this work can
> be demoralising as well as exhausting. But in the course of applying for
> unpaid leave (and the difficulty of making arrangements in my absence),
> I felt a snap: I call it feminist snap. My relationship with the institution
> was too broken. I needed a real break: I had reached the end of the line.
>   That snap might sound quite violent, dramatic even. Resigning in
> feminist protest—and making public that you are resigning in feminist
> protest—does get attention. It can be a sharp sound; it can sound like
> a sudden break. In my case, that break was supported by many of my

colleagues; but not by all. One colleague describes my action as "rash," a word used to imply an action that is too quick as well as careless. Snapping is often a matter of timing. A snap can feel like a moment. But snap is a moment with a history: a history can be the accumulated effect of what you have come up against. And just think: you have to do more, the more you do not get through. You have had hundreds of meetings, with students, with academics, with administrators. You have written blogs about the problem of sexual harassment and the silence that surrounds it. And still there is silence. To resign is a tipping point, a gesture that becomes necessary because of what the previous actions did not accomplish. The actions that did not accomplish anything are not noticed by those who are not involved in the effort. So the action that spills a history, so that it falls out, so there is a fall out, is deemed rash.

Well maybe then: I am willing to be rash.[2]

On May 30, 2016, Ahmed resigned after working as a professor for twenty years. Without needing to negotiate anything with her university, she could continue to speak out against sexism in academia and beyond, amplifying her feminist work.

Snapping is one way to respond to an impasse in the university—a situation that seems impossible to move past. Ahmed confronted the impasse of sexism (intertwined with those of racism and heteronormativity, among others). Her response of snapping contrasts sharply with her university administrators' response to these impasses: pushing everyone to move on. Those who refuse to move on are, in Ahmed's words, "deemed rash," as their action "spills a history."

Corey Menafee also famously snapped at his university. On June 13, 2016, he decided the window had to go. During his work break, the thirty-eight-year-old African American service worker at Yale University's Calhoun College dining hall used a broomstick to smash a stained-glass window that depicted enslaved people of African descent (Figure 1). Afterward, he explained how, two weeks prior to his action, a visitor to Yale talked with him about the image:

> It was reunion weekend, [a Yale alumnus] came in with his 10-year-old daughter. . . . [H]e mentioned that image was there way back, like, 10 years ago when he was there as a student, and he said it's still there. I mean, *you can only imagine the type of emotions that run through an African-*

FIGURE 1. Corey Menafee and the stained-glass window depicting enslaved people at Yale University. Courtesy of *Democracy Now!*

American, if I can say that, seeing a picture of two slaves—two actual slaves picking cotton.[3]

After he was arrested and charged with a felony, Menafee resigned from Yale and gave several interviews with local and national news outlets. The nationwide outcry against Yale pressured them to drop the charges and to rehire him. But they did so only on the condition of a gag provision, preventing Menafee from making "any further statements to the public" about his action and the administrative response.[4] The Yale administration sought to bury the controversy that Menafee's act, and his speaking about it, had brought into the public spotlight. Yale's vice president of communications, Eileen O'Connor, claimed the reason for the gag provision was "so that everyone can now move on." Despite their silencing him, what he already said about the event remains public. Reading Menafee's words, although "you can *only* imagine," you can still *try* to "imagine the type of emotions that run through an African-American" when he (Menafee) sees this glorified image of slavery, and when he sees the name of the slaveholder and colonialist John C. Calhoun on a Yale University building, his daily workplace.

The typical stories about racism and sexism in higher education portray them as "ugly histories" from a buried past that one has to dig up. By contrast, Ahmed's and Menafee's snaps show that these histories continue to be lived in the present. This book takes the baton from Ahmed and Menafee, and from all those who are "willing to be rash." I have snapped at the university, also, in my own way. When I was in graduate school, the academic life felt contradictory: we faced hyper-competitive pressure to climb up the professional ladder while the number of secure jobs dwindled. Discussion of mental illness, and of cracking under the pressure to compete, was stigmatized. When a fellow graduate student committed suicide, I snapped. I decided to use my dissertation, and now this book, as opportunities to study the object of my snapping, the university, to "spill its history." I am writing about what it means to snap *in* and *at* the university—to become undone along with others whom the university has undone. Together, we can unravel the university's secrets. Together, we can make places for studying where violence isn't hidden under masks of happiness and between the lines of romantic stories.

The controversy between Menafee and Yale raises questions that motivate this book. Menafee reached an impasse about racism in the university. His response was to destroy the offending object, and this opened up a broad public discussion. Yale responded by narrating a crisis of public relations. They sought to shut down the critical studying that Menafee's action had incited. Unmasking higher education's normative narrative of uplift, community, and romance, Menafee had exposed some of its hidden violence. What does it mean to talk about Menafee and studying together, given the ways that the university represents service labor and studying as irreconcilable? Considering Yale's gag provision on Menafee, how does Menafee's studying threaten the university's normative mode of study, that is, education?

This book argues that education is just one possible mode of study among many alternatives. Modes of study are bound up with different modes of world-making—ways of making ourselves, politics, economies, communities, cultures, and so forth.[5] I argue that the education-based mode of study supplements modes of world-making that are associated with modernist, colonial, capitalist, statist, white-supremacist, heteropatriarchal norms. In the course of political struggles between conflicting modes of world-making, education has been presented as the best and only option for study. Because it is romanticized in this way, the possibilities of alternative modes of study have become almost unthinkable. Against the grain, this book takes aim at the romance of education.

The book's argument unfolds through, first, showing how the romance of education is endemic in contemporary debates about the impasse of higher education. The education romance is part of what I call an epistemology of educated ignorance that hinders study of the complex controversies in this impasse. I show how movements for educational equity and justice tend to naturalize romantic stories about education, thereby not only defeating their own purposes but also expanding the racialized and gendered carceral regime. The dominant tendency in university studies has been to present the problems or crises of higher education as *analytical* and *moral* questions that could be resolved through rational debate and persuasion. This approach tends to take on an expert position—what Walter Mignolo calls a "zero-point" position "above" the world—from which one can analyze and moralize.[6] Adopting such a position has depoliticizing effects, because it forecloses consideration of how one's own position is implicated in producing the problem.

As an antidote, I argue that we should see the impasse of higher education as rooted in *political* questions about conflicts between alternative modes of world-making that are co-constitutive with certain modes of study and self-making. Seeing one's own body and place as thoroughly situated within these political conflicts, the knowledge that one produces about these conflicts is necessarily political. *All* approaches to the impasse are political, including the moral and analytical approaches that attempt to hide their politics behind a veneer of objective expertise. I argue not merely for an *openly* political approach to the impasse but also for a *fanatical* political approach, one that commits oneself as a partisan to particular sides in the many struggles that striate the terrain of universities. As a partisan of abolitionist, decolonial, feminist, anticapitalist movements myself, I offer in this book a theory that can be useful for penetrating the vectors of these movements more deeply into the hearts of universities.

This book wagers that a critical genealogy of education can open our imaginations to new possibilities. Taking my impetus from critiques of U.S. universities as colonial-capitalist institutions in need of decolonization,

I trace the origins of ideas about education that the British settlers brought with them to the colonies. From spilling this "critical history of the present," we can learn how the romantic narrative of education today is entwined with colonial-capitalism.[7] The book's middle chapters give critical genealogies of key elements of the education-based mode of study. The end of the book builds on this analysis of the problem with the romance of education to offer possible solutions. I highlight examples of alternative modes of study and contemporary struggles to expand them against and beyond education. For clarifying the stakes of these struggles, I argue that we need to engage with the hidden histories of alternative modes of study that grappled with the tensions of the university's "undercommons"— that is, studying *in but not of* as well as *against and beyond* the dominant institutions.[8]

In this introduction I give a taste of the book's key concepts— "education romance," "modes of study," "educated ignorance," "impasse," and "undercommons"—by using them as frames for illuminating the controversy between Corey Menafee and Yale. I connect these concepts with Ahmed's theory of affective economies to describe how Menafee's alternative mode of study presents a threat to Yale. Then, I elaborate on the concept of mode of study, including descriptions of how Menafee's studying is part of broader movements of Black radical study, and of how Yale attempts to recuperate Menafee's threat. I clarify how different modes of study are bound up with different modes of world-making. To explain the origins of this book, I narrate my own path from education romance toward critical research on education's impasses. Finally, I give an overview of the book's chapters.

SMASHING THE UNIVERSITY'S RACIST
WINDOWS TO SPILL A HISTORY

Before Menafee took on the gag provision, he described in interviews the emotions that ran through him when he saw the stained-glass window:

> You know, it's a picture—it was a picture that just—you know, as soon as you look at it, it just hurts. You feel it in your heart, like, oh, man—

like here in the 21st century, you know, we're in a modern era where we shouldn't have to be subjected to those primitive and degrading images.... [I]t was a small piece of glass that was no bigger than a tablet. It was—it depicted a male and a female, both appearing to be African-American, standing in a field of white crops, what appear to be cotton, with baskets over their heads. And I believe one of the figures were actually smiling, which is like so condescending, because looking back on slavery, like, it wasn't a happy time for African Americans.[9]

I took a broomstick, and it was kind of high, and I climbed up and reached up and broke it. . . . It's 2016, I shouldn't have to come to work and see things like that. . . . I just said, "That thing's coming down today. I'm tired of it."[10]

I was aware of all the controversy behind the name John Calhoun and what he represented. However, I don't want to go ahead and necessarily say that that contributed to what I did. I just simply got tired of looking at that image. I don't know, you just get fed up. It gets to a point where it's like, enough's enough. I don't know. I think it's like Edgar Allan Poe's "The Tell-Tale Heart." It was sitting in the corner of the room ticking away subconsciously—somewhere in my subconscious.[11]

His words burst with emotions: *tired of it, fed up, it just hurts, you feel it in your heart, primitive and degrading, so condescending, The Tell-Tale Heart.* Menafee and Ahmed share academic fame for having snapped at their universities, for different but related reasons: protesting institutional racism and institutional sexism, respectively.[12] Their snaps also both involved their resignations from their universities, but in different ways. Ahmed's resignation was intentional, whereas when Menafee broke the window he was not intentionally resigning but was refusing Yale's plantation-ness. He resigned because it was the option he and his union were offered through negotiations with Yale's human-resources officials.

Ahmed's theory of "the cultural politics of emotions"—which she developed in and through her struggles with universities—can help us understand Menafee's action. Ahmed reframes emotions, not as residing in subjects or objects (seen in common expressions such as "I *have* a feeling" or "the book *is* sad"), but as movements, associations, and circulations of objects and signs that ripple across and between bodies.[13] What we see as the boundaries and surfaces of bodies—as individuals and collectives— do not preexist emotions but rather are formed through the circulation of the objects of emotions. Readings of pain, fear, love, hate, shame, and other emotions can bind a group together as a community, framing people either as internal members or as excluded others.

Ahmed describes emotions as productive of the impression of surfaces of individuals and collectives through *"intensifications of feeling."*[14] In his allusion to Poe's "The Tell-Tale Heart," Menafee describes his subconscious as a "room." From working in the building for six months, Menafee had accumulated psychic pain in relation to the window, like a covered-up-but-still-beating heart, "sitting in the corner of the room ticking away subconsciously."[15] He came to see the building's surface as tied with his identity, with the walls of its rooms representing his body's own surface. The stained-glass window shows an image to viewers both inside and outside. Seeing the window over and over from the inside, from the "room" of his "subconscious," intensified his feeling of pain, reproducing the impression of the window as homologous with the surface of his body. Further, imagining external viewers of this image—such as from talking with the visiting Yale alumnus and his ten-year-old daughter—intensified Menafee's sense of pain, from empathizing with them as they dwelled critically on this image, which he saw as part of himself. An intensification of his pain produced his desire to break the surface—to remove the object of his pain and to reorient his body in relation to the pain.

Menafee's feeling of pain is related to his memories, both personal and historical.[16] In interviews, Menafee does not relate his action to his personal history, and due to the gag provision we cannot ask him to elaborate. He grew up in New Haven with its inequalities and segregations of race, class, and town-and-gown. He graduated in 2001 from a historically Black university, Virginia Union University, "founded in 1865 to give newly emancipated slaves an opportunity for education and advancement."[17] He then returned to New Haven, worked for a few months as a substitute teacher in New Haven's segregated schools, and then worked for nine years in a service position at elite, white-dominated Yale University.[18] Menafee attributes a main source of his pain from the image to its misrepresenting the emotions of the enslaved African Americans as "actually smiling." He finds it "so condescending" that this image whitewashes the violent history of slavery, presenting it as "a happy time." His sense of indignation might have been heightened by the movement to change the name of Calhoun College. Four months after he broke the window, at a protest with the Change the Name Coalition, he gave a speech, saying, "We no longer want the name Calhoun casting a shadow on our university."[19] The 2001 report "Yale, Slavery and Abolition" described how John C. Calhoun had been a student at Yale with his tuition paid by profits from enslaved people's labor, went on to gain wealth and political power as a slave plantation owner, and became a statesman who wielded "enormous political influence on the preservation of slavery."[20] In 1930, Yale University decided to name "Calhoun College" in his honor. Profits from slave labor provided much of the capital for Yale's first scholarships, early buildings, and endowment, and Yale's campus was itself a site of slave labor.[21]

The attempts to unearth this history of Yale's ties to slavery have been entwined with labor struggles. The report "Yale, Slavery and Abolition" was written by three graduate student labor organizers. Menafee might have seen his action as continuing the history of worker resistance at Yale. According to historian Zach Schwartz-Weinstein, "the long, submerged history of property destruction and direct action by Yale employees" includes the November 1969 incident of a thirty-year-old Black dining hall waitress, Colia Williams, throwing a glass of water at a white manager who was harassing her, the 1971 actions of striking workers who "slashed the wiring and tires of university vehicles," and the 1977 firebombing of a university safety office during a thirteen-week walkout, which was one of approximately twenty strikes on Yale's campus from the 1940s to the present.[22] Although Menafee's action did not take place during a strike, his labor union supported him against the charges and fought for his rehiring.

In addition to considering Menafee's motives for breaking the window, we can ask about Yale's motives for silencing him. Why would the administration find Menafee's words so dangerous as to impose a gag provision on him? How could the public speech of one dishwasher threaten a university with a $25 billion endowment and over 4,400 faculty members?[23] The answer lies in the contagious power of emotions. With the media amplifying his voice to a national stage, Menafee invited a national audience to "imagine the type of emotions that run through" him and other African Americans when they see images of enslaved people misrepresented as "actually smiling." He invited listeners to empathize with him—to connect with the circulating emotions that run between, across, and through him, his fellow service workers, Black students at Yale, and others who feel indignation at racism. Yet, through empathizing with Menafee's pain, an audience does not actually feel *his* pain.

Ahmed highlights "the impossibility of feeling the pain of others," as "empathy remains a 'wish feeling,' in which subjects 'feel' something other than what another feels in the very moment of imagining they could feel what another feels."[24] She calls for an "ethics of responding to pain" that "involves being open to being affected by that which one cannot know or feel. . . . [T]he ungraspability of my own pain is brought to the surface by the ungraspability of the pain of others."[25] She also promotes a *politics* of responding to the pain of others. Heeding the call of "a pain that can't be shared through empathy" entails "a demand for collective politics, as a politics based not on the possibility that we might be reconciled, but on learning to live with the impossibility of reconciliation, or learning to live with and beside each other, and yet we are not as one."[26] Making such ethical and political responses to Menafee's pain would require grappling with the impasse of racism at the university, such as by participating in the critical mode of study practiced by Menafee and others in the Change the Name movement. Ahmed's call for a *politics* of responding to the pain of others resonates with my argument that we should interpret the impasse of higher education in terms of a *political* question: provoking the audience to ask themselves, Which side am I on? My concept of "mode of study" can help clarify the conflicting sides in this political struggle as well as the stakes involved in choosing a side. Will you choose to be an accomplice with Menafee and the Change the Name movement's struggles to dismantle institutional racism in universities, or will you side with the administration's attempts to maintain the dominant order? Will you participate in Menafee's mode of study, which combines direct action—such as breaking a window—with critical reflection on, and organizing around, Yale's racist history and present?

This political approach contrasts sharply with how Yale's administrators responded to the impasse brought up by Menafee's action. Their response presented an interpretation of this impasse as a moral and analytical question, attempting to depoliticize it by obscuring the sides and stakes of the conflict. They deployed moralizing language with their claims of opposition to "violence" and support of "non-violence." They sought to redirect concern about Yale's white-supremacist history into normal circuits of education within the university—as if the problem can be solved through more education. Their moral and analytical rhetoric aimed to make us *turn away* from Menafee's pain so that—in the words of their vice president of communications—"everyone can now move on."[27] To make everyone move on from reflecting on his pain—short-circuiting political questions about how to respond—they used two affective strategies: first, normalizing an emotional economy of happiness, safety, and fear; and second, appropriating his pain through claims of shame, generosity, and reconciliation. These strategies sought to neutralize Menafee's challenge to Yale's dominant, education-based mode of study.

One aspect of Yale's normalized emotional economy is seen in the stained-glass image's representation of the slaves as happy—a performed happiness that masks the violence of an exploitative situation. For contemporary service workers, this affective economy is continued in performance reviews that evaluate whether employees, such as dining hall workers, appear happy and friendly when interacting with customers. For academics, this is seen in academic norms of civility and collegiality that suppress and stigmatize expressions of anger.[28] For students, the prescribed happiness is seen through their romantic relation to education: they are framed as heroes in a romance narrative of climbing the educational ladder, overcoming obstacles on the way toward a happy life after graduation. Yale's response to Menafee's action is a way to restore this romance of education and its associated performances of happiness.

A second aspect of this normal affective economy is seen in the Yale administration's narratives of safety. In the romantic narrative of education, the protagonist is the Yale student. Service workers like Menafee are supposed to contribute to this narrative by creating a protected space in which the Yale student can learn. Menafee's action ruptures the romance of education. He presents a mode of study that is both alternative and threatening to Yale's education-based mode of study. Menafee's response is studied (e.g., his reference to "The Tell-Tale Heart"). He is not only a college-educated man but is also engaged in the wider body of thinking around the movement to grapple with Yale's legacy of slavery. He shows how study and the desire to do violence to certain kinds of property are not diametrically opposed. As such, this makes him a teacher of students in a way that the university does not want. Yale's attempt to gag him is also an attempt to obscure how studied he is—to have him take on the appearance of an uneducated person whose only response can be a violent one rather than one that comes from a place of study. According to Yale vice president Eileen O'Connor, "a stained glass window was broken by an employee of Yale, resulting in glass falling onto the street and onto a passerby, endangering [her] safety," and in a follow-up interview O'Connor said "she doesn't know for sure if the glass fell on the passerby or in front of her, but 'it was scary enough nonetheless.'"[29] In his response, Menafee contests the university's framing of him as a threat to students: "I didn't commit any acts of violence against anyone or any living thing. I didn't be belligerent, or yell. I just broke the windows." Through metonymic slides, the administration's narrative slips between objects—from the threat to a passerby of the falling glass, to the whole situation framed as "scary," to Menafee himself—sticking them together as objects of fear.

Ahmed notes that fear is not only about an unpleasant experience in the present but also "an *anticipation* of hurt or injury" in an imagined future.[30] The future-oriented and individualizing character of fear counteracts Menafee's studied connection of Yale's present with its past, his call for collective unforgetting of Yale's legacy of slavery as its "Tell-Tale Heart." Further, through the administration's narrative attaching the signs of "scary," "danger," and "threat to safety" to Menafee's body while gendering the passerby as female, they draw on stereotypes—associations of Black men with criminality, particularly with sexual danger to white women. These stereotypes serve to intensify an audience's referencing of the object of fear onto Menafee, rendering his body as "a site of insecurity."[31] Through framing his response as violent and unstudied, the university attempts to restore him to the role of servant and make clear that he is not a teacher of students. Thereby they seek to neutralize the threat that he poses to the education-based mode of study.

MODES OF STUDY: EDUCATION AND ITS ALTERNATIVES

In my analysis above of Menafee's disruption of Yale's normal order, I have introduced the concept of "mode of study." Inspired by Gustav Landauer's argument that the state is a relationship and that we dismantle it by relating to one another differently, I contend that when new concepts allow us to think differently about the university, we can enact new ways of relating in and beyond it.[32] In order to open up imaginative possibilities, we can view education as only one mode of study among many possible modes. By understanding how education has become the currently dominant mode of study through a contingent, conflict-ridden history, we can broaden our imaginative horizons.

To explain the concept of modes of study, I elaborate its elements. I see study, generally, as an activity in which people devote attention to the world. This sustained attention modifies their capacities and dispositions for understanding the world. A mode of study is a way of composing the *means* and *relations* of study. I see this distinction between means and relations as a fluid one, posited here for analytic purposes. The means of study are the various actors involved in any activity of studying. These actors include both *who* is studying as well as *what* they are studying with—the tools, objects, and techniques with which they study. There are infinite possibilities for such means, but some examples that might seem obvious to a contemporary reader include pens, paper, books, classrooms, chalkboards, computers, exams, grades, the Internet, laboratories, teacher salaries, student tuition, school and university buildings, and divisions between classrooms. The means of study also might include collectivities of students and teachers themselves. Using Bruno Latour's division of movements of association into processes of collection and composition, we can ask two key questions about these means of studying: *Which* means are collected together, and *how* are they composed together—that is, how are they related with each other?[33] We can imagine infinite possible collections of different means of studying, as well as infinite possible ways of composing the relations between them.

Compositions of the relations of study can be analyzed on multiple scales. On a meso scale of everyday human-to-human practices, they might refer to the relations between people involved in studying practices, such as between students, teachers, school police, and school administrators, and the relations with their tools for studying, such as classrooms and computers. On more micro scales, these relations of study entail affective, imaginative, and evaluative practices and processes, such as students feeling joy in studying their favorite subject or feeling shame in receiving a bad grade. On more macro scales, the relations of study might include transportation of students between their homes and schools, funding and accreditation of schools by local, state, and federal governments, and rankings of schools and universities.

The means and relations of study are collected and composed in various ways. Focusing on composition, I argue that we can generalize across different modes of composing collections of the means of study. This is what I mean by the term "mode of study": a theoretical abstraction that refers to a generalized, idealized way of composing the relations among collected means of studying. Differently composed relations of study limit or enable who can access the means of study and how they can study with them. For example, when teachers are positioned as experts, they tend to control the means of study in a classroom and to limit when and how different students can access those means. Differently composed means of study create enabling or limiting conditions on the formation of relations of study. For example, the mass-production of books with printing presses enabled studying with books among a wider populace. Charging higher prices for those books, or writing them in inaccessible language, limits who can study with them.

A mode of study is a generalized way of composing the means and relations of study in any given place and historical moment. Considering the infinite potential ways of describing and delimiting the collections and compositions of different means and relations of studying, there are no necessary ways of describing different modes of study. In other words, any definition of a particular mode of study is relative to the political motivations of whoever is designating it—an idealized abstraction constructed for particular political purposes. For my purposes, I give general concepts of different modes of study through identifying particular patterns across histories and geographies.

I define the education-based mode of study as entailing seven main features that have powerful effects for composing the means and relations of study:

a vertical imaginary—students rise *up* the levels of schooling (e.g., pre-K through twelfth grade through *higher* education)

a romantic narrative—students face obstacles, and overcome them as heroic individuals, along their journey up education's levels

relations of separation between students as producers and the means of studying—the teacher enforces this separation and regulates relations across it

techniques of governance—students' subjectivities are shaped with dispositions of obedience to the teacher's authority as an expert

a zero-point epistemology—the teacher's expert knowledge is seen as universally valid, from a position above any particular bodies and places in the world

an affective pedagogical economy of credit and debt—students are disciplined to desire honor and avoid shame in the eyes of their teachers and fellow students, often taking the form of grades on exams

binary figures of educational value and waste (e.g., the success vs. the failure, the college-bound vs. the remedial, the graduate vs. the dropout)

This book's chapters 2, 3, and 4 present critical genealogies of some of these features, showing how they emerged from political struggles. Different practices called "education" exhibit these features to varying extents. Some, such as mass education with standardized testing in most U.S. public schools and charter schools, exhibit these features more than others, such as Montessori-style education and democratic education. The education-based mode of study is also distinct from the global set of formal educational institutions, such as schools, colleges, and universities. Many different modes of study are happening in practices and institutions that we might describe as "educational."

Now that we can comprehend education as a specific mode of study and not a universal one, I can explain the aim of this book more clearly: to help us diagnose the problems with the education-based mode of study, understand its contingent historical emergence, analyze its relationship to alternative modes of study, and explore possibilities for some of those alternatives. Key controversies in the politics of study are about the conflicts between promoters of different modes of study—in association with different modes of world-making—as they struggle for access to, and composition of, potential means of study. Examples of modes of study alternative to that of education include the modes of study in Indigenous communities, in Black radical social movements, and in other traditions of movement-embedded studying. For example, in France's May 1968 rebellions, students' and workers' practices of organizing were bound up with studying that gave them capacities to occupy and collectively manage universities and factories.[34] Another example is that, according to Indigenous Nishnaabeg scholar Leanne Simpson, studying in Nishnaabeg communities entails practices that break from the features of the education-based mode of study. Rejecting the separation of students from the means of studying and refusing the zero-point epistemology, the Nishnaabeg ground practices of studying in a complex "compassionate web" of more-than-human relationships.[35] Through centering Indigenous storytelling as a mode of study, Indigenous people narrate the meaning of their lives as interwoven with the land, wherein "land" takes on a capacious meaning to include wetlands, sea, air, mountains, cities, soil, and the animals, plants, and ancestral spirits who are seen as cohabitating and studying with humans.[36] A more-than-humanist perspective on studying can also include micro scales within human bodies, such as with the "sympoetic" compositions of bacterial and human cells in the production of emotions.[37] Simpson criticizes academia for co-opting Indigenous study projects into the trap of "reconciliation" that maintains settler colonialism; instead, she calls for appropriating academia's resources for a "radical resurgence project" that intertwines land-based Indigenous study with anticolonial resistance movements.[38]

Corey Menafee also participated in an alternative mode of study—Black radical study. His direct action of breaking the window must be seen in the context of the spread of the Movement for Black Lives from the streets onto campuses in 2015 and 2016, which has drawn attention to universities' racial inequities, especially with the decrease of affirmative action while systemic racism continues to fester. Led by Black students, these protests sent shock waves of revolt across U.S. campuses. The students' demands—articulated in different ways in more than eighty statements from different campuses, including Yale—challenge racism in its overt, institutional, structural, cultural, and strategic forms.[39] Their struggles have forced institutional changes, from the adoption of task forces on racial equity to the ouster of college presidents.[40] By connecting the Black Lives Matter message to campus issues, these insurgent students have amplified the complexity of narratives about higher education's impasse.

An important public forum for debate about this impasse was hosted in the *Boston Review* under the title "Black Study, Black Struggle" in March 2016.[41] A key controversy in this debate was whether universities can be engines of social transformation or if, instead, such a function should only be seen in the work of political education and organizing from outside the university. Robin D. G. Kelley articulates this controversy in strategic terms between, on the one hand, a strategy of pushing the university through struggle to live up to its enlightened ideal, and on the other hand, the undercommons approach, which Kelley, drawing on Fred Moten and Stefano Harney, defines as "a subversive way of being *in* but not *of* the university."[42] Rejecting the idea that the university could ever become an enlightened space, devotees of the undercommons refuse to narrate the university's structural racism as a crisis that administrators could resolve through reforms of "more diversity, better training, a culturally sensitive curriculum," and increased "safety and affordability." Instead, the undercommons strategy aims to steal and repurpose the university's resources for collective study, acting as a "fugitive network." While the university's means of study are normally devoted to the education-based mode of study, the "guerrilla intellectuals" of the undercommons seek to redirect these means into an alternative network of Black radical modes of study. Insurgent students can grapple with the impasse of the university in their own autonomous study groups. Thereby, they not only aim to transform the existing university but also, through their study, they prefigure a liberated university.

The debate in this forum brings up controversial questions around the relations between study, labor, reform, and revolution. *Who* is in the undercommons? How do the different ways that people are "in" or "outside" the university condition their participation in the undercommons? How does the undercommons relate to different space-times within and beyond the university, from the classroom and cafeteria to the public sphere and marginalized neighborhoods? How do people's different positionalities as studiers and laborers of various kinds—as students, service workers, contingent faculty, tenure-stream faculty, or people unaffiliated with the university—affect their roles in studying and organizing together for reform and/or revolution?

In order to engage these complex questions, I contend that we need to interrogate an ambiguity contained within the "Black Study, Black Struggle" debate, namely, between study and education.[43] Kelley draws from Harney and Moten both the theory of the undercommons and their advocacy of study. In an interview, Harney and Moten have also made a distinction between study and education.[44] Picking up on their attempt at a more nuanced theory, I offer the concept of modes of study. With this concept we can distinguish between the modes of study in the formal classroom, in service workers' everyday conversations and organizing, and in autonomous study groups. We can imagine possibilities for breaking from the education-based mode of study in these different situations. The concept of modes of study allows for engaging with, rather than burying, controversies over how the different positionalities of students, faculty, service workers, and people beyond campuses are related with inequalities of access to the means for study and conflicts between their different modes of study. For example, the education-based mode of study is co-constituted with universities' "unequal temporal architectures" in which tenured professors' privileged experiences of engaging in "slow scholarship" are interdependent with oppressive, "sped-up" labor conditions for many others in the university—service workers who maintain the professors' offices, students who take on extra jobs and debt to pay tuition, and contingent faculty who teach more classes.[45] When the latter are working to enable the tenured class's conditions for studying, their possibilities for exploring alternative modes of study are limited. Conversely, movements on campus—such as for Black liberation and

Indigenous resurgence—can open up spaces on campus that enact more equal temporal architectures and facilitate alternative modes of study. With a political theory of study, I offer framings for these movements to affirm their modes of study in association with their projects for making a new world.

RECUPERATION OF ALTERNATIVE MODES OF STUDY

A key danger these movements face is that their alternative world-making projects tend to become absorbed into the dominant world-making project. My concept of modes of study allows for a more nuanced view on how this recuperation occurs. Institutions built around the education-based mode of study are *parasitic* upon alternative modes of study. Rather than being based on a homogeneity of their mode of study, these institutions' success is dependent upon their ability to appropriate and recuperate alternative modes of study *up to a point.*

To elaborate this argument about recuperation with a concrete example, I return to Corey Menafee. To stabilize their normal educational order, Yale's administration tries to recuperate his alternative (Black radical) mode of study. Their attempt to maintain a normalized affective economy of the university includes their politics of shame, which has two interrelated aspects: first, shame is "brought onto" the Yale community by an illegitimate Other; and second, Yale brings shame "onto itself."[46] When Menafee is framed as a violent threat, he experiences shame—seen in his act of apologizing. The administration frames his response as having "expressed deep remorse about his actions." Ahmed notes how this kind of shame is experienced "as the affective cost of not following the scripts of normative existence."[47] Menafee violates Yale's liberal norm for dealing with conflicts, namely, through ostensibly nonviolent discussion. Conversely, this norm frames direct actions—such as in Yale's history of service worker strikes—as violent. By seeking an apology from Menafee, the administration shifts guilt and shame onto Menafee, and thereby diverts attention away from one of his objectives with Black radical study: to inspire the collective "unforgetting" of, and critical reflection on, Yale's legacy of slavery.[48]

At the same time, the administration tries to co-opt Menafee's action into their preferred mode of acknowledging their legacy of racism. This entails a second sense of Yale's politics of shame. The administration incorporates Menafee's action into an official narrative of how Yale has brought shame "on itself," exposed as "failing" a liberal multicultural ideal. The administration performs an act of "generosity" by giving Menafee his job back and presents this "reconciliation" between Yale and Menafee in connection with Yale's attempts to heal the wounds of slavery. They represent their efforts to deal with this painful history as forms of healing for the Yale community.[49] In Yale's narrative of reconciliation with their legacy of slavery, they claim the pain of Black bodies as their own, recuperating their pain as a means for affectively intensifying people's subscriptions to the identity of the Yale community.[50] This reconciliation narrative deflects attention from Yale's continuing expansion into New Haven's Black neighborhoods, an expansion for which slavery laid the groundwork.[51] Their performance of a moral reconciliation might trick their audience to "move on," to turn away from the political controversy that Menafee's snap revealed. This controversy is between conflicting modes of world-making that are co-constituted with certain modes of study.

THE CO-CONSTITUTION OF MODES OF STUDY AND WORLD-MAKING

My critique is aimed neither at the term "education" nor at educational institutions, but rather at the education-based mode of study. My concept of modes of study is similar to the Marxist concept of modes of production, which is defined as a configuration of means (i.e., forces) of production and relations of production. But, unlike orthodox Marxists, who envision "natural progress" through changing modes of production (e.g., from feudalism to capitalism to communism), I do not theorize any necessarily developmental, progressive, or teleological relations between different modes of study. Also, instead of using the term "modes of production" I prefer "modes of world-making." The former tends to carry the orthodox Marxist baggage of a dualistic worldview (i.e., material base vs. ideological superstructure), whereas "modes of world-making" implies a monist worldview with ideas and materiality on the same immanent plane of existence. By asserting that modes of study and modes of world-making are co-constitutive, I am discouraging a dualist or transcendent view in which adopting a certain mode of study could give a vantage on the world from a point outside and separate from the world.

Relations between certain modes of study and certain modes of world-making are relatively congruent or dissonant. A key example of this, which I will elaborate in the book, is the supplementary relation between the education-based mode of study and the capitalist, modernist/colonial mode of world-making, particularly through theorizing the education-based mode of study as part of the processes of creating the preconditions of capitalism, what Karl Marx described as "so-called primitive accumulation . . . the historical process of divorcing the producer from the means of production."[52] Another example is how modes of study in particular Indigenous people's communities, such as the Nishnaabeg mentioned above, are congruent with their modes of life. A mode of study can vary in the extent that it is normalized and institutionalized. It can be a marginal mode or a minor, counterhegemonic mode, or a major, hegemonic mode. The latter I also call a "regime of study." The elements of the education-based mode of study began emerging as marginal practices in the feudal mode of world-making (a process described in chapter 3). Along with the rise of the statist, modernist/colonial, capitalist mode of world-making, more elements of the education-based mode of study emerged and congealed with each other, becoming more normalized and institutionalized as a hegemonic regime of study (the subject of chapter 4).

To further clarify the education-based mode of study, we need to disentangle the typology of *modes of study* from the question of one's *stance toward any particular mode*. My critique of the education-based mode of study is not aimed only at this mode of study but also at the romanticized stance that people tend to take toward it—with their moralizing, reparative, and melodramatic narratives about it. This distinction gives a double meaning to the title of this introduction, "Against the Romance of Education." First, I am against the romantic narrative that is *part of* the education-based mode of study (the view of students as heroically overcoming obstacles as they climb up education levels). Second, I am against taking a romanticizing stance *toward* the education-based mode of study. My critique is not of the romanticizing of modes of study per se. In fact, I am a romantic about some (but certainly not all) alternative kinds of modes of study, but in our current historical conjuncture I find the education-based mode of study unworthy of romance. Likewise, for any alternative mode of study that I am more romantic about now, I recognize that it can be liberating now but probably not forever. The next section explains why I am a fanatic for some modes of study that are in conflict with the education-based mode.

EDUCATION AS IMPASSE OR ROMANCE: SITUATING THE AUTHOR

I've felt ambivalent about education for a long time. I love to study, and I've succeeded at education, but something about it seemed rotten. On paper, my trajectory from kindergarten through the PhD was near perfect. My parents sent me to a private Montessori school, where I was encouraged to explore my own interests and to study cooperatively with my peers. When my parents divorced, school was my refuge from familial turmoil. But when I transferred to a public school in fifth grade, its lectures, exams, and grades felt stultifying. I was a white, middle-class kid in the honors track of mostly white, suburban schools in the segregated city of York, Pennsylvania—a dying industrial town known for race riots and white flight. I loved studying, but York's schools were shaping kids for the predictable American dream of a patriarchal family, a manicured lawn, and lifelong work. I was at an impasse.

To escape, I subscribed to the romantic story of education. I jumped at the chance to leave for college a year early. My high SAT scores got me a full scholarship at the University of Southern California. I wrote myself into a romantic narrative of a heroic individual climbing the educational ladder: "rising up" through the K–12 grades, graduating rather than "dropping out," and entering "higher" education. The romantic genre framed my ambivalent relations to education in a way that allowed me to escape the impasse I had faced in York. The romantic story portrayed the student, myself, as engaging in a quest, climbing up education's levels, overcoming obstacles (such as exams and graduation requirements) at each step, and rising toward an image of the good life defined by success, security, independence, maturity, and happiness. The romance framed my grappling with the challenges along the way as an internalized struggle between forces of good and evil, with evil personified as education's Others—the failure and the dropout.[53] I feared becoming such Othered figures. But I found ways to overcome these obstacles—such as by escaping to college a year early on a full four-year scholarship—thereby temporarily deadening my ambivalence about education and allowing me to enjoy my new situation at a higher level of education.

I wanted to be independent from my parents, so I chose the major that had the highest starting salary post-college: chemical engineering. At college, by conforming to the norms of the education-based mode of study, I was on a path to become a successful engineer. But from hanging out with film and humanities majors and listening to punk rock and hip-hop, engineering began to feel unfulfilling. I was at another impasse: I needed a career, but I feared becoming a tool for the status quo. To find a way to grapple with my dissident feelings, I added a philosophy major, staying an extra year to graduate with two degrees, while taking on student debt. Philosophy gave me the opportunity to come to terms with the sense of precarity and unfreedom that I felt. I also learned that I wasn't alone. The feeling of precarity is widespread among the American population in the early twenty-first century: a mess of confusion, disorientation, anxiety, and apathy, mixed with concerns about our future relations with what we need and care about in life—our employment, health, family, housing, food, and so forth.[54] Through introducing me to critical theories of capitalism and the state, philosophy allowed me to dwell on the underlying causes of this feeling of precarity—phenomena such as outsourcing, deindustrialization, intensified labor exploitation, expensive health care, immigration control, racial and economic segregation, the state violence of police and prisons, industrial pollution, anthropogenic climate change, the corporatized politics of liberal democracy, and the decline of labor unions, among others. Through philosophy, I began to find some bearings for how to endure and adapt in the impasse.

With student debt looming, after college I got a job as a sanitary engineer at Los Angeles's largest sewage treatment plant. Each day at work, several million people's wastewater flowed under my feet. Bacterial and chemical processes purified the water before it flowed into the ocean. After work I would go surfing. Bobbing on the waves, I reflected on how humans collaborated with bacteria to turn the wastewater into clean water, allowing the beach to remain a playground. Despite my awe at this technological miracle, my philosophy background motivated me to study how the industry I worked in was complicit with global inequalities. The rich city of Los Angeles can afford advanced wastewater treatment technologies, while people in the Global South suffer from polluted water that causes millions of deaths every year. I felt an impasse again: I wanted to do something about this inequality, but found the industry more concerned with questions of efficiency and profitability. With my office hidden in the city's vast bureaucracy, I stole time to study the political-economic questions that were ignored in our work. I also stole time to apply for graduate school. My philosophy degree gave me an escape route to a place with more resources for critical study, the University of Minnesota's departments of philosophy and political science.

As I moved on from my engineering career to begin graduate school, I became more and more aware of the lives and struggles of people around me. I learned of perspectives that my education had never addressed, including the stories of campus workers whose often-hidden labor is essential for making the university work. In the fall of 2007, nearly thirty-five hundred clerical, technical, and health care workers in the American Federation of State, County, and Municipal Employees (AFSCME) union at the University of Minnesota went on strike, demanding a wage increase to keep up with the cost of living. I joined other students and workers in solidarity actions. It was, in many ways, this experience that showed me how much I had to gain from *studying* outside of education.

Earlier that year, I was unsettled when a grad student friend in my department committed suicide—at a university with a long trend of lack of support for students' mental health. This shook my loyalty to and identification with the university. *I snapped at the university.* My sense of an impasse became focused on the university itself. I could no longer escape my impasse through the romantic story of education. That romance had died along with my friend. At the same time, I took inspiration from my friend's empathy with communities of anger. Before he died, he was studying how Indigenous peoples resist the ongoing structures of settler colonialism. Picking up his desire to learn how to be a white settler accomplice with movements for decolonization, I began to inquire into the relations of colonialism and universities.

I became drawn to people who were resisting the soul-crushing features of our own university, built on land stolen from the Dakota peoples. During the AFSCME strike, I joined strike supporters in organizing protests, occupying a board of regents meeting, and holding a four-day hunger strike. Despite our efforts, the administration didn't give the union a better contract.[55] Yet through our struggle we had built strong relationships that we did not want to lose. We channeled our desires for change into a forum for reflection on the strike and on what to do next. One of the presenters at the forum was from the Experimental College of the Twin Cities (EXCO), a free, anarchistic university that had an organizing group based out of a local liberal arts college, Macalester. Seeing resonances between our struggle at the university and the one that had founded their project—against a shift to a more elitist admissions policy—some of us decided to found a new chapter of EXCO at the university, as a free, open, egalitarian project for modes of study alternative to education. We used student groups to appropriate funds and spaces from the University of Minnesota and Macalester for EXCO classes, building an alternative university within the cracks of higher education.

I learned as much through studying in EXCO classes as in graduate school. Through study groups on anarchism, feminism, Marxism, and university politics, we built relationships that gave life to projects against and beyond the university, including a grad student union, a social center, and the decolonization-focused groups Unsettling Minnesota and Teachers against Occupation. I came to understand the university as a terrain of struggle. This terrain penetrated my own subjectivity, as I felt a tension between surviving in academia and resisting it. After three members of my PhD committee moved to other universities, one of them asked if I was planning to drop out. I wasn't. But this question sparked a line of self-inquiry. Why was I seen as "dropping out" when I felt more like I was being *pushed* out? Did my friend who committed suicide "drop out" of grad school? Would it be better to drop out than to struggle with precarity like my friends who had earned PhDs but were un- or under-employed in the brutal academic job market? Looking back, I wondered why leaving my white, suburban high school a year early for college was considered praiseworthy while kids in the mostly Black and Latinx, working-class, inner-city school were pushed out, criminalized, and stigmatized as "drop-outs." How were our different education and life trajectories bound up with each other? "School dropouts" and "contingent faculty" seemed connected as figures of "waste" for the education industry. Having left my career in the wastewater industry due to its inequities, how could I now justify pursuing a career in an unjust system of education?

Grappling with these questions brought my relations with education to an impasse. To study this impasse, I embarked on critical research about education. Studying began to peel away my layers of "educated ignorance" about my complicity with an oppressive system of education. Instead of seeking an escape from this impasse, I built relationships with others who were studying their own impasses around education. I found that other people have different understandings of the impasse, and different stories of how they came to it, endure in it, or escape from it. For my research, I interviewed thirty-five people engaged in organizing within, against, and beyond universities.[56] Coming from different positions as undergrads, grad students, and faculty, they shared various experiences of their ambivalent relations to education. In addition to tensions around feelings of anxiety, depression, and shame in relation to education, these organizers experience another, interrelated set of tensions. Their critical feelings about the education system and their desires to organize against it are in tension with their desires to accept the status quo so as to compete and succeed, or at least survive, within it.

Through studying and organizing in EXCO classes, I met people who told very different stories about their experiences of an impasse with education. Some introduced me to alternative framings of school non-completion. One of my co-studiers in an anarchist reading group said that he had "risen out" of high school, not only rejecting the stigma of "dropping out" but also affirming his refusal of the education system. The EXCO classes fostered modes of study outside of, and alternative to, education. I came to wonder: Could our different modes of study in these EXCO classes enable modes of world-making alternative to the dominant ways of world-making through education in settler-colonial, racial capitalism? Could alternative modes of study help challenge and even abolish the status quo? I took these questions as a spur for my research.

Rather than assuming the inevitability of the education-based mode of study, I examined its historical contingency. I found that modes of study within the institutional situation of schools emerged at various times in different cultures, such as in Egypt around 3000 B.C. In Europe, practices of study occurred in schools and universities for centuries prior to the birth of the modern concept of education, with the first universities emerging in the eleventh century A.D. and the first monastic schools in the sixth century A.D.[57] The first use of the term for "education" in French was in the late fifteenth century, and in English in the early sixteenth, concurrent with the rise of capitalism, colonialism, and the state.[58] The education-based mode of study has become so foundational to the other institutions of the liberal-capitalist, modernist mode of life that it acts as a systemic blind spot, not only for modernity's boosters but also for its critics.

OVERVIEW OF THE BOOK

To elaborate how narratives of crisis are tied with the romantic story of education, chapter 1 examines contemporary debates on higher education. The impasse of higher education can be engaged in a variety of ways, but most authors of recent books on higher education politics in the United States respond to the impasse as a crisis. Rather than treating the impasse as a political question about conflicts between alternative modes of world-making and study, they treat it as a moral and analytical question to be resolved through rational persuasion. Narratives of crisis imply a moral distinction between past and future and ask, Where did we go wrong? The genres of jeremiad and melodrama give simplified ways of narrating the answer, which set up a prognosis for how we can improve. However, these narratives repeat the education romance, thereby suppressing motivations to grapple with the impasse and reproducing an epistemology of educated ignorance. This problem is evident in the growing field of critical university studies, whose calls for fighting privatization and neoliberalism via a return to a public ideal of higher education fail to grapple with, and take a stand on, the impasse of ongoing settler-colonial and racial-capitalist structures in universities. By contrast, some recent student movements have engaged in alternative modes of study around this impasse, rejecting crisis managers with the call of "We are the crisis!" Taking inspiration from them, I describe how the modernist blind spots of crisis, security, and education reinforce each other in a self-enclosed logic. This problem spurs the book's inquiry into a critical genealogy of the education-based mode of study.

The crisis narrative has supplementary relations with other education narratives. In chapter 2, to intervene at a point of interconnection between these supplementary ideologies, I give a critical genealogy of the narrative of school dropout crisis. The political origins of the "dropout problem" narrative are in the early 1960s United States with the liberal-capitalist modernist project promoted by the Ford Foundation and the National Education Association. In response to threats from the left and the right—as well as from migrants' alternative modes of study and world-making—liberal capitalists created color-blind institutions that focused on "urban problems," including the "dropout." Narratives around the dropout include imagined vertical life trajectories tied with a certain emotional economy—imagining life as a dropout produces shame and fear, while rising up as a graduate produces pride. This emotional economy constructs and stabilizes the boundaries of key entities in the liberal-capitalist imaginary: the individual, the community, and the nation. The dropout problematic creates a terrain of intervention for liberal-capitalist governance that is framed as an individualized process of disposal and salvaging. In the 1960s, the Ford Foundation's "dropout" project dovetailed with its promotion of an end to free tuition and commodifying of higher education. With the rise of liberal and neoliberal versions of multiculturalism from the 1970s through 1990s, the framing of dropouts as "culturally deprived" was replaced by non-cultural descriptions, such as "educationally disadvantaged" and "at risk." But the narrative of the "dropout crisis" retains its effect of focusing on governance of individuals, families, schools, and communities while diverting attention from structural racism.

The next two chapters explore the origins of further key elements of the education-based mode of study. Chapter 3 details the history of struggles between conflicting modes of life and their associated modes of study during the emergence of capitalism. I examine how, in thirteenth- to sixteenth-century Lower Germany, communities of women in the cities, particularly in beguinages, created new modes of life, spirituality, commons, and enclosure entwined with new modes of study. In opposition to the beguines' horizontalist mode of study, others developed more verticalist modes, particularly the institution of ascending levels in schools associated with the Sisters and Brothers of the Common Life. Splitting schools into ascending levels and narrating an ideology of spiritual ascent for an individualized self gave the schoolmasters means for managing the crisis of disorder among the increasing number of students in their schools. Along with the colonial dispossession of land, plundering of colonized people's labor and resources, and patriarchal repression of rebellious women, the institution of school levels spread throughout Europe, contributing to the creation of the preconditions for capitalism.

To elaborate on education's role in the rise of capitalism, chapter 4 describes how education was used in reactions to resistances in sixteenth- and seventeenth-century England. The first part of the chapter focuses on the emergence of the term "education" in 1530s England. People's rebellions pushed King Henry VIII's regime into a widespread crisis of legitimacy. The political technology of education served as a narrative solution when coupled with a constellation of binary, individualized figures—for example, "idle" people with "bad education" versus "hardworking" people with "good education." The rising liberal, colonial, patriarchal, capitalist project was entwined with political theorists' development of the education-based mode of study. To examine an emblematic example of these theorists, I analyze how John Locke frames the Others of modernity—the poor, women, slaves, and natives—in co-constitutive oppositions with the figure of the self formed through education. Locke revises the conception of the self from an essentialist view to one constructed through experiences. He prescribes education for shaping these experiences in ways conducive for self-governance. The teacher should manage the student's self-formation with modernist/colonial narratives and a household-based emotional economy—shame, pride, fear, and anxiety—that creates a system of credits and debts. This mode of accounting gives teachers educational tools for suppressing subversive collaborations across class, gender, age, and race.

Building on insights from the earlier chapters' critical genealogies, chapter 5 returns to the undercommons approach to contemporary struggles on the terrain of higher education. My coauthor, Erin Dyke, and I present reflections and analysis from several years of militant co-research with an alternative study organization called the Experimental College of the Twin Cities. Using the concept of "modes of study" to frame our analysis, we show how this project's participants developed new ways of thinking and relating that enacted alternatives to the education-based mode of study, intertwined with alternatives to liberal-capitalist modes of subject-formation and governance. For example, a course on "Radical Pedagogy" engaged participants in anarchist modes of study, and courses on "Dakota Decolonization" and "Unsettling Minnesota" engaged non-Indigenous settler descendants with Indigenous people's modes of study. This account highlights limits and possibilities for projects with undercommons relations to universities, stealing resources for supporting alternative modes of study.

In the conclusion I apply my book's theory of universities as terrains of conflict between alternative modes of study and world-making. Returning to the phenomenon of snapping in and at the university, I ask, Why doesn't everyone who experiences exploitation and oppression snap? I hypothesize that our anger at the university is continually mollified by the epistemology of educated ignorance. We fall back on romanticized views of higher education, where some ideal—the academic vocation, the public university, academic freedom, tenure, the liberal arts, slow scholarship, and so forth—is framed as in crisis and in need of defense. As an antidote, we need to engage in more thorough critical genealogies of *all* of the elements of this epistemology. Seeing this book as the beginning of a broader, collaborative research project, I call for further genealogies of these romanticized ideals about higher education. By showing how these ideals emerged as moralizing crisis responses to struggles, we can unsubscribe from these narratives and expand our horizons to alternative modes of study and world-making. Going beyond critical university studies, I call for not only an abolitionist university studies but also an *abolition university*, one that aligns itself with modes of study in abolitionist movements within, against, and beyond the university as we know it.

Academic study does not have to take the form of reified expertise within the education-based mode. Instead, academics and non-academic movement participants can collaborate in continually unsettling flows of teaching, knowledge, study, and organizing. As we kill the romance of education, we can bring to life new modes of studying and remaking the world together.

1

"We Are the Crisis"

STUDYING THE IMPASSE OF UNIVERSITY POLITICS

Student resistance can expand our horizons to another world. The following is an excerpt from a manifesto written by students who occupied Campbell Hall at UCLA on November 19, 2009:

> And there are those of us who have also said: yes, I am in love with this movement and yes I must fight for this movement, no matter what comes of it. This event without a name.
>
> For those of us who have made that decision, tossed those dice, all we can say is this: *there is more ecstasy in this world than in the one we left behind.* There is more ecstasy because, like falling in love, the old world means nothing now, because what you thought was impossible suddenly becomes the very thing you can throw your arms around, lose yourself in, speed off with to the far edges of the earth.
>
> And if sweat is soaking your face, if your fingers are shaking, if your lips have gone dry, if you are more confused and excited than ever, ask yourself this: *Am I perhaps in love with this movement as well?*
>
> And if we can venture a tentative name for our love, a name that belongs to none of us as individuals, yet belongs to all of us, together, it would only be this: *We are the crisis!*
>
> —"WE ARE THE CRISIS: The Student Movement
> and the Coming Decade"[1]

Over the course of three days in November 2009, students occupied spaces throughout the University of California system. On November 18, students at UC Santa Cruz occupied Kresge Town Hall "to create an organizing space against the budget cuts," which entailed tuition hikes of 32 percent, among other injustices.[2] UC Santa Cruz students also occupied an administration building for four days. Concurrently, students at UCLA held a sit-in to disrupt the regents' meeting, leading to fourteen arrests. On November 19, students at UCLA occupied Campbell Hall and renamed it Carter-Huggins Hall in honor of Bunchy Carter and John Huggins, Black Panthers who were murdered in the building in 1969. The students issued a statement but made no demands. Instead, they proclaimed: "We demand nothing. We will take, we will occupy. We have to learn not to tip toe through a space which ought by right to belong to everyone."[3] Two students were arrested. On the same day, students at UC Davis occupied the main administration building on campus, resulting in fifty-two arrests.

The standoff at UC Berkeley on November 20 highlighted the movement's desires. Students occupied Wheeler Hall for twelve hours, leading to massive police repression and forty-three arrests. Two of those arrested, Amanda Armstrong and Paul Nadal, wrote about their experiences in an essay titled "Building Times: How Lines of Care Occupied Wheeler Hall."[4] They spoke of the "ways in which the time of the University is being turned against us": reduced course offerings, especially in the arts and languages, and the firing of thirty-eight custodial workers, which

FIGURE 2. Banners at student occupation of UC Santa Cruz graduate student commons, September 24, 2009. Photograph by Wes Modes.

"effectively forced all remaining custodians to do more work in the same amount of time, to endure an accelerated pace of labor." Further, raising tuition by 32 percent forced students to take on increased loans, compelling them "to sell our labor, day in and day out for an indefinite period, to those who hold capital. . . . Debt alienates us from the temporal substance of our lives. It becomes the privation of our present and future being." They also spoke of how, against the university's temporal oppression, their reclamation of space was "a seizing of time," not only destabilizing the status quo but "opening up lines of care and solidarity." Massing their bodies together, they held the doors tight, looking around to see "arms stretched high and eyes unwavering to the tumult" of the police trying to force their way inside. "Unexpected alliances" formed with people streaming to the occupation from the campus and surrounding communities. After allies created a second barricade that hemmed in the police's own barricade of the building, they threw provisions to the occupiers over the heads of the police, making their "lines of care" visible.[5]

Inspired by students' occupations of buildings at the New School and NYU in 2008 and 2009, the wave of protests across California in the 2009–10 academic year involved at least two dozen occupations of university buildings amid a surge of rebellious activity, including walkouts, marches, sit-ins, hunger strikes, and illegal dance parties. In trying to draw public attention to their struggles, the protesters confronted university administrators' rationalizing and moralizing crisis narratives, proclaiming during the occupation of Wheeler Hall, "We won't pay for your crisis!" (a slogan borrowed from the "anomalous wave" social movement in Italy). In the words of Armstrong and Nadal:

> University buildings stood as though only to absorb into their walls the waves of dissenting voices, but the uproar of our protests grew so loud as to make even the tiniest screw heads inside tremble. The university administrators, deliberating behind closed doors, however, seemed unmoved by our calls for justice. Crisis begets difficult choices they say. And through the screen of crisis, their fatal and fatalistic plans pass off as expert determinations of what must be done. "When you have no choice, you have no choice," says U.C. President Mark Yudof, after his endorsement

of the Regents' vote for a system-wide 32% tuition increase. His words, we note, do more than authorize hikes and cuts; they seek to suppress and flatten the seeds of change onto the deadening temporality of the inevitable.[6]

The protesters fought the administration's crisis narratives in two main ways. They revealed the administrators' "screen of crisis" as a cover for tuition hikes, increasing student debt, and labor speedup. They also put into question the crisis framing itself. Some students used the counter-narrative of "We are the crisis" to affirm themselves both as *causing* declared "crises" for the universities, the state, and capitalism and as *refusing to bow* to those who sought to manage the "crises."[7] The "We are the crisis" narrative unsettles the assumptions behind narratives of crisis that seek to manage threats to the dominant mode of ordering the university, an order enmeshed with the political project of liberal-capitalist modernity.[8] The call of "We are the crisis" means not only that *we* reject *your* crisis narrative but also that we *distinguish* our world-making project from your world-making project ("the old world")—framing these worlds as in political conflict with each other, and *affirming* how our world pushes your world into crisis. Yet the call of "We are the crisis" shares with other crisis narratives a basic assumption: that higher education in the United States today is at *some* kind of impasse. Crisis narratives offer moralizing escape routes from the impasse, while narratives of "We are the crisis" call for continual study of political controversies in the impasse.

In this chapter's first section I show how crisis narratives frame the impasse in terms of moral-analytical questions, which are narrated in the genres of melodrama, jeremiad, and consumer guide. In the second section I show how these narratives share common framings of the romance of education for populating the characters in their stories. These moralizing narratives depoliticize the impasse, diverting attention from political questions about conflicts between alternative modes of study and world-making on the terrain of universities. I theorize this depoliticization as an "epistemology of educated ignorance": ways of knowing that hinder thought about critiques of, and alternatives to, the education-based mode of study. The intertwined narratives of crisis and education suppress attention to the perspectives of people who are marginalized from education and of people who engage in resistance to education.

In order to break out of this epistemology of educated ignorance, we need to amplify the voices that it silences. In the third section of this chapter I present perspectives of people who have been treated as the Others of education as well as people who have organized to change universities. For recognizing and affirming their voices—treating them as legitimate sources of political-theoretical analyses—my concept of "modes of study" provides a useful framing. In the final section of the chapter I articulate some of the political questions raised with alternative modes of study, such as how Indigenous and Black radical modes of study raise controversies over the composition of the means, relations, and ends of study, particularly in their conflicts with the modernist/colonial world-making project. These political questions are intertwined with ethical questions such as who the "We" are in "We are the crisis," and of how we should compose our relations with each other in our alternative modes of study and world-making.

ESCAPING THE IMPASSE: GENRES OF CRISIS NARRATIVE

Debates about education are competing stories about a story. Publicly, people tell different narratives about the history, present, and future of education. How audiences receive a narrative depends on whether it resonates with the stories they tell about their own lives, stories in which education is often a big part of the plot: the schools we attended, the schools we wished we could attend, whether we graduated or dropped out, whether we went to college and took on debt from student loans, whether we worked to pay off that debt, continuing friendships with old classmates, reminiscing about favorite teachers, regretting certain educational paths we were pushed down or chose not to take, and so on. How we narrate our personal stories of education—and situate them in the broader stories of our lives—varies greatly depending on the positions we came from, the positions at which we end up, and our struggles along the way. Those who graduated from high school at the top of their class, went on to an elite university, and used their degree to enter a high-paying career might highlight and affirm their experiences of education as a foundational part of their life's narrative. Those who were pushed out of high school, stigmatized as a dropout, and treated as a criminal for hustling just to get by in an informal economy might weave their memories of education into their life's narrative as experiences of shame and disrespect, experiences they would rather forget.

Generalizing beyond particular stories, we can ask how certain features of the narratives resonate with certain features of the audience, their desires, expectations, and dispositions. Widespread among the American population today are states of unfreedom and precarity. Without having the time, energy, or capacities to describe the complex underlying sources of these feelings, attempts to understand them can be frustrating and confusing. To dwell with these reflections is to take on the challenge of grappling with an impasse.

Talking about "the impasse" in general can be confusing, because it elides three interrelated phenomena. One is a person's embodied experience of being in an impasse. Another is reflection on this experience. A third is generalizing from those reflections by describing them in language that is communicable across people who experience an impasse. These three phenomena are interrelated through action. With experience of an impasse, common emotional responses are anxiety, vulnerability, precarity, and unfreedom. Reflecting on these emotions might destabilize belief in fantasies of the good life—for example, economic security, a nuclear family, and democratic citizenship—that used to give meaning to their sense of self. According to Lauren Berlant, narratives of the impasse show what people do to adapt and survive in response to such destabilization—how they search for some kind of re-stabilization, a new equilibrium.[9] Most approaches to writing about the problems with education start out with a brief engagement with the impasse. However, they short-circuit such engagement through offering the reader, in Berlant's terms, a "cruelly optimistic" line of escape from the impasse via crisis narratives.

"Modes of impasse" is a conceptual toy for playfully thinking about different ways to grapple with the impasse of the present. One mode is through crisis narratives, which frame the present in terms of a crisis with a moral distinction between past and future, asking, Where did we go wrong?[10] Seeing crisis narratives as one possible mode of impasse among others puts into question their apparent necessity. Then, we can open our horizons to many alternative possible modes of engaging the impasse of the present.

Public narratives about education can help people either take on this challenge of grappling with the impasse or escape from it. By positioning themselves as actors in the narrative, people can find a new source of meaningful guidance for their lives. Education is an especially sensitive focus of concern in two main ways. First, it is seen as a main process through which people are supposed to gain better understandings of the world. If we have doubts about understanding education itself, our confidence in understanding anything else in the world is shaken. Second, education is a key transitional process in many of the other hegemonic narratives about people's life trajectories—from childhood to adulthood, from dependence on the family to independence as a worker, from exploited work to a fulfilling career, from criminality to responsible citizenship. These features make education a confluence point for many of the anxieties that people have about other areas of their lives.

People's ambivalent emotional relations with education motivate them to tell stories of anxiety, crisis, precarity, or injustice and to be receptive to such stories. Books about the problems of higher education, seeking to give guidance for anyone facing its impasse, draw selectively on these stories, weaving some of them together into a larger metanarrative while neglecting others. Most recent books on university politics narrate the impasse of higher education as a crisis—a situation that Abigail Boggs and Nick Mitchell refer to as "the crisis consensus."[11] A recent example is Robert Samuels's *Why Public Higher Education Should Be Free*, which proclaims a crisis in the first sentence: "Universities are in crisis because they have lost their central identity."[12] Another example is Goldie Blumenstyk's *American Higher Education in Crisis?* Her title's question is answered affirmatively: "Yes. Higher education is most assuredly in crisis."[13] At least a dozen other recent books about American higher education have "crisis" in their title.[14]

Narratives of crisis project images of time as abstracted from space and as having a distinguishable, sequential past, present, and future.

They combine these images with a moral imperative, asking, Where did we go wrong between the past and the present, and how can we fix the problem for a better future? To give simplified ways of telling a story of where we went wrong and to set up a prognosis for how we can do better, these crisis narratives are composed with certain genres: the jeremiad (lamenting the loss of a past practice or ideal) and melodrama (a story of villains, victims, and heroes).[15] The genre of consumer guide translates such prognoses into guidance for individuals to achieve success. Most writers on higher education, and on education generally, weave together these genres to narrate the impasse as a crisis and to offer guidance for navigating it. Despite their different ways of combining these genres, they share a narrative on the microhistorical level of an individual life: the romance of education, that is, a person's ideal life trajectory as ascending the levels of education toward autonomous self-governance. This romance provides the narrators with a shared subject form to be cast with a variety of actors in their metanarratives for different political projects.

Examples of combinations of melodrama and jeremiad are legion in leftist narratives about higher education. For example, Suzanne Mettler's *Degrees of Inequality: How the Politics of Higher Education Sabotaged the American Dream* gives a jeremiad about a "tragedy that has befallen the U.S." since the 1980s with higher education policies that "have deteriorated or gone off course," thereby leading to a decline of the possibility of pursuing "the American Dream" through higher education.[16] She combines this with a melodrama about the villains of political partisans, plutocracy, owners and shareholders of for-profit colleges, and universities that shift costs onto students. Their victims are students who suffer inequality of access, low graduation rates, and crushing debt, as well as taxpayers who finance for-profit colleges' federal student aid. The heroes are the reformers of higher education who counteract the neoliberal policy developments and who maintain the legacy of mid-twentieth-century public policies that "ushered in a golden age of educational opportunity."[17]

This theme is also seen in a recent book in the field of critical university studies, Christopher Newfield's *The Great Mistake: How We Wrecked Public Universities and How We Can Fix Them*. He proclaims a "crisis within public universities."[18] He narrates this crisis with a progressive jeremiad, seen

in the subtitle of his book, as well as in his assumption that higher education is "a public good socially defined," an ideal that should be renewed.[19]
His subscription to the romance of education is also seen in his ideal of
"collective enlightenment" as a solution for "the planet's problems."[20] He
portrays a melodrama with enemies of "politicians, bankers, *and* university officials" who "have tacitly worked together to generate the student
debt explosion," as well as the "policy choice" of privatization, which
has wreaked havoc on the victims of students and faculty.[21] The heroes
in his story are those academics and policy-makers who can understand
and amplify the narrative of "university education as a public good," and
thereby, motivate public investment in higher education that will create
a "virtuous cycle" of economic benefits.[22]

While both left and right narratives combine jeremiads and melodramas in order to foster political mobilization for reform, some writers take a
less overtly political approach. They deploy another genre, the consumer
guide, which aims to help individuals succeed within the status quo. An
example of this is Jeffrey Selingo's *College (Un)bound*, a best-seller by an
editor of the *Chronicle of Higher Education*. The book begins with a brief
narrative of crisis that combines a jeremiad and a melodrama. Selingo
engages the reader's interest by raising tensions between the hopes of a
"revolution" in higher education from new technologies and the dangers
of losing "the critical role higher education plays in preparing the whole
person to be a productive citizen in a democratic society."[23] Rather than
grappling with this impasse, he falls into timeworn genres of storytelling.
He narrates a melodrama of administrators as villains with "ego-driven
desires . . . to keep up with competitors and rise in the rankings," as well
as faculty members who "cling to tradition despite incentives to experiment."[24] Students and their parents are cast as victims of increasing tuition
and debt while their degrees lose value. But they can also become heroes
through appreciating the "revolution" brought on by "disrupters" who
introduce new technologies for making campuses "unbound," such as
massive open online courses (MOOCs) and data-driven "personalized
education." He combines this melodrama with a jeremiad about how
"colleges have lost their way in the last decade," with corporatization
leading them to lose "focus on what had been and should be their primary

mission—teaching students and researching the big discoveries."²⁵ Instead
of returning to past higher education practices to realize these past ideals,
Selingo's melodramatic narrative prescribes an embrace of technological
"disruption" as the best way to adapt to higher education's future.

This acceptance of an inevitable future is implied in the subtitle of
Selingo's book: *The Future of Higher Education and What It Means for
Students*. Rather than interrogating different perspectives on the historical, political, and economic conditions that resulted in the corporatization of universities, Selingo presents one image of this history as if it is
definitive. For example, he says nothing about the historical impact of
the Black freedom movement on expanding access to higher education in
the 1960s and 1970s and about the anti-Blackness of conservatives who
implemented neoliberal policies in response.²⁶ In fact, he says nothing at
all about historical and contemporary racism in higher education.

Rather than grappling with contested interpretations of history and
visions of what is to come, Selingo deploys reified images of past and future, co-constituted with a race-neutral image of a static individual in the
present, one who is "bound" for college. Selingo's title, *College (Un)bound*,
plays off of an ambivalence between two meanings of "(un)bound" in
relation to "college." On the one hand, it refers to the image of a person
on an ascending, individualized, and individualizing trajectory into higher
education—that is, as "bound" for it. On the other hand, "unbound"
refers not to the possibility of persons rejecting that normative trajectory
but rather to how, with disruptive technologies, "the traditional college
is becoming unbound—its students less tethered to one campus for four
years and its functions, from courses in a fifteen-week semester to majors,
no longer in a one-size-fits-all package."²⁷ Through deploying this double
meaning, Selingo articulates a particular interpretation of the impasse
around higher education, framed from a perspective that highlights certain
tensions while obscuring others. However, neither reading of "(un)bound"
puts into question the individualizing trajectory of education. Instead,
he pitches his book as a consumer guide for an audience of neoliberal
self-entrepreneurs to make more profitable choices about "unbound"
higher education.

Prescribing ways for students, parents, faculty, and administrators to cope and succeed as individuals within neoliberal capitalism, Selingo and other techno-evangelists for higher education offer a neoliberal consumerist response to, and escape from, the impasse of the present.[28] The neoliberal consumerist approach eschews any sort of broad historical narrative as a basis for prescribing reforms. Yet it does share a narrative with most leftist approaches to higher education, a narrative on the microhistorical level of an individual life: the *education romance*. Each of these approaches affirms the life trajectory of a person rising through some process of education, however defined. Taking the romantic narrative of education for granted provides a stabilized subject form to be filled with a cast of actors in their metanarratives. These seemingly divergent political projects prescribe a common concept, education, for how a person should tell a major portion of the story of their life.

THE ROMANTIC NARRATIVE OF EDUCATION:
AN EPISTEMOLOGY OF EDUCATED IGNORANCE

In public discussions about education in the United States, it goes without saying that some kind of formal education is a necessary good—a sure path to a good life for each and a good society for all. A general story of education tends to be abstracted from any particular personal stories— neglecting the differences among them—and presented as a necessarily good thing. Consider how institutional and popular discourses of education embed this positive valuation in their imagery of a person's normative educational trajectory: "rising up" from pre-K to grade 12, graduating as opposed to "dropping out," entering "higher" education, and continuing into the highest realm of "masters" and "doctorates." The romantic story of a heroic individual climbing the educational ladder higher and higher, while overcoming obstacles at each rung, toward the good life—to success, security, autonomy, independence, maturity, and happiness—is almost never questioned.

Who promotes the romantic story of education, and why? To give examples, I offer two vignettes. The first is from the College Board, the U.S. nonprofit organization that prepares and administers the SAT and Advanced Placement (AP) Program. Their "You Can Go!" campaign aims to motivate people to apply for college by presenting profiles of student "success stories": "These college students worried something would hold them back, but they made it. See how." The following vignette is of Jonathan W., an African American sophomore at a public two-year college, with a family income in the $20,000–40,000 range.

His obstacle

After playing varsity football in high school, Jonathan was ready to take his game to the college level and he looked into athletic scholarships. But when his grandmother died, he was no longer so sure about his college plans. "She had passed and I took it hard, so I put everything off. She couldn't even get to go to my graduation . . . so it really just messed me up."

Without any financial support from family, Jonathan also knew any further education would be his own responsibility. "I had a burden on myself to pay for college. I didn't have extra help."

How he overcame it

Even though he didn't go to college right away, Jonathan was driven by two things: the promise he'd made to his grandmother to further his education and the desire to prove something to others. "I just wanted to succeed . . . My biggest fear was failing, so I've done everything in my power to not fail." . . .

He also wanted to stay close to home for emotional support in case he needed it, so for him it was the perfect fit.

Jonathan wasn't embarrassed to ask about financial aid. "I went in with confidence. I needed help, but knew once I received help I was going to take college seriously. That's how I looked at it." He took the time to learn the process and evaluate all the forms of aid. He approached the financial aid office at his college for guidance. They gave him information on grants and he went online and applied.

Life at college

Jonathan finds the work in college much more intense than in high school. He balances his studies with a part-time job at an airline, which helps pay extra expenses. "I don't think college is hard; it's time-consuming. If you can manage your time, you can do well."[29]

The next vignette is from the website of an online college, Rasmussen College, called "College Success Stories: 5 Students Like You Who Made

It Through." This story is about Krystl Taylor, a white woman who is characterized as "the young parent":

> Navigating college life while fresh out of high school can be a challenge, especially at a large university. When you add the responsibilities of being a parent to that challenge, it is easy to see how some might struggle. Nursing student Krystl Taylor learned all about that experience when she first enrolled in college.
>
> "I was one of the few students married with kids," Taylor says. "I felt kind of alone because there weren't a lot of students that could relate to my life."
>
> Taylor eventually left the larger state school for Rasmussen College, where the flexibility of online classes eased the logistical issues that come with raising a family and attending school.
>
> The staff has also gone above and beyond to provide her with the one-on-one support that was lacking at her previous school—one instructor even provided her with a walk through of a subject late on a Saturday night. Taylor is expected to graduate in 2014, thanks in part to that support. The significance in graduating isn't just the degree, but the example she has set for her children.[30]

In each vignette, the authors draw selectively on the student's personal experiences in order to compose a particular narrative. Conversely, they exclude or neglect other parts of those students' experiences. The narrators' criteria of inclusion and exclusion are shaped by their organizations' purposes. The College Board is trying to motivate students to apply to college generally, and Rasmussen wants students to apply to their college. Their websites compose sets of narratives in ways that exclude students with life stories that would go against these purposes. They have no stories of people who avoided college while still enjoying a good life. Nor do they include stories of people who had bad experiences in high school or college that they never overcame or that irreparably scarred them, such as bullying, sexual abuse, or mountains of student debt. Such stories might turn off potential students—they might kill the romance with education.

These vignettes exemplify the romantic genre of stories about education. This is seen in *how* the narrators frame their stories. In the College

Board's snapshot of Jonathan, his story is framed with the linear sequence of, first, the student facing some obstacles (with accompanying video clips categorized as "costs" and "feeling overwhelmed"), then learning to overcome those obstacles, and finally enjoying life at college. In the narrative from Rasmussen College, Krystl faces the obstacles of "the responsibilities of being a parent" and feeling isolated at a large state school. She overcomes them by leaving for Rasmussen College, where she enjoys "the flexibility of online classes" and "one-on-one support" from teachers. She also anticipates the pride she will feel upon graduating from "the example she has set for her children." The romantic genre is seen in how the narrators frame the students' processes of grappling with their *ambivalent relations to education.* They express desires for the expanded possibilities that can come from attending college, but they also share anxieties and fears about it.

In each story, the romantic aspect entails framing the student's tensions in a certain normative way. Each student is portrayed as engaging on a quest with an internalized struggle between forces of good and evil. The narrators do not use the term "evil"; rather, they use the imagined Others of education—the figures of the failure and the dropout—to stand in for the opposite of what is perceived as good. The romantic narrative frames the students as anxious of becoming such Othered figures. This framing allows for a linearly sequenced and vertically imaged narrative: the students feared that the obstacles they faced would make them into a failure or dropout, but they found a way to overcome these obstacles, thereby deadening their affective tensions and allowing them to enjoy their present situation at a higher level of education.

The simplifications of these narratives make them more easily digestible for their audience, to help them imagine themselves in the students' shoes. The romantic narrative's simplifications are composed from other elements that set the scene for the characters' actions: views of the self, autonomy, space-time, and morality. The simplifying elements draw upon views prevalent in commonsense imaginaries: a view of the self as unified, bounded, and desiring security; a view of autonomy as individualized and atomized; a view of time with a sequential past, present, and future and abstracted from spatially located bodies and places; and a view of morality as reducible to a binary of good versus evil, with evil personified as Others.[31]

Narratives of crises in education harmonize with the education romance through their shared reliance upon these background assumptions. The imaginary of a unified, bounded self and atomistic autonomy allows for framing people's ambivalent relations to education in a certain way. Subscribing to this lens shapes how one interprets and acts upon that ambivalent relation. Rather than exploring the manifold possibilities for interpreting this relation, the commonsense framing subsumes it under a view of an ambivalent self—that is, a self seen as carrying the ambivalence internally within its spatially defined boundaries and as having to grapple with it through one's own individualized autonomy. Framing the self as *ideally* bounded, secured, unified, and individually autonomous, any relations that would disrupt these supposedly ideal qualities are portrayed as negative. Affects produced through this negative framing—such as anxiety about the stability of the self's boundaries—discourage exploration of the ambivalent relations and, instead, encourage subscription to framings that evade and suppress these relations.

An audience that subscribes to this imaginary of the bounded self is more likely to accept crisis narratives wherein the self is seen as in crisis. Acting as blind spots in the commonsense imaginary, narratives of crisis and the romantic story of education complement each other. The crisis narrative frames a moral distinction between past and future, asking, Where did we go wrong?[32] This question diverts people's attention away from possibilities for them to study their ambivalent relations with education in the present impasse. Through the lens of a crisis narrative, the responsibility for such studying might be abandoned to crisis managers, who are seen as qualified to manage the ambivalent relation through their expertise, which supposedly gives them knowledge about the past and prognoses for the future. Alternatively, one might anoint oneself as the manager of one's own crisis. Either option makes one more likely to subscribe to the romantic story of education: either to legitimate the crisis managers' expert credentials or to frame education as the pathway for oneself to gain capacities for self-management. Either option involves reproducing subscriptions to the imaginary of education, crisis, security, and the commonsense views of self, autonomy, space-time, and morality. By recirculating this imaginary, people suppress their reflections on their ambivalent relations to education. Subscribing to these images encourages them to forget the ambivalence in favor of pursuing one of its sides: reinvestment in education. Conversely, this imaginary prescribes an ideal of security in choosing to avoid the alternative path of becoming one of education's Others, a failure or a dropout.

Crisis narratives involve the romance of education in multiple, interconnected ways. First, education stories entail romantic narratives on an individual level, as described, for example, in the above vignettes from the College Board and Rasmussen College. Second, education itself is romanticized—that is, the education-based mode of study is treated as natural, inevitable, and progressive while neglecting alternative modes of study. Third, the university itself is framed as a subject—a romantic hero—in narratives about the American nation, such as "democracy's college." Fourth, certain groups of people, such as faculty, are portrayed as potential heroes for revitalizing the university (often so that it can take on its own romantic role in the national narrative). The latter is seen in the melodramatic narratives in books that treat the impasse of higher education as a crisis. These potential heroes are portrayed as being capable of rational, moral persuasion to take on their role as heroes. The first and fourth forms of romance are interconnected: the potential heroes are framed as having been made into rational and moral actors through education.

Examining the connections between these four forms of education-romance narratives, we can better understand how the education-based mode of study is co-constituted with a certain mode of world-making, particularly that of liberal-capitalist modernity. In the self-referential circularity of these romance narratives, the boundaries of actors at multiple scales (individual, university, and nation) are constructed through narratives that cross-reference each other. This allows for a perpetual distraction from reflection on the contradictions and failures of the modernist world-making project. These narratives construct an epistemology—a way of knowing—that perpetually diverts attention from—that is, (re)produces ignorance of—critical perspectives on the modernist world-making project. They constitute an epistemology of ignorance, a particular education-focused one, that complements the epistemologies of white ignorance and settler ignorance that (re)produce ignorance of modernity's dark undersides of coloniality and white supremacy.

W. E. B. Du Bois once critiqued "the deliberately educated ignorance of white schools."[33] Borrowing his concept, I see an "educated ignorance" produced by the narratives of crisis and education romance in the genres of jeremiad, melodrama, and consumer guide. These narratives serve to short-circuit studying of the impasse and to offer simplified solutions to the crisis. Because of this simplifying, short-circuiting of reflection, I see these narratives as part of an "epistemology of educated ignorance." I coin this phrase as a variation of Charles Mills's theory of an "epistemology of white ignorance."[34] In general, an epistemology of ignorance is a way of *knowing what not to know* in order to maintain some dominant way of being in the world, whether white supremacy, colonialism, patriarchy, capitalism, or—as I argue—the education-based mode of study. An epistemology of *educated* ignorance is not only a lack of critical perspectives on how education is bound up with forms of oppression, but also what Linda Alcoff calls "a substantive epistemic practice" or "a pattern of belief-forming practices" that creates the effect of systematic ignorance about the oppressive features of the education-based mode of study.[35]

The epistemologies of educated ignorance and white ignorance supplement each other. I see a prime example of this in the work of a canonical philosopher of education, John Dewey. In his analysis of Dewey's work, Frank Margonis finds that Dewey has "structured silences" about racial segregation, U.S. imperialism, and the doctrine of Manifest Destiny. Despite his stand against the racial reasoning that underlies "intelligence testing and vocational tracking in schools," Dewey's "discussions of 'cultural pluralism' exhibited a remarkable—yet common—obliviousness to the social processes of racial segregation that explained what Du Bois called the 'color line.'"[36] I contend that Dewey's white ignorance is intertwined with his subscription to an epistemology of educated ignorance. In *Democracy and Education* he calls for a renewal and universalizing of public education but he neglects to say anything about the racial segregation that severely limits the extent to which such an ideal could be realized.[37] His only mentions of "race" refer to the "human race" as a whole rather than the specific problems of white supremacy, racial inequality, and segregation in America. In his romantic promotion of public education he ignores, and thereby naturalizes, how the racially segregated and unequal education system reinforces racial and economic inequalities and hierarchies in society more broadly. Attending to people's experiences of the oppressive sides of these segregations, inequalities, and hierarchies provides a basis for putting the education romance into question.

KILLING THE ROMANCE BECAUSE ACADEMIA IS KILLING MY FRIENDS

For the stories of crisis and education romance to circulate, their audience must identify with the heroes of the stories and distinguish themselves from the Others of education. But what would happen if we took the perspective of those who are treated as Others? What if we took seriously the Others' own ambivalent relations to education? We might see the braided narratives of crisis and education romance begin to unravel.

For perspectives of people who tend to be stigmatized as the Others of educational success, I draw vignettes from a blog called *Academia Is Killing My Friends*. Most of the submissions are anonymous. The blog's creator describes its genesis:

> I am a final year PhD student in the Social Sciences. Last year a fellow PhD student committed suicide after being harassed by a lecturer. I got angry and made this site. This site is a response to the cultures of violence, fear and silence I have witnessed and experienced in my academic community. Sexual harassment, mental illness and unpaid labor are the accepted and expected norms. Abusive academics are well known and yet remain in the community. We are powerless and afraid of backlash, unemployment and failure. All of this gets worse as public spending is cut and universities become increasingly neoliberal institutions. This site is a "fuck you" to the silence and fear. It is, I hope, a space where we can share our stories of abuse, exploitation and suffering in academia.[38]

The following are two anonymous stories from this website. The first is about experiences in graduate school:

My supervisor discriminated against me because I was a mother. When I decided to start a family during my PhD my supervisor told me mothers couldn't be good academics. When I ignored her she demanded I hand in work until 3 days before my due date. I went back baby in arms at 3 weeks, finishing my master's with honors and diving into my PhD. She spent the rest of the year telling me I was dumb and pregnancy and motherhood had ruined my academic brain. I finally dropped out of the program because I was at the point of a nervous breakdown and had to prioritize my daughter. It was a great decision.[39]

The second is about the experiences of an undergraduate:

When I was an undergraduate, I wanted nothing more than to join a lab, get my PhD, and do something to contribute to science at large.

I managed step one, and joined a small molecular bio lab at my university as an undergraduate researcher. Immediately, the professor running the lab expected me to be there 10 hours a day, 6 days a week. I wasn't being paid, of course. I didn't get my own project, either. Any paid work I needed to do, he expected me to do around the time I was supposed to be working for him.

That wasn't all. I was constantly getting comments from the professor, like, "You really need to exercise more," and "This experiment is so easy, even you should be able to do it." Constantly. Day in, and day out. . . .

As a direct result, I developed pretty severe anxiety and depression issues. I was on the verge of a complete breakdown and it became apparent even to the professor I was working for.

His reaction was, "Have you tried exercising more?"

I ended up not going into academia at all. I'm almost certain I would have gone on to grad school if I'd gotten into a less terrible professor's lab, but now even the thought of going back into research puts me on the edge of a panic attack.[40]

These narratives present experiences that disrupt the romantic genre of education stories. They begin with a similar premise: presenting students who have ambivalent feelings about education, desiring success while feeling anxiety, fear, and shame. But in opposition to the romantic narratives, they do not frame the students' negative emotions as mere obstacles to be overcome. Instead of subscribing to a linear, vertically rising narrative, these students continue to grapple with their past emotional experiences in the present. Unlike a romantic narrative in which the protagonist amplifies her "good" qualities by distinguishing herself from an Other, in these stories the narrator takes on the role of someone who might be figured as Other, such as a dropout.

The students in these stories do not accept such a normative framing. Instead, they problematize it by describing relations of co-constitution between those who, in dominant discourses, would be framed as Other and those who would be framed as "good." They mess with the romantic binary of good versus evil. In the first vignette, a person who has achieved the valued level of a PhD, the supervisor, incites the young mother's feelings of anxiety by calling her dumb and shaming her for having a child, thereby contributing to her leaving graduate school. Rather than accepting a stigmatizing label of "dropout," the young mother affirms her exit: "It was a great decision." In the second story, the professor running the lab submits the undergraduate lab researcher to body shaming, belittling, and overwork that causes anxiety and depression, thereby killing the undergraduate's desire to attend grad school.

Reflecting on such stories can be the basis for people to take an alternative approach to grappling with their ambivalent relations to education—an alternative to the romantic story that treats their negative feelings about education as obstacles to be overcome. While the romantic story requires background scenery of the commonsense imaginary of the self, autonomy, space-time, and morality, the reflections in these vignettes gesture toward an alternative imaginary. Through framing their own selves and their capacities for action as co-constituted in relation with those of other people, their stories imply relational views of the self, autonomy, and ethics.[41] Likewise, in their descriptions of time—"When I ignored her she demanded I hand in work until 3 days before my due date"; "the professor running the lab expected me to be there 10 hours a day, 6 days a week"— they gesture to a relational view of time as grounded in particular bodies and places, in "temporal architectures" that relate the temporal privileges of some as interdependent with the oppressive temporal experiences of others.[42] Eschewing the romantic story's simplistic moral binary of good versus evil, their stories invoke a messy, complex view of responsibility that calls for grappling with intertwined ethical and political impasses.

Academia Is Killing My Friends presents "a space where we can share our stories of abuse, exploitation and suffering in academia."[43] Normally, people try to grapple with these experiences on their own, which can reinforce their feelings of isolation, anxiety, and depression. This blog offers part of an antidote with its space for sharing experiences and expressing empathy with each other. Yet it is merely a beginning for building the kinds of relationships necessary to change the institutional conditions that underpin these horrible experiences. Some of these stories run the danger of overemphasizing the actions of individuals—such as a cruel PhD supervisor or a toxic professor—highlighting a few bad apples at the neglect of institutional conditions. Focusing only on narratives of those who are marginalized and oppressed as Others—and on the particular individuals who are oppressing them—can lead to cynicism about possibilities for more systemic change. For broadening our imaginative horizons, we need also to listen to stories of those who take radical perspectives on the institutions, asking political questions about how to organize to change them.

ORGANIZING WITH AMBIVALENT RELATIONS TO EDUCATION

For this book I interviewed thirty-five people engaged in organizing within, against, and beyond universities. Coming from different positions as undergrads, grad students, and faculty, they shared various experiences of their ambivalent relations to education.[44] In addition to the ethical tensions from the above vignettes around feelings of anxiety, depression, and shame in relation to education, these organizers experience another, related set of political tensions. Their critical feelings about the education system—their motives to organize for systemic change—are in tension with their desires to accept the status quo so as to compete and succeed, or at least survive, within it. Collectively organizing to change education institutions creates friction with their individualized ascent up the levels of the education imaginary's normative trajectory. How people are situated in ways particular to their bodies and places—with respect to structures of labor, race, gender, class, sexuality, ability, nationality, and so forth—strongly conditions their experiences of these ethical and political tensions. The following vignettes of such experiences are told from three different labor positions: graduate student, contingent faculty, and tenure-track faculty.

At the time of my interview with Carolina Sarmiento in 2012, she was a graduate student-worker at the University of California, Irvine, and a community organizer at the Mexican Cultural Center in Santa Ana, California. She discussed the tensions she experienced as a woman of color whose life intersects multiple worlds.[45] She expressed the difficulties of building relationships across the divisions between the university and the working-class, 95 percent Latinx community of Santa Ana where she had grown up. She addressed the challenges of community-engaged projects for university students,[46] and she spoke to the tensions that she grappled with "individually, as a Chicana student":

> I think it's tough because a lot of the things that I've done that are most valuable haven't been through the classes but have actually been through mentorships with other Chicanas who feel completely lost in the university system. So, your TA hours are packed with people of color who have questions about what it means to be at the university. It becomes a lot of mentorship. . . . Getting through the system as a woman of color, trying to talk to your advisors about how important your community work is—you need to find an advisor that's willing to guide you despite the fact that you're paving this really different road than what they want you to do. You're gonna do all these community meetings all the time, and I spend half of my time at this collective community space, and I find that of more worth than my PhD.

After finishing her PhD, Carolina gained a tenure-track faculty position where she continues to grapple with these tensions; as she said, "I don't think it's gonna stop even if I become a professor."

Most faculty do not enjoy the privileges of a tenure-track position. Contingent—that is, non-tenure-track—faculty make up over 70 percent of instructional staff appointments in U.S. higher education (not even counting the many PhD holders who cannot find employment and are eventually pushed out of academia).[47] As contingent faculty, they experience the tensions of higher education differently from those on the tenure track. On the one hand, their long professionalization process—years of graduate study and having other professionals certify their capacities through exams and degrees—habituates them to aspire to an academic career. On the other hand, they find their professional capacities systematically undervalued in the precarious, competitive, stultifying, and exploitative conditions of adjunct life.

The following excerpt is from an interview with Matthew Evsky (pseudonym), who was working as an adjunct at the City University of New York and organizing with the Adjunct Project at the time of the interview.[48] He speaks to the tensions between contingent faculty and tenure-track faculty in their union, the Professional Staff Congress (PSC). Their bargaining unit of twenty-five thousand people has a majority of contingent faculty, but they are relatively disempowered within the union.

> The situation in the PSC is that you have a large group of people who are not becoming members, but of that group of people, it's overwhelmingly contingents. Why? Obviously all the reasons we can imagine: you just arrived on a campus, you don't have an office, you don't have any support, you don't know if you will be a worker there later on. I haven't been on every campus, but from my experience at Queens, there is not a lot of general grassroots-type organizing by the PSC that would put you in contact with other organizers. So, you have this huge group that is well-represented in the bargaining unit, but under-represented in the membership, and that process gets starker the higher up in the ranks that you go in the PSC.

Contingent faculty need a union to improve their labor conditions, but those very conditions hinder their participation in a union. Organizers must grapple with this tension.

For faculty who enter the elite realm of tenure-track positions, despite having relatively greater security of employment, their tensions are still multiple and complex, especially for those who participate in political organizing. In an interview, George Ciccariello-Maher spoke about the tensions he experienced while attempting to engage in different types of struggles across the university-community divisions when he was a graduate student-worker at UC Berkeley.[49] After moving to Philadelphia to become an assistant professor at Drexel University, he continued to navigate between his roles of working in academia and organizing with radical collectives. He noted that the capacities to negotiate such tensions require remembering that "the best education is the struggle" and to avoid subscribing to "academic alibis":

> I think, first and foremost, academia is a job, and I think our first fuck-up is when we forget that—when we think that it's, like, the expression of our species being, or when we think that education is the future. I teach at a university in which students go here, they study, and then they go get a job. Of course I think it's great to engage in pressing them, in making them look at things a little more critically, and definitely seizing onto a few of them and pulling them in a more radical direction. But, I would be fooling myself if I confused this with my political work. Unfortunately, people fool themselves every day by doing precisely that, and I think, as I said earlier, it's an alibi to not do actual political work, to not engage in struggle.

Ciccariello-Maher is not rejecting the potential importance of classrooms as spaces where political work can happen, but rather he argues that "we need to be more direct about separating our jobs from our political work." Since our interview, George has become embroiled in controversies over his political public speech, such as a tweet critical of the neo-Nazi idea of "white genocide." In December 2017 he resigned from Drexel, explaining that, "after nearly a year of harassment by right-wing, white supremacist media outlets and internet mobs, after death threats and threats of violence directed against me and my family, my situation has become unsustainable."[50] He implicitly critiqued Drexel for bowing to right-wing "pressure, intimidation, and threats" and called, instead, for "making our campuses unsafe spaces for white supremacists."

The above stories give different perspectives of people organizing within, against, and beyond universities. Their experiences not only disrupt the romantic education narrative but also point beyond education to alternative modes of study. By grappling with their experiences of ambivalent relations to education, these organizers break out of the commonsense imaginary that forms the background for the education romance—the bounded, security-desiring self (in contrast with Others), atomistic autonomy (in contrast with collective dependency), dichotomized space-time, and a binary morality. Instead, they engage in relational ethics and politics, breaking out of these dichotomous ways of imagining.

Through collectively organizing within, against, and beyond the university, they create alternatives to the commonsense imaginary. For opening our horizon of possibility to alternative imaginaries, we can reflect on their experiences as the basis for disrupting the taken-for-granted narratives of crisis and education. To explore these possibilities, I offer new conceptual "toys," such as "modes of study."[51] Rather than relying on "expert" academics who narrate "crises" of higher education, the concept of modes of study allows for framing organizers as sophisticated theorists of their own struggles. They raise and engage with political questions about the conflicts between the education-based mode of study and its alternatives. Thereby, they counteract the tendency of education theorists to bury these conflicts.

POLITICAL QUESTIONS ABOUT CONFLICTING MODES OF STUDY

Despite their radical aspirations, critical theorists of education have perpetuated the education romance and other elements of an epistemology of educated ignorance. Some have begun to put the education romance into question, but they remain limited in the extent of their critique. They tend to present some definition of "education" or "learning" or "study" as an *ideal* mode of study without attending to the political conditions from which that ideal emerged and in which it would be applied. Thereby, they depoliticize and dehistoricize the concepts of education, learning, or study and obscure their own political projects. As an antidote, my concept of modes of study offers a way beyond their limitations with a political theory that de-romanticizes education and destabilizes epistemologies of educated ignorance.

The concept of modes of study allows for a deeper infusion of political questions into discussions that usually center the concepts of education or learning. For analyzing any practice of studying, the lens of modes of study enables raising many political controversies about the composition of different means, relations, and ends of study. At a micropolitical level, controversies can be raised about a studying practice with respect to its participants' interacting processes of cognition, which Charles Mills distinguishes as "perception, conception, memory, testimony, motiva-tional group interest, and . . . differential group experience."[52] Questions about these processes could include the following: What political forces shape the participants' perceptions and conceptions? Why are some things remembered and others forgotten? Whose testimony counts as legitimate? How does the differentially situated character of the participants' group membership—by gender, sexuality, race, class, and so forth—affect their conceptions? Revealing such controversies can open myriad possibilities for resistance in everyday life.

By contrast, a focus on education or learning tends to depoliticize, suppress, and foreclose engagement with these controversies, because these abstractions presuppose ready-made answers to how the means, relations, and ends of studying should be composed. "Education" and "learning" are both *humanist* concepts: they imply and center the human subject as the one who is educated and learns. This humanist framing is associated with certain modernist dichotomies—for example, human versus animal and social versus natural—that provide shortcuts around engagement with controversies about any practice of studying. These hu-manist concepts are key parts of the epistemology of educated ignorance. Critical theorists of education have taken some steps toward dismantling this epistemology, but they still perpetuate aspects of it.

A trailblazer of popular education, Paolo Freire, is explicit about the association between different forms of education and different political projects. He sets out preconditions for undoing the epistemology of educated ignorance: recognizing the political character of any mode of study and being explicit about the politics of the mode of study that one promotes. He opposes the approach of "banking education"—in which teachers "deposit" their narrative in the students—with his approach of "problem-posing, dialogical education," in which all participants are simultaneously both students and teachers. He frames these approaches as bound up with conflicting political projects of oppression and liberation ("humanization," "revolutionary futurity"), respectively.[53] In criticizing "banking education," Freire also breaks away from some other elements of the epistemology of educated ignorance, especially the belief in a hi-erarchical relationship of the authority of the teacher's knowledge over that of the students. Yet in his promotion of dialogical education, Freire remains wedded to a concept of education that is associated with the political projects of humanism and modernity/coloniality. This is seen in some modernist distinctions that he deploys, such as between human and animal, distinguishing the former as capable of treating the self as an object of reflection.[54] He uses modernist abstractions such as "full humanity," "authentically human," and "authentic education" that serve as shortcuts to an ideal normative vision while short-circuiting engagement with complex political controversies about the means, relations, and ends of studying.[55] Perhaps unwittingly, his use of these abstractions sets up a need for an "educator of educators," that is, one who has the expertise to teach this complicated jargon to aspiring dialogical educators.

More-recent critical theorists of education share Freire's adherence to some elements of an epistemology of educated ignorance. For example, one of the most renowned contemporary philosophers of education, Gert Biesta, continues to romanticize education in his recent book *The Beautiful Risk of Education*.[56] Biesta gets caught in tautological and paradoxical formulations (e.g., "the language of learning tends to obscure those dimensions that make education educational"),[57] because he is stuck in a humanist framing of politics and study. Similar to Freire, Biesta relies on an anthropocentric view of politics, with a distinction of humans from animals as political, "speaking beings."[58]

Another example is an important recent book in the critical philosophy of education, Jan Masschelein and Maarten Simons's *In Defense of the School: A Public Issue*.[59] The authors theorize the school as a terrain of political struggle in which the ruling class has attempted to tame the school's "democratic and communistic dimension."[60] Yet the authors undercut their engagement with the complexity of these controversies by falling back on normative concepts of the school, study, and education.[61] The depoliticizing effect of such idealized concepts is seen, for example, in their promotion of the school as a "modern institution" while obscuring the history of the key role of schools in colonization (e.g., Native American boarding schools) as the underside of the construction of the so-called modern world.[62]

Another recent critical theorist of education, Tyson Lewis, develops

in *On Study* a more nuanced concept. Despite his admirable historiciz-
ing and politicizing approach to describing the educational project that
he opposes,[63] Lewis neglects to take such an approach to the educational
project he promotes. He gives different articulations of "study," but all
have some kind of positive normative valence. Lewis defines studying as
a "paradoxical state" between "education for subjectification" and "learning for desubjectification," which has the effect of returning "the studier
to a pure experience of impotentiality."[64] By describing oppositions with
other concepts *within* the concept of study itself, Lewis's concept includes
normative elements that foreclose description of political controversies.

Rather than internalizing such oppositions into the concept of study
itself, I present my concept of modes of study as a tool for describing
oppositions between alternative modes of study. The normative, idealized concepts of study in Lewis and in Masschelein and Simons, like the
idealized concepts of education in Biesta and Freire, lead them into the
problem of *wishful thinking*. By promoting an idealized concept without
engaging the political conditions of emergence and application of that
concept, they fail to consider the obstacles for people to subscribe to
that concept. Readers of their books might find their ideals of study
and education appealing, but they will be puzzled about how to bridge
the gap between the reality they experience and the authors' proposed
ideal.

The epistemology of educated ignorance relies on the assumption
that there is no alternative to education. Rejecting this assumption is the
first step to break free from educated ignorance. A group of marginalized theorists has rejected this assumption—marginalized from education studies partly because they pose a threat to those with professional
investments in the education system. A recent important work in this
tendency is Madhu Suri Prakash and Gustavo Esteva's *Escaping Education:
Living as Learning within Grassroots Cultures*. Building on the work of Ivan
Illich—famous for his *Deschooling Society*—as well as Mahatma Gandhi,
Paul Goodman, John Holt, and the Zapatistas, Prakash and Esteva begin
to break away from the epistemology of educated ignorance. They give a
critique of education and they distinguish an alternative mode of study,
"living as learning in grassroots cultures." They describe how education

is bound up with "the nonsubsistence economy—national, international, and global—whether liberal, socialist, or neoliberal . . . the very economic system that wipes out other economies—of household, commons, and community; sustaining, thereby, the educators' mythopoesis: that there are no authentic alternatives TO education; that education is a universal good; that, therefore, the educational system, currently broken, must be reformed and revamped."[65] Further, they give accounts of the political conditions of emergence and application for their proposed alternatives, such as with Gandhi's *Nai Talim*, a kind of teaching and learning that "keeps alive his people's subsistence economy," and the Zapatistas, who are "reclaiming their commons and liberating themselves from the specific oppression they are suffering at the local level."[66]

My book takes the baton from Prakash and Esteva's *Escaping Education*, building on their and others' attempts to promote alternatives *to* education. One of my main contributions is to theorize more carefully— and more usefully for praxis—the distinction between education and its alternatives. A shortcoming I diagnose in *Escaping Education* is the same flaw that I noted with other critical theorists of education: they promote a particular mode of study as a normative ideal ("living as learning within grassroots cultures") while insufficiently engaging the controversies about the contrasts and conflicts between that normative ideal and the form of education that they oppose, thereby short-circuiting the possibility for such engagement by associating their normative ideal with a constellation of normatively positive concepts.[67] They often rely on assumptions of a naturalized opposition between positively and negatively valued concepts, such as "localization" versus "globalization" and "commons" versus "enclosure." They thereby foreclose study of the politically constructed histories of these ideas and prevent reflection on how in some cases the valences of these binaries might be switched.[68] Their normative abstractions short-circuit further study of the complexity of controversies involved in the situations they examine. This leads Prakash and Esteva to give overly positive assessments—wishful thinking—about the prospects for political victories of the groups they promote, such as the Zapatistas. By contrast with their normative concept of "living as learning," my conceptual toy of "modes of study" is open to either negative or positive normative valences. This allows for more nuanced, deeper engagement with the controversies involved in the relations between what I call modes of study alternative to education and modes of world-making alternative to modernity/coloniality.

Reading accounts of Black radical and Indigenous modes of study—such as those described in the introduction with the Movement for Black Lives and land-based study in Nishnaabeg communities—can unsettle the assumption that education is the only possible mode of study. Yet more than merely exposure to alternatives is necessary for unsettling education in an enduring way. Our addictions to education have become deeply ingrained through subscribing to the epistemology of educated ignorance: not only belief in the necessity and goodness of education but also a constellation of practice-guiding beliefs that support this core belief. In order to denaturalize, politicize, and historicize some of the key narrative elements of this epistemology of educated ignorance, in the next three chapters I engage in critical genealogies of the education-based mode of study. Each chapter focuses on a different aspect of this mode of study, including naturalized beliefs about the dropout as the educated person's Other, the imaginary of ascending levels of schooling, and the mode of accounting in a pedagogy of credits and debts, now institutionalized with graded exams. With Sara Ahmed's description of the "feminist snap," these are some of the histories that spill out when we refuse to move on from the experiences of those who have snapped in and at the education system.[69]

This book's title, *Beyond Education: Radical Studying for Another World*, calls for an approach that grapples with the impasse of the present without relying on tired genres of storytelling. This approach entails not only disrupting crisis narratives but also practicing a mode of study that is *unbound* from the assumptions of the education-based mode of study. To study unbound is to engage with the world in a continual, expansive way against education's systematic short-circuiting of study with its exams, expertise, and preparation for governance. It is to study unbound from reified images of time, knowledge, and subjectivity that are entailed in the imaginary of the education romance. In the following chapters I offer tools for understanding how study has become bound within the education imaginary. Revealing the contingent history of the education-based mode of study can destabilize its appearance of necessity and open our horizons to alternative possibilities. To riff off Karl Marx's incitement to "workers of the world": we students of the world have nothing to lose but our educational chains.

2

Disposing of Threats

THE "DROPOUT" NARRATIVE AS
CRISIS-MANAGEMENT TOOL

Concern with the problems of school dropouts and their detrimental effects on other aspects of our society reached serious national proportion during the second year of the operation of the Project on School Dropouts. President John F. Kennedy specifically referred to the problem in his State of the Union message, in his education message, in his acceptance of the report on vocational education, and finally at a nationwide press conference held on August 1, 1963. At this time he referred to it as a "serious national problem," and then announced that he was allocating $250,000 from his special emergency fund to school systems for the purpose of hiring guidance counselors to visit school dropouts and potential dropouts, in order to get them to return to school.
  —Daniel Schreiber, Project: School Dropouts,
  Second Annual Interim Report (1963)

The Black people in America are the only people that can free the world, loosen the yoke of colonialism, and destroy the war machine. As long as the wheels of the imperialistic war machine are turning there is no country that can defeat this monster of the West. But black people can make a malfunction of this machine from within. Black people can destroy the machinery that's enslaving the world. America cannot stand to fight every Black country in the world and fight a civil war at the same time. It is militarily impossible to do both of these things at once.
  —Huey Newton, "In Defense of Self-Defense" (1967)

During and after World War II, Black freedom and anticolonial movements came into conflict with the liberal-capitalist establishment, creating what Howard Winant calls "a racial break," a shift in the dominant norms of public discourse such that explicitly racist narratives were no longer seen as legitimate and were displaced by formally anti-racist narratives.[1] In the United States, the military service of Black men in World War II and their return as veterans created a new context that amplified the Black freedom movement's critiques of racism. Internationally, in geopolitical competition with Soviet Communism, evidence of the United States' domestic racism sullied its projected image of American democracy. The social scientist Gunnar Myrdal narrated this racial break as a "crisis" for the liberal-capitalist establishment, as the "American dilemma" of how to respond to the "Negro problem" in a way consistent with the ideals of "modern democracy."[2] The response of the establishment, guided by Myrdal's work, was to reassert the world-making project of liberal-capitalist modernity and repackage it with a formally anti-racist framing, in contrast with white-supremacist framings. This inaugurated what Jodi Melamed calls the "racial liberalism" phase of "formally anti-racist, liberal-capitalist modernity."[3]

But these were not the only possibilities. The very movements that were pushing the establishment into crisis were also enacting world-making projects *alternative* to both white-supremacist modernity *and* formally anti-racist liberal-capitalist modernity. The U.S.-based civil rights and Black freedom movements made connections with transnational anticolonial movements, articulating visions of alternative projects, such as Black nationalism, against U.S. imperialism abroad and "internal colonialism" at home.[4] Interrelated with these overtly political movements in the 1940s, 1950s, and 1960s were movements of migration—of Black, Puerto Rican, Mexican, and poor white peoples and their cultures—across national borders, from rural to urban areas, and from the American South to cities in the North and West. The confluence of these political, migratory, and cultural movements disrupted the dominant mode of world-making in the cities in the late 1950s and early 1960s, frustrating attempts of urban governance according to liberal-capitalist, modernist principles.

In response, the liberal establishment narrated what it called an "urban crisis." This narrative was continuous with Myrdal's earlier narrative of an American dilemma but adapted to the particularities of urban migration. The liberal establishment prescribed new solutions for crisis management, constructed through a lens of modernization.[5] These solutions were framed as achievable through technocratic reform of systems and behavioral adjustments of individuals, assimilating them into the dominant white, American, liberal-capitalist, modernist culture. These social-engineering approaches—for systems and individuals—converged in the reformers' focus on education. Modernization theory prescribed expert technocrats and leaders who have gained their expertise *through education*. So, when the focus of this reform was on education institutions themselves, this provided mutually reinforcing legitimations for liberal-capitalist modernity. New education institutions were created through these reforms, including dropout-prevention programs and vastly expanded community colleges.

The expert-driven, modernist mode of crisis management was one approach to the impasse of racism in America and globally. Its promoters sought to portray it as the *only* option. But Black freedom, anticolonial, and migrant movements enacted alternative approaches to the impasse. Rather than limiting their approaches within an epistemology of educated ignorance, they grappled with the impasse through movement-embedded study. Against liberal-capitalist narratives of urban crisis, these movements asserted, "We are the crisis." The Black freedom movement rejected the universalizing claims of Western, liberal-capitalist modernity that depended upon modernist/colonial dichotomies such as rural versus urban, traditional versus modern, nature versus society, value versus waste, and space versus time.[6] The Black freedom movement disrupted and enacted alternatives to these dichotomous ways of seeing and shaping the world. For example, Black migrants to Oakland, California, integrated rural, past traditions from the South, such as armed self-defense, with the conditions of urban struggles in the present, leading to the development of the Black Panther Party.[7] Through movement-embedded study they grappled with the impasses they faced in pushing the racial break toward a mode of world-making alternative to liberal-capitalist modernity. At the same time, these movements engaged with the existing institutions of both K–12 education and higher education, seeking to appropriate their resources for movement-embedded study. Their horizontalist mode of study implicitly disrupted the vertical hierarchies of the education system, which in response were intensified and expanded with new education institutions.

This chapter takes the baton from the Black freedom movement. I reveal how interconnected narratives of modernity/coloniality and education shaped postwar liberals' construction of key institutions of the K–12 and higher education systems. To illustrate how these phenomena transformed the project of formally anti-racist, liberal-capitalist modernity while maintaining its core logic, I focus on the historical construction of school-dropout prevention.[8] In response to challenges to the liberal-capitalist modernist project from the left, the right, and migrants' cultural alternatives, such as the blues of working-class African American peoples, liberal capitalism needed to adapt in order to accommodate both left-wing and right-wing demands, as well as to dispose of the threat of migrants' alternative modes of world-making. For this purpose, the discourse around dropout problems and prevention—including narratives of "cultural deprivation" that homogenized, depoliticized, and devalued migrant peoples' cultures—served as a management tool to discipline and contain Black, Brown, and poor white people. This discourse discouraged them from rebellion and delegitimated their modes of study and world-making while assimilating them into liberal-capitalist modernity. The dropout narrative associates an emotional economy with the vertical imaginary of education: imagining the motion of dropping down toward becoming a dropout produces shame, fear, and anxiety, while imagining rising up toward becoming a graduate produces pride and desire. The dropout narrative diverts questions about responsibility for urban problems away from structural racism and the liberal-capitalist political economy and toward individuals, families, communities, cultures, and schools. As part of a wider epistemology of educated ignorance, the dropout narrative limits the kinds of questions that can be asked about responsibility for the *disposals* of young people across tracks within schools, across segregations between schools, and into carceral institutions.

Dropout-prevention programs have played a key role in the modernist project, as a humanist complement to this project's colonial, violent underside of the expansion of policing and incarceration. The dropout narrative contributed to an increased norm for high school graduation and for attendance in higher education. The deployment of this narrative changed over time as part of the liberal-capitalist establishment's response to the revolutionary struggles of the Black freedom movement, a response that enacted a shift to a new phase of liberal-capitalist modernity, from racial liberalism to liberal multiculturalism. The institution of dropout prevention persists in modified forms today as a key element in the most recent phase of this world-making project, neoliberal multiculturalism.

THE RISE OF THE "DROPOUT PROBLEM": DEFENDING LIBERAL-CAPITALIST MODERNITY

Key promoters of U.S. postwar racial liberalism constructed the school dropout as a "national problem" or "crisis" in the early 1960s. The Ford Foundation and the National Education Association (NEA) were principal funders of Project: School Dropouts, a five-year program (1961–66) that spread the "school dropout problem" narrative to schools and governments at all levels, including the Kennedy and Johnson administrations.[9] The project's creators described it as "a consultation and clearinghouse" for raising awareness of the dropout problem and for offering solutions. In his final report for the Ford Foundation and the NEA, the director of the project, Daniel Schreiber, boasted of having achieved these aims:

> The word, the school dropout, quite often only dropout, has moved from the textbooks to the news and editorial pages of our newspapers and magazines. More people are aware of the problem and its possible solutions than ever before in history [sic] of our country. The *Project: School Dropouts* played a major role in bringing this to fruition.[10]

Project: School Dropouts succeeded in widely circulating this narrative, making it an enduring fixture of American discourse. The graph in Figure 3 shows the sharp rise in usage of the phrase "school dropout" to have been coincident with the period of the project, with an approximately tenfold increase in its usage in U.S.-published books.[11] By contrast, another term for problematizing young people, "juvenile delinquent," has relatively declined in usage since the 1960s.

Why was the "dropout problem" narrative constructed and spread in the early 1960s? One possible explanation, given by Sherman Dorn in his book *Creating the Dropout*, is that "the appearance of the dropout problem

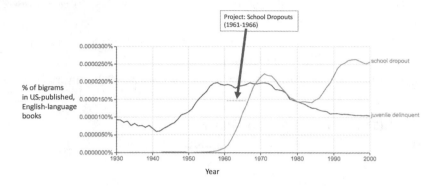

FIGURE 3. Ngram graph showing the rise in usage of the phrase "school dropout" during the period of Project: School Dropouts. Source: Google Books ngram viewer.

makes sense best as a reflection of the growing expectation of high school graduation."[12] The rise in graduation rates created a new norm of an expectation for high school graduation, such that the "dropout problem" was an expression of "criticism of the fact that that [high schools] did not keep everyone until graduation." This explanation falls short, however. If the graduation rate had gone over 50 percent by the early 1950s and the age-specific norm for graduation emerged then, Dorn's explanation cannot account for why the dropout problem narrative did not spread until the early 1960s.[13]

To understand what motivated promoters of the dropout narrative to spread it in the early 1960s, we have to situate it in the context of intertwined domestic and international threats to postwar racial liberalism. Domestically, the dropout problem was narrated in association with, in James Conant's phrase, how America was "allowing social dynamite to accumulate in [its] large cities."[14] (Figure 5 shows a political cartoon making this association.) Promoters of liberal-capitalist modernity, such as the Ford Foundation and the NEA, saw their project as under attack from multiple political forces—from the left, the right, and people whose politics were more difficult to read within the hegemonic political spectrum. In the Cold War the U.S. government and allied capitalists narrated threats from Communist countries internationally. Anticolonial

FIGURE 4. "Target . . . Dropout" ad from Project: School Dropouts *Newsletter*, September 1963. Microform reel 0255, PA 61-208, "National Education Association of the United States (06100208), 1961 June 01– 1964 May 31," Finding Aid 732E, Grants, Ford Foundation Records, Rockefeller Archive Center.

movements were overthrowing colonial regimes in Africa, Asia, and Latin America, untethering those regimes' alliances with capitalist countries and flirting with Communist alliances. As an indication of the international character of the Ford Foundation's use of school dropout programs to promote liberal-capitalist modernity, at the same time it was funding Project: School Dropouts in the United States the foundation was also funding a project to address the problem of school dropouts, or "early school leavers," in Uganda in 1961. In the justification for the latter project, it said that "'school leavers' have thus become a problem of great concern to African governments . . . they may determine how 'socialistic' these societies become."[15] This quote indicates a key concern of proponents of racial liberalism: to oppose socialism and promote liberal capitalism.

FIGURE 5. "Social dynamite" political cartoon associating the "dropout problem" with urban unrest. From Project: School Dropouts *Newsletter*, September 1963. Microform reel 0255, PA 61-208, "National Education Association of the United States (06100208), 1961 June 01–1964 May 31," Finding Aid 732E, Grants, Ford Foundation Records, Rockefeller Archive Center.

Domestically, the liberal capitalists sought to suppress what they saw as oppositional forces, including Communist organizations, labor unions, and civil rights movements. The Black freedom movement was calling for the dismantling of structural racism, including through the attainment of civil rights, desegregation, and racial equality. Civil rights struggles became increasingly militant in the late 1950s and early 1960s, such as with boycotts and sit-ins at segregated restaurants and schools.

Liberal-capitalist modernity was also under attack from the right. McCarthyite anti-Communist witch hunts associated the civil rights movement with Communism. In the early to mid-1950s the Ford Foundation had come under attack from the right for promoting desegregation through its Fund for the Advancement of Education.[16] It was subjected to right-wing congressional investigations of the Cox and Reece committees, seeking to associate the foundation's civil rights activities, as well as that of other liberal foundations, with Communism. Conservatives, especially in the U.S. South but also in the North, sought to reassert a white-supremacist form of the capitalist modernist project against the foundation's formally anti-racist liberal-capitalist vision of modernity. This Second Red Scare put the Ford Foundation on the defensive, and it shifted away from desegregation in the late 1950s.

In portraying the threats to the liberal-capitalist establishment, I want to avoid the tendency to subsume all of the political forces at play into a simplifying, linear spectrum of left versus right. That framing can obscure the political character of liberal capitalism behind a facade of neutral centrism. Conversely, it can depoliticize those modes of world-making that present alternatives to the three options portrayed in the dominant representations of the political array in the Cold War context: representations of the left as statist Soviet-style Communism, of the middle as liberalism, and of the right as conservatism. Internationally, decolonization movements were creating alternative world-making projects that burst the limited imaginative horizons of these three options, such as the Third World Project developed through international communication and meetings like the Bandung Conference in 1955.[17]

Parallel to decolonization in Third World countries, people were migrating internationally into the United States—such as with the *bracero* program that brought in an estimated 4.5 million Mexican contract laborers—and domestically across regions of the United States, especially from the South to the North and West.[18] These migrants were also enacting modes of world-making that presented alternatives to liberal-capitalist modernity, whether or not anyone explicitly framed them in such a political opposition. With the "autonomy of migration" approach, I theorize the migrants' autonomous movements as creating threats to the liberal establishment through an often "imperceptible politics" in which resistance more often took the form of "hidden" rather than "public transcripts."[19]

Rather than recognizing and validating the autonomy of the migrants, the liberal establishment narrated these threats as a migrant crisis. The liberal establishment perceived at least three kinds of threats: from the political right, from the political left, and from migrants, who were illegible in the dominant political representations. In response to the latter representational problem, they framed the migrants with new concepts, such as "gray areas" and "cultural deprivation." These concepts had political motivations and effects, but their promoters sought to portray them as apolitical. In an effort to undo this historical deception, I have two interrelated goals in the next two sections. First, I describe the political forms of the migrants' autonomous activity, focusing on working-class African Americans' "blues epistemology," as an alternative mode of world-making and study. Second, I reveal how the liberal establishment reacted to this migrant autonomy with depoliticizing representations of migrants as culturally deprived. Their narratives supplemented the liberals' creation of new institutions, with intensified enclosure and bordering practices, as counterattacks against the threats from migrants.

Migration and the Blues Epistemology as Autonomous First Strikes

During the Cold War, marginalized, non-aligned peoples enacted minor world-making projects that presented alternatives to the major, nation-state-focused projects. Much earlier, an alternative world-making project emerged from enslaved people's struggles against the plantation regime, a project that geographer Clyde Woods calls the "blues epistemology" of African American working-class intellectual traditions and social organizations.[20] Woods portrays a central narrative in American history as an epic conflict between "the plantation bloc" and "the blues bloc." The blues epistemology was developed initially by the enslaved Black southern working class, emerging "in spite of, and in opposition to, plantation powers," as a "distinct and evolving complex of social explanation and social action." The blues epistemology not only entails blues music but is a holistic, interactive "complex of language, music, and performance."[21] Although having its roots in enslaved people's modes of communication through music,

> the blues emerges immediately after the overthrow of Reconstruction. During this period, unmediated African American voices were routinely silenced through the imposition of a new regime of censorship based on exile, assassination and massacre. The blues became an alternative form of communication, analysis, moral intervention, observation, celebration for a new generation that had witnessed slavery, freedom, and unfreedom in rapid succession between 1860 and 1875.[22]

The plantation bloc's Counter-Reconstruction movement continued through the twentieth century with the southern enclosure movement. The plantation bloc transformed the Delta region "from capital-scarce, labor-intensive plantation production to capital-intensive, labor-surplus neo-plantation production."[23] One-third of the sharecropping families were evicted between 1930 and 1950, expanding the pool of wage laborers and thereby putting downward pressure on wages. Those who refused work were treated as vagabonds, jailed, and put to work in prison farms. In response to the breakdown of their communities, institutionalized violence, and horrifying work conditions, millions fled the South, with 10 percent of the South's Black population leaving during the 1940s.[24] Many sought refuge in northern cities such as Detroit, Cincinnati, New York, and Chicago: "between 1940 and 1950, the Black population in Chicago nearly doubled, from 277,000 to 492,000."[25]

An earlier wave of southern Black migrants had already brought the blues with them to Chicago, where "the blues found a comfortable home in the clubs, house parties, and other social events held in the predominantly Black South Side."[26] During the Depression, the Chicago blues continued to capture working-class African Americans' experiences of the challenges they faced, with songs such as "Broke Man Blues," "Collector Man Blues," "Hobo Jungle Blues," "Mean Old Master Blues," and "Starvation Blues." With the Depression a new "urban-industrial blues" sound emerged, as "the decline in record issues led many musicians toward experimentation and away from the formulaic blues preferred by the record companies."[27] In this experimental mode, liberated from "a commodified form of commercial entertainment," the blues were what William Barlow calls "a living cultural tradition nourishing an ethnic group hard pressed by poverty and discrimination." The blues artists became even more rooted in, and interdependent with, the local Black community's support and sustenance: "They played for their friends and neighbors at rent parties, at never-ending jam sessions on the sidewalk of State Street, or in their own homes."[28] The blues epistemology transgressed the boundaries of the white-dominated industrial city, cutting across the spheres of work, play, and study, public and private.

The blues epistemology was also contagious across boundaries of different artistic forms. Blues-grounded jazz musicians "engaged in radical experimentations in instrumentation and composition."[29] Chicago-based writers, most famously Richard Wright, "extended the blues epistemology into literature." Wright, a native of Jackson, Mississippi, described his aim of in-depth exploration of African American working-class lives as "depict[ing] a character in terms of the living tissue and texture of daily consciousness."[30] He saw the blues as both an embodiment of the "African American working-class perspective on daily life, work, and exploitation" and "a method to investigate these relations, an epistemology and the foundation for social action."[31]

The blues were what I theorize as an alternative mode of study to the mode dominant in the white world's education system. In opposition to the latter's boundaries between different spheres of life, isolating study to the school and universities, "Wright relied upon the blues epistemology to undermine the increasingly rigid boundaries being erected around forms of social action, social inquiry, artistic production, and moral discourse."[32] This blues mode of study was practiced by Wright and many others in "the Blues School of Literature," such as Margaret Walker Alexander, Ralph Ellison, and Saul Bellow. They found infrastructural, counter-institutional support in the Chicago Writers Project and the South Side Writers group, connected with the National Negro Congress. A blues movement was also influential in Black churches with the gospel blues.[33]

The world-making project of the blues epistemology involved modes of study alternative to the education mode. Blues musicians experimented with musical forms, while jazz musicians, fiction writers, and poets inflected their creative works with the blues. Much of the resources for this studying were collected and composed in institutions autonomous from the dominant institutions of the white world. Yet practitioners of the blues epistemology also sought to contest the white-dominated public schools for control over their means of studying. The public schools were terrains of struggle between alternative, conflicting world-making projects—the blues epistemology versus the white, settler-colonial, capitalist project—in association with alternative modes of study. Black teachers in the public schools taught Black students through modes of study that intersected with the blues epistemology.

African American teachers intermingled outside the schools through informal friendship and community networks as well as through more formal, autonomous African American institutions. They developed curricula in Black history, literature, music, and arts, inspired by the Chicago Negro Exposition, the South Side Community Arts Center, the DuSable History Clubs that met at libraries, and the Association for the Study of African American Life and History.[34] At DuSable High School, Walter Dyett taught thousands of young musicians, some of whom became famous jazz musicians. The Afrocentric, Afro-futurist jazz musician Sun Ra recruited many of his band members from Dyett's students.[35] Samuel Stratton taught history at DuSable and ran the DuSable History Clubs, which uncovered and discussed African American history in ways that affirmed contemporary African Americans' resistance to white attempts to suppress and devalue their cultural heritage.[36] Madeline Morgan, also a history teacher in Black public schools and a close collaborator of Stratton's, developed an alternative Black curriculum that she implemented in her own school, where, "to many black students, the units served as much needed affirmation of their presence as an integral part of the American story."[37] Morgan pushed for the curriculum's adoption in other schools, both Black and white, in Chicago and nationally. Margaret Burroughs, a "teacher, artist, poet, and activist," founded the South Side Community Arts Center in 1940, a key African American cultural institution, and the Ebony/DuSable Museum of African American history in 1961.[38] After

World War II, with the repression of leftists in the Cold War, Burroughs, like much of the African American left in Chicago, focused "on art and education even more intensely as a means of maintaining a presence in the African American community within the constraints of McCarthyism."[39]

Black parents and students were making demands on the schools and governments for more resources for these alternative modes of study within schools, whether through desegregation, more teachers, or better facilities. School-focused protests in Chicago from the 1930s through the 1950s included advocating for Black representation on the school board, calls to build new schools, petitions, letter-writing campaigns, touring the schools, protests by the Citizens Schools Committee and the Parent Teacher Associations, picketing and boycotting of the inferior-quality portable school buildings in 1936—which successfully pressured the school board to build a new school—and even burning down the portable school buildings.[40] These demands for resources for a blues mode of study, as assertions of Black autonomy in schools, were what Damien Sojoyner calls a "first strike": "Black culture as an agent of social transformation has always been a first strike against violent modalities of white supremacy."[41] To depoliticize and suppress this movement, which had transgressively mixed political and cultural activities, the white power structure in charge of the schools established new enclosures. Such enclosures of Black cultural forms "to limit Black freedom" have a long history, "exemplified by the passage of laws during the eighteenth and nineteenth centuries in the mainland colonies and the Caribbean that were aimed at preventing Blacks from playing music or congregating together, and a strict surveillance of Black spiritual practices."[42] I contend that, in reaction to Black cultural assertions in the 1950s, these enclosures took the forms of ongoing white violence to maintain segregation and the creation of new institutions to limit and enclose spaces for Black autonomous modes of study.

Liberal Reaction: Gray-washing the Blues, Depoliticizing Migration, and Internalizing Borders

On the domestic front, the liberal-capitalist elites had to respond to threats from the movements of migration, from the cultural spaces of the blues epistemology, and, interrelated, from the anti-racist struggles of the civil rights movement. With their concession to the right wing of avoiding desegregation, they needed to develop new forms of racial liberalism that could accommodate the threats from these movements without fundamentally challenging liberal-capitalist modernity. Naomi Murakawa defines "postwar racial liberalism" as "the historically grounded understanding of the American race 'problem' as psychological in nature, with 'solutions' of teaching tolerance and creating colorblind institutions . . . 'rather than as a systemic problem rooted in specific social practices and pervading relations of political economy and culture.'"[43] Racial liberalism eclipsed alternative frameworks for conceiving of race: both the conservatives' "biological racism" and the leftists' "structural racism, which situated domestic racism and colonialism abroad in an integrated critique of global capitalism."[44] Jodi Melamed describes racial liberalism as the first phase of "formally anti-racist, liberal-capitalist modernity," which has persisted to the present while shifting into phases of liberal and neoliberal multiculturalism.[45]

From the mid-1950s to the early 1960s, racial liberalism's articulation of America's "race problem" took different forms, but generally these narratives focused on projects for urban areas and prescribed solutions framed in color-blind and individualizing terms. In the mid- to late 1950s these color-blind projects included programs on the contrasted figures of "juvenile delinquents" and "talented youth," sponsored by the Ford Foundation, the Carnegie Corporation, and the NEA.[46] The narrative of "delinquency" aimed to stigmatize young people who might act subversively against the liberal-capitalist order, while those labeled as "talented" were framed as valuable for this order.

Yet the promoters of these frames found that they were insufficient for suppressing and managing anti-racist rebellions and migrant movements. The term "delinquent" has only negative connotations. If it becomes associated with a certain group of people, such as Black people, they can respond by saying, "Don't stereotype us." In the notes from a meeting of the top officials of the Ford Foundation's Gray Areas and Great Cities programs, this rationale was made explicit:

Mr. Hunter explained the importance of avoiding the approach through labeling certain youths as "potential delinquents," and Mr. Nelson rephrased this by asserting the principle that we should work on the environmental factors rather than on the individual. Mr. Ylvisaker added . . . [that] we will make no grants that might perpetuate the stereotypes which already burden the people in the gray area.[47]

This view coheres with racial liberalism's framing of stereotypes as racist, while neglecting structural racism. Similarly, the NEA claimed to avoid this problem by responding to critiques of narratives of the delinquent for using stereotypes. It criticized others for "cashing in on 'delinquency'" as a scapegoat for wider problems, because "today's youth is largely a product of his environment, and must be judged according to the culture of which he is a part."[48] The NEA continued to use the framing of "the delinquent" but claimed to be giving a social-scientific analysis of environmental factors along with it.

The NEA and the Ford Foundation sought more nuanced terms for describing racial tensions without explicitly dealing with institutional racism. They claimed to avoid stereotyping through shifting their focus away from the individual and toward environmental factors, including "culture" and "atmosphere." The turn to cultural explanations for racial differences had academic sources, with the first documented use of the terms "culturally deprived" and "disadvantaged" in an address to school psychologists at the American Psychological Association's annual meeting in 1955.[49] The NEA picked up these terms and used them in its publications, such as *Delinquent Behavior: Culture and the Individual* (1959) and *Education and the Disadvantaged American* (1962). The Ford Foundation used these terms as well, such as in its "Project on the Culturally Deprived," in which Ben Willis, Chicago's segregationist superintendent, took a leading role.[50]

In the late 1950s through early 1960s, the Ford Foundation's Gray Areas and Great Cities Projects involved grants amounting to over $30 million for projects focused on "urban problems" in six cities and the state of North Carolina. These programs' narratives were initially laced with the color-blind (covertly racist) framing of "culturally deprived." "Gray areas" was also a color-blind concept. The Gray Areas program avoided tackling racism through focusing on migrants in general, not on people of color specifically.[51] The program's officials lumped together white Appalachian migrants with Black southern and Puerto Rican migrants to the northern cities. They labeled as "gray areas" the places to which the migrants tended to move, particularly the ring between the center city and the suburbs. The director of the Gray Areas project, Paul Ylvisaker, later said that this was "strategic because if you could conceive of an overarching process within which one could deal with the *Verbotens* of race relations and so forth, and where you weren't talking black immediately, which raised all the hackles, then you had much more chance of getting a program accepted."[52] They wanted to avoid racial language for political reasons. In focusing on the "urban problems" of these new migrants, they avoided political-economic questions, including about the motivations for these groups to migrate, such as unemployment from declining agricultural economies as well as racial discrimination and segregation. Thereby, they deflected critique away from liberal capitalism.

At the same time, Ford Foundation officials denigrated the cultures of the migrants by describing them as "culturally deprived" and "disadvantaged" in contrast with the northern urban white cultures. Their focus on culture implicitly recognized the threat of autonomous African American culture—bound up with the blues epistemology—as a world-making project alternative to, and in conflict with, their dominant world-making project. Their denigration of Black culture served as a counterattack against the strength of Black cultural formations that were tied with the political organizing of the Black freedom movement against racist institutions. With Black teachers engaging in autonomous Black modes of study with students, the public schools become terrains of conflict between these alternative modes of study and world-making.

Concurrently, the liberals' rhetoric of "cultural deprivation" sought to depoliticize and obscure this political conflict. By avoiding the language of race with their color-blind rhetoric and by homogenizing all migrants' cultures together as an Other to the dominant (white) culture, they portrayed the existence of all cultures on a linear scale of modernist development, with white culture at the evolutionary pinnacle. Thereby they foreclosed the possibility of imagining alternative models of development, or alternatives *to* modernity, such as the blues epistemology. They aimed to devalue, delegitimize, and disrupt the diverse cultures of the migrants, to make them abandon their cultures in favor of assimilation into the dominant, implicitly white, productivist, heteropatriarchal culture of liberal-capitalist modernity. Their descriptions of cultures deployed modernist/colonial language, such as seen in these statements from discussions among Gray Areas project officials:

> [The programs] seek to encourage urban communities to fashion more effective ways *to speed the transition of the urban in-migrant and slum resident* of low educational achievement and inadequate work skills to full economic, social and cultural participation in the urban community.[53]

> Paul Ylvisaker sees the grey area project as a new frontier for the Foundation, indeed *a frontier for society.*[54]

The "gray areas" were treated as "frontiers" in which to colonize and modernize the cultures of the "urban in-migrant and slum resident." Willis's Chicago Gray Areas projects are one example of how these modernizing programs were enacted to avoid and delay desegregation.

In combination with programs focused on specific cities, another part of the Gray Areas programs was Project: School Dropouts, which took as its model Daniel Schreiber's New York City–based Higher Horizons project from the mid- to late 1950s. Project: School Dropouts continued Higher Horizons' centering and reifying of the vertical imaginary of education (see Figure 6). "Rising up" to "higher horizons" through education is assumed to be good, equated with adding value through discovering and realizing "human talents," in contrast with the "falling down" of the "dropout" as bad, equated with waste. Schreiber repeatedly highlights this verticalist, humanist, modernist dichotomy of waste and value as the normative grounding for the Higher Horizons project, which he cites as the model for Project: School Dropouts. For example:

> [Higher Horizons'] main premise was that, regardless of what past records and I.Q. scores might indicate, many human talents—human lives, in fact—were going to waste. . . . Far too many young lives, with all the

FIGURE 6. A political cartoon that illustrates the vertical imaginary of education, from the Project: School Dropouts *Newsletter*, September 1963. Microform reel 0255, PA 61-208, "National Education Association of the United States (06100208), 1961 June 01–1964 May 31," Finding Aid 732E, Grants, Ford Foundation Records, Rockefeller Archive Center.

potential and real talents and capabilities they embody, are being wasted and crushed. The redemption of these lives requires inventiveness and energy and dedication. It requires the school be constantly re-examined and re-thought, organized and re-organized. This is the large and formidable challenge that each potential dropout presents to us.[55]

In order to associate the cultures of migrants with "wasting" of "all the potential and real talents and capabilities," Schreiber and the NEA described them as "culturally deprived."[56] Thereby, this framing denigrated the migrant *groups'* cultures, while portraying the potential for salvaging the valuable talents of *individuals* through using education to assimilate those individuals into the dominant culture.

Figure 7 illustrates some of the key members of the actor-network that circulated the "school dropout problem" narrative and shows the network's dramatic growth between 1960 and 1964. I use the term "actor-network" to frame this figure in order to highlight the material forms of representing and circulating the dropout narrative—such as newsletters, speeches,

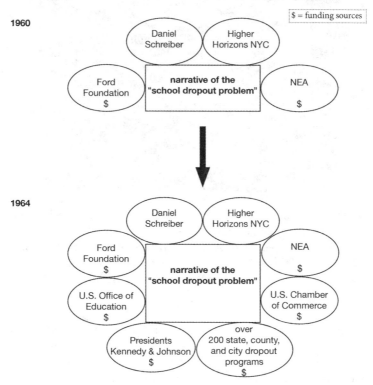

FIGURE 7. Expansion of the actor-network promoting the "school dropout problem" narrative from 1960 to 1964.

consultations, documentaries, newspaper articles, and pamphlets—as themselves actors in this network.[57] The NEA hired Schreiber, proposed Project: School Dropouts, and partly funded it. The Ford Foundation provided the majority of the funding and situated the project as part of its broader Gray Areas and Great Cities programs, which included other dropout-focused projects in specific cities. The Ford Foundation and the NEA acted as a kind of "shadow state," promoting narratives that influenced the official state on multiple levels.[58] The project acted as a "clearinghouse," disseminating information to spread the dropout narrative and receiving and filling more than fifteen thousand requests for material.[59] In the project's four years, Schreiber traveled to forty-five states, putting on conferences and workshops and consulting with school and city leaders. Over two hundred dropout programs, projects, and studies were started through state, county, and local governments.

The promoters of the dropout narrative influenced the federal government as well, inspiring the Kennedy and Johnson administrations to adopt the narrative. Their powerful platforms amplified the narrative to a national audience. On August 1, 1963, President Kennedy referred to "school dropouts" as a "serious national problem" and allocated $250,000 for dropout-prevention programs.[60] Other federal institutions picked up the narrative. The U.S. Chamber of Commerce put on a nationwide "stay-in-school" campaign and created a new division in its Education Department, the Division of Manpower Development and Training, with programs in areas of "'dropout,' youth employment, retraining and guidance."[61] The U.S. Office of Education's Cooperative Project on Pupil Accounting worked with Schreiber to create and fix a new definition of "school dropout": "A DROPOUT is a pupil who leaves a school, for any reason except death, before graduation or completion of a program of studies and without transferring to another school."[62] They spread this definition to state and local school systems through publishing it in their Pupil Accounting Handbook and including it in mailed newsletters. Stabilizing definitions is a key element of problematization by the actor-network: gaining hegemony over the meaning of words and over the normative valences associated with the words. They sought to depoliticize conflicts over the meaning of the word "dropout," such as by avoiding discussion of alternative framings of a school non-completer as a "pushout" or "riseout."

Alternative Actor-Networks for Making Another World

The promoters of the dropout narrative were forming an actor-network for a certain geopolitical world-making project, one in tune with postwar racial liberalism. By contrast, other people, especially those who were part of the civil rights movement and practicing the blues epistemology, were forming actor-networks for alternative world-making projects. Accordingly, they narrated alternative framings for problems in urban areas. Clashes between these alternative world-making projects took place in many cities across the United States. A prominent example was Chicago, one of the main sites for the Ford Foundation's Gray Areas and Great Cities programs, starting in 1960, and a recipient of its funds for dropout programs.[63]

To provide a sense of what one of these dropout-prevention programs entailed, I highlight a program in Chicago called "Experimental Work and Study Program for Potential and Actual School Drop-outs." Chicago Public Schools superintendent Ben Willis wrote a proposal to the Ford Foundation, which approved a grant of $50,000 for the program on May 22, 1961.[64] The program involved a collaboration between Chicago Public Schools and a department store company, Carson Pirie Scott & Co., that employed potential and actual dropouts in one of its stores. In his project proposal, Willis stated the wider purpose of the program as addressing the country's "serious problem" of the high unemployment rate of "young people who dropped out of school," which creates threats that "the vitality of the nation will be undermined, and our social and economic life will be jeopardized." The aims of the program are "to make these young people employable and, hopefully, to encourage them to return to school." The proposal entailed a plan for "a five-day, eight-hour-per-day program of work-study for approximately 50 unmarried boys and girls, sixteen years of age and over, who have already dropped out of school and are unemployed or who are still in school but appear to be potential drop-outs prior to high school graduation." Highlights of the program included a "one-month pre-employment program of instruction in the schools," "a regular training program of one week by the store," a one-year work program with at least minimum-wage compensation, "supervision on the job and related classroom instruction by a teacher-counselor and by store personnel," "school credit toward high school graduation," and "allocation of a portion of each week's earnings for savings or investment as part of a program of economic education."[65]

The aspects of giving school credit for work-study as well as seeing savings as a kind of "economic education" show that the program was designed to have an effect of disciplining the young people into obedient subjects for liberal capitalism—as hard workers, efficient consumers, and "productive and responsible citizens."[66] In an interim report on the program, the assistant training director from Carson Pirie Scott & Co. said, "We do not believe the youngster can benefit and learn about the dignity of the honorable 'World of Work' unless he is exposed to the crude facts of life for at least three months," before he can request "a possible change of jobs."[67] This makes clear the program's imperative to inculcate young people with a capitalist work ethic.

Seeing this Chicago program as a solution to the dropout problem requires that we treat schools as a means for tracking poor, mostly Black students into low-wage, service-sector jobs. The internal discussions of the program rarely mention race and class. The program does not analyze the reasons why students drop out but rather presents an approach to adapting and adjusting them into the labor market—that is, as a way to reduce the negative impact of dropouts on the economy. This "solution" was devised in consultation between public school officials, the Ford Foundation, and business leaders. Notably absent was any consultation with leaders of the civil rights movement, despite the fact that struggles for desegregation and racial equality were raging in Chicago at the time of the program.

The civil rights movement's calls for integration were bound up with efforts to create spaces and expand resources for Black modes of study. As a living cultural foundation for their protests in the streets, they were practicing the blues epistemology in many spaces, including the schools, such as with Dyett's jazz music training and Morgan's alternative Black curriculum. Protesters took on the superintendent of Chicago Public Schools, Ben Willis, who had defended de facto segregation. As a measure to delay integration, he expanded poorly resourced, cramped Black schools with trailers that came to be called "Willis Wagons." To protest this continued segregation, on October 22, 1963, the Coordinating Council of Community Organizations staged Freedom Day, a school boycott in which 250,000 students did not attend school and around 20,000 protesters marched in the streets (see Figure 8).[68] Instead of making "the dropout" a central focus of problematization, the civil rights movement focused its critique on the problems of structural racism, especially racial segregation and inequality of resources for schools and housing.[69]

The dropout narrative circulated publicly more strongly than the structural racism narrative. One reason is that critics of structural racism had to undo people's habituated subscriptions to a broader web of narratives that legitimated racist ideas in seemingly color-blind ways, such as the homogenizing, depoliticizing narrative of migrants as culturally

FIGURE 8. Protest during the Chicago school boycott, October 22, 1963. From the documentary *'63 Boycott* by Kartemquin Films.

deprived. Another reason is that racial liberalism's actor-network had greater financial wealth and political power for deploying its preferred narrative. In the memos and meeting notes from the Ford Foundation and NEA's Project: School Dropouts, more communication was about financial matters than about social, political, or ethical issues. A generous budget purchased media, books, and pamphlets, paid the salaries of personnel for the groundwork of building community participation and buy-in, and paid secretaries to maintain a bureaucracy around dropout projects in each city. By contrast, Black freedom movement groups seeking to dismantle structural racism had much less funds and had to do much of their organizing on a voluntary basis. Thus they could not afford, for example, to fund a "consultation and clearinghouse" campaign for pushing an alternative narrative of structural racism as the source of racially unequal rates of school non-completion.

THE DROPOUT AS A CRISIS-MANAGEMENT TOOL
FOR LIBERAL-CAPITALIST MODERNITY

Migrants were (and still are) the crisis. When Black, Brown, and poor white people migrated from the South to cities in the North and West and organized to improve their living conditions, they created a sense of crisis for promoters of liberal-capitalist modernity. The liberal establishment's crisis narrative shifted from "American dilemma" in the 1940s to "urban crisis" from the mid-1950s through the 1960s. The migrants brought into the cities their desires for world-making projects—such as working-class African Americans' blues epistemology—alternative to both white-supremacist and liberal-capitalist forms of modernity. They pursued their desires by organizing for desegregation, for redistribution and control of resources, and against race- and class-based inequalities. Their resistance and alternative modes of study hindered the smooth functioning of the cities' education systems. To the extent that these systems operated according to white-supremacist modes of ordering, the migrants threatened racial "pollution" of white education spaces. To the extent that these systems operated in a formally anti-racist, liberal-capitalist modernist mode, the migrants' demands threatened to expose the shallowness of racial liberalism's anti-racism and to debunk the myth of meritocracy that underlies the ideology of the American dream. They used the resources of schools as means for studying in modes that were co-constitutive with their organizing, such as in Morgan's alternative Black curriculum, diverting resources away from use in the education-based mode of study for producing obedient, assimilative subjects and workers and toward use in studying that shaped young people with capacities to affirm Black culture and history and to resist structural racism. The migrants also challenged the order of labor control in liberal capitalism, as desegregation could build relationships across the racial divides that hinder the working class from uniting against the capitalist class.

To say that "the migrants are the crisis" is uncontroversial. The controversy lies in how we interpret this phrase. Promoters of liberal capitalism saw the crisis of migration as one to be managed and resolved. Promoters of alternative world-making projects saw the crisis as one to be *amplified*. Liberal capitalists sought to offload their crisis onto the migrants themselves, making individualized Others pay for their crisis. The narratives and institutions around the dropout were a tool for this mode of crisis management. It was, and still is, a highly effective tool for defending and expanding the liberal-capitalist project—for directing questions about responsibility for urban problems away from the liberal-capitalist political economy and onto individuals, families, communities, cultures, and schools. Yet it also failed, and continues to fail, to completely control the desires and movements of the migrants and their descendants.

Theoretical Interlude 1: Rubbish and the Disposal of Value

The migrants' desires point toward alternative imagined life trajectories, modes of study, and world-making projects. They desire resources for studying, relating, and laboring together in ways that exceed the limits the liberal capitalists sought to impose.[70] Through drawing attention to segregations in education and housing and to inequalities and discrimination in employment and government, the migrants put into question the value scales of the liberal-capitalist modernist mode of representational order. This mode of order seeks to define school, housing, work, and government as discrete regions of life with fixed assumptions about value scales within them. As the 1970s movements Wages for Housework and Wages for Schoolwork argued, the liberal-capitalist order relies upon an ideological distinction between the sphere of "production" as a place of waged work and spheres of "reproduction," including the home and school, as places of non-work activities and, hence, as not requiring wages.[71] The Black freedom movement's critiques destabilized the liberal-capitalist assumptions by highlighting structural commonalities across these regions of life, particularly how capitalism and structural racism intertwined to produce inequalities, segregations, and discriminations. Their critiques were based upon their practical experiences of working-class Black modes of study alternative to education, such as with the blues epistemology, which intertwined these spheres of life. In order to stabilize the boundaries between these regions of life and to reassert the value scales within them, the dropout narratives frame a region of flexibility for affirming the liberal-capitalist order of value.

The dropout figure serves as a stabilizing door between the value scales of school and work. Drawing on Kevin Hetherington's theory of disposal, rather than seeing the rubbish bin as the archetypal conduit for the disposal of value, *the door* is a better metaphor.[72] Hetherington builds on Michael Thompson's distinction between three classes of objects: durable objects (high status and value), transient objects (lose status and value over time), and rubbish (little or no status and value).[73] Rubbish has a dynamic role as a blank, fluid space between durable and transient objects, as a conduit or door for objects to move back and forth between these states while maintaining an appearance of separateness between them. By describing the dropout as a kind of rubbish door, I use this theory of disposal to describe how the dropout narrative plays a stabilizing role between school and work.

The Dropout as a Rubbish Figure for
Stabilizing the Liberal-Capitalist Order

The dropout discourse links seemingly disparate narratives of automation and urban crisis. In Project: School Dropouts a recurrent narrative is fear of reduction in the value of labor due to automation. The Ford Foundation's proposal for the project defined one of its main rationales as follows: "The technological revolution, especially with the impact of automation, is rapidly diminishing the relative number of jobs available for the unskilled."[74] This narrative of a diminishing need for unskilled labor complements the narrative of the urban crisis of migrants. The project's proposal also included the rationale that this "growing unemployed youth group" would result in "unhealthy social unrest—a disgruntled, disillusioned, and unsatisfactory segment of our society." At the same time, the automation narrative diverts attention away from the origins of the urban crisis in the migrants' autonomous activity—that is, in their organizing for civil rights, appropriating resources of schools for Black modes of study, and moving across state lines, urban/rural boundaries, and urban segregations. The automation narrative implies that part of the agency creating the crisis is in the progressive forces ("the technological revolution") of liberal-capitalist modernization.

In the automation narrative, the value of the worker decreases (as a transient object). Conversely, this narrative describes the value of the graduate as increasing (as a relatively more durable object). For facilitating the complex processes of disposal and salvaging of value back and forth between these figures of the worker and the graduate, the dropout serves as a door-like figure of rubbish. This figure facilitates this process in a smooth, friction-reducing way because of its depoliticizing effects— that is, diverting attention away from the political controversies over alternative, conflicting modes of study and world-making in schools, which have alternative interpretations of the value of a graduate and a worker. As attending to these controversies could disrupt the fantasy of an apolitical, measurable value for these figures, the dropout figure's door-like function helps to reassert that fantasy. In relation to the narrative of "automation making the job market worse for job-seekers who have less formal education," the dropout figure allows for flexibility in the value of the diploma-endowed graduate. With an increasing number of graduates in a tighter job market, the graduate shifts from a durable object to a transient object with decreasing value.

The dropout figure allows for affirming the relatively durable value of the diploma, such as through deploying statistics of higher employment rates for graduates compared to dropouts. The graduate figure's appearance of measurable value partly comes from its association with other positively valued discourses, such as "talented youth" and "merit" (see Figure 9). The graduate's appearance of value also comes from narrating it in contrast with framings of the dropout in association with other discourses—delinquency, criminality, dependency, social burden, deviance, and so forth—that imply a kind of waste or by-product of the education system with zero value or as the abject Other of value. Further waste narratives in Project: School Dropouts came from associating migrants with terms such as "cultural deprivation" and "cultural disadvantage." By contrast, these narratives frame whatever leads to the opposite of the dropout as having some positive, homogeneous value that can be possessed by an individualized person.

The dropout is framed with a two-sided potentiality. Its image is

FIGURE 9. The two-sided potential of the dropout, with a vertical imaginary, metonymic slides, and emotional economy.

composed with negative and positive potential life trajectories: as a potential delinquent in the community *and* as having potential talent realized through education in schools. Its two-sided framing straddles the school-community relation. This creates a terrain of intervention for governance, framed as an individualized salvaging process, while distracting attention from political-economic problems, such as structural racism. The dichotomies of waste versus value in the dropout narrative are made relatable to people through populating them with imagined, human figures who can be interpreted in relation to certain "emotional economies."[75] Imagining the motion of dropping down toward becoming a dropout produces emotions of shame, fear, and anxiety. Conversely, imagining the motion of rising up toward becoming a graduate produces pride and desire. These affects are intensified by metonymic slides between the graduate and dropout figures and other figures, images, and signs. The graduate slides into association with the talented youth, which is tied with fears and anxieties about unemployment in a time of automation, as talents are needed for learning new skills in the high-tech economy. The dropout is associated with the delinquent, which is tied with fears of crime, poverty, and the social dynamite of unrest in urban communities.

This emotional economy constructs and stabilizes the boundaries and surfaces of entities in the liberal-capitalist imaginary.[76] Believing that you have to *choose* between these two imagined potential paths of "graduate" or "dropout"—and imagining potential pride or shame—is co-constitutive with viewing oneself as an autonomous, bounded, responsible individual. The dropout is framed as bringing shame *onto* the community (as an illegitimate Other).[77] With the narrative of a "national dropout crisis," the nation is constructed as bringing shame *onto itself*, for failing to live up to its ideals. Through resolving the dropout crisis, pride in the nation can be restored, thereby reaffirming its boundaries. Certain "experts"—teachers, administrators, and a new category of expert, the dropout prevention specialist—are framed as managers and potential resolvers of the dropout crisis on multiple scales: for the nation, the city, the school, and the individual student. These experts are framed as apolitical, objective deciders about whether and how the student can access and use the means of studying. The framings of crisis and expertise depoliticize these expert figures' history of complicit involvement in constructing the boundaries of segregated school districts and tracking within schools, and the inequalities of resources for studying across these boundaries. Further, these narratives obscure these figures' complicity in constructing the boundaries of individualized students themselves, particularly through their participation in this emotional economy, such as through teachers instilling fear, anxiety, shame, and pride in students by subjecting them to exams and grades.

Through linking discourses of talents and delinquency, dropout narratives reinforce and expand the liberal-capitalist world-making project that includes those subject-formations. Through distracting attention from structural racism while highlighting criminogenic features of delinquency, narratives of the dropout complement the *criminalization* of Black people—that is, associating criminality with Blackness. Conversely, dropout narratives reinforce what I call the *talentization* of white people, that is, assuming that white people inherently possess valuable talents. These multiple forms of subject-construction are what make dropout narratives not merely a kind of stereotyping but also part of an ontological, world-making project.[78]

The dropout, as a rubbish figure, creates a region of flexibility for the disposal of value through association with dropout-*prevention* discourses and programs. In dropout-prevention narratives, the dropout serves as a stabilizing door between the value scales (the regions of fixed, stable assumptions about value) of the figures of the student and the worker. In the liberal-capitalist imaginary, the worlds of school and work are constructed as two modes or spheres of life that rely on *fixed assumptions* for the stability of their value practices. The world of school derives its value scales partly from the vertical imaginary of education, with students competing to earn grades on exams and for classes that allow them to rise up the levels of K–12 in school and possibly up further to higher education. Liberal-capitalist narratives frame the life stage of school/youth as dependent and as a developmental transition to adulthood and work. These narratives contrastingly frame the idealized life stage of work/adulthood as atomistic, fend-for-yourself ("self-made man"), and independent. Cutting against these narratives, critical genealogies of the dependence/independence dichotomy show how identities figured as dependent (native, slave, housewife, welfare recipient, student) have been historically constructed in contrast with identities of independent figures (e.g., wage workers who "freely choose" to sell their labor power and adopt a Protestant work ethic).[79]

Theoretical Interlude 2: More-Than-Humanism and Actor-Network-Theory

The dropout narrative works as a tool of crisis management through a disposal and salvaging process that stabilizes the liberal-capitalist modernist mode of representational order. These processes take place, partly, on the micro-political terrain of subjectivity. Some aspects of the self are treated as disposable and others as salvageable. It is difficult to understand this process when viewed through the liberal-capitalist modernist imaginary, which suppresses the possibility of, in Donna Haraway's phrase, "staying with the trouble" of a fractured self.[80] Instead, this imaginary idealizes a unified, bounded self, which is seen as in crisis whenever deviating into a fractured form, to be resolved as quickly as possible through self-crisis management.

For a way out of this imaginative dead-end, I draw inspiration from modes of world-making alternative to modernity—such as Indigenous ways of life—with alternative conceptions of the self. Indigenous authors have theorized how Indigenous peoples' different views of the self are bound up with alternative modes of study that break out of modernist/colonial binaries, such as individual versus society and nature versus society. For example, Nishnaabeg scholar Leanne Simpson theorizes the self as situated within complex webs of more-than-human relationships, inextricably tied with the land, as "the land is context and process for coming to know."[81] Also, drawing on actor-network-theory, with a more-than-humanist view of the self, seemingly human affects are framed as part of actor-networks involving associations of human cells and non-human bacterial cells inside a person's body, and in relations with other human and non-human actors in emotional economies that circulate across the boundaries of the body.[82] These perspectives offer more nuanced ways of talking about the emotional economy involved in the dropout discourse. The second hyphen in "actor-network-theory" indicates that theories and other kinds of representations of actor-networks should be seen, not as separate from the actor-networks, but as themselves part of the actor-networks—that is, people subscribe to them, interpret the world through their lenses, and continue their circulation.[83] I use this view to describe in more detail how migrant people's desires exceed the liberal-capitalist, modernist norms, how these "excessive desires" create "crises" for the modernizers, and how the modernizers use the dropout narrative as a tool to depoliticize, manage, police, discipline, and suppress these desires.[84]

(De)Stabilizing Controversies over Transitions between School and Work

The dropout narrative mediates how a person moves between the figures of student and worker. The dropout acts as a conduit for the transient value of the student to decrease while transforming into a worker with a different articulation of durable and transient values. The worker's labor power is seen as having transient value, as their skills lose value over time, such as with automation, and hence in need of further education, possibly requiring a return to school or university. The dropout, as a rubbish figure or door, serves a key depoliticizing function by stabilizing and suppressing any *controversies* that could arise during these transitions between student/school and worker/work. Such controversies could include questions of wider ethical-political responsibility for the loss of a person's value *qua* student or worker, as well as questions about alternative interpretations of value in alternative modes of world-making.

People undergoing these transitions could raise such controversies on the basis of their affective experiences. Interrogating these controversies could entail raising questions about the responsibility for the valuing and wasting of different aspects of the student's subjectivity; where/when does the disposal process begin and end, and who/what is responsible for these disposals? The dropout framing creates epistemological limits on whether and how these questions are asked, highlighting certain controversies as relevant while burying other controversies. These epistemological limits are part of what I described in chapter 1 as an epistemology of educated ignorance. The epistemological limits are interwoven with ontological limits through the emotional economy of the dropout discourse that constructs the boundaries of entities in the liberal-capitalist imaginary. This discourse's circulating emotions of shame, pride, fear, and anxiety are mutually co-constituted with subscriptions to liberal-capitalist ways of studying, knowing, and imagining the world.

Alternative framings of school non-completion, such as "pushout," can disinter the questions buried with the dropout framing.[85] Someone who adopts the pushout frame might ask, Who or what is responsible for pushing the student out of school—the student, the school, structural racism, the state, or the capitalist political economy? These are controversies that could arise by describing the student's desired life trajectories that are excessive to the normative trajectories in liberal capitalism (i.e., becoming a productive worker, heteropatriarchal family member, and obedient citizen). Yet, the pushout framing might also limit these imaginative possibilities, because its focus on an individual who is pushed out obscures and depoliticizes how the school itself is involved in the construction of students *as individuals*. In other words, the pushout framing seems to take for granted a pre-constituted individual, and thereby it forecloses the possibility of devoting critical attention to how the education-based mode of study is part of processes of "primitive accumulation," that is, the creation of the preconditions for capitalist relations through constructing relationships of separation between individualized producers and the means of production.[86] Thus, as a complement to a pushout framing I suggest adopting a framing of schools as terrains of struggle between alternative, conflicting modes of world-making in association with alternative modes of study. For example, a student might desire to use the school's means for studying to gain capacities—via alternative modes of study, such as autonomous Black or Indigenous modes—for facilitating self-organization of their community, which would require deviating from liberal capitalism's normative life trajectories.

Narratives of the contrasting figures of dropout and graduate serve to suppress such excessive imaginal trajectories. With micro-political actions of disposal and salvaging of the student's fractured subjectivity, the dropout narratives devalue such excessive desires as wasteful. With an emotional economy of fear, anxiety, pride, and shame, these narratives frame excessive desires as pathways toward becoming the rubbish figure of the dropout with a disposable life in the world of precarious work, unemployment, poverty, and incarceration. Conversely, these narratives affirm and endow with value and positive affects those desires that accord with liberal-capitalist modernist norms—that is, as pathways toward graduation and a smooth transition to the world of work.

More-than-humanist theories can help describe how the student's affective experiences are constituted in relation with other-than-human actors, on multiple scales. Zooming in to a scale micro to the human body, bacterial actors relate with human cells to co-produce affects of pride and desire for some imagined life trajectories, but also affects of fear, anxiety, and shame about other possible trajectories. Conversely, subscribing to the dropout narrative serves to suppress affective relations with alternative modes of world-making, such as affects of love, solidarity, desire, and friendship in Black radical movements and the blues epistemology. Zooming out to more macro scales, a person could subscribe to representations of institutions and places—such as tracking in schools, segregation across neighborhoods, and incarceration in juvenile detention, jails, and prisons—that could limit their possibilities for imagining their life trajectories. By subscribing to representations of such institutions and places as immutable, necessary, natural, and apolitical, people limit their abilities to imagine pathways for themselves through these institutions. They also limit their imagined possibilities for raising questions about ethical-political responsibility in the histories of those institutions and places. For thinking critically about these imagined limits, a more-than-humanist perspective can attribute collective agency to the student in association with not only humans but also these other-than-human actors, including bacteria, tracked schools, segregated neighborhoods, and carceral buildings. Further, such a perspective allows for framing the *representations* of these actors as themselves actors that materially circulate, such as through the mass media, textbooks, and teaching. If subscribed to, these representations become the frames through which a person interprets the world.

The dropout narrative limits critical engagement with these representations through its association with education. The dropout narrative's disposal/salvaging process centrally deploys the vertical imaginary of the education-based mode of study. This narrative highlights the vertical transitions in education—with a norm of avoiding the "drop" of dropping out and aiming to rise "up" the K–12 grades and possibly to higher education. Affiliating one's desired life trajectory with such a vertical rise, and fearing the drop, can create a fetish for this vertical movement, especially in association with the capitalist economic imaginary of rising up the class ladder. Fetishizing these vertical movements distracts attention from the *horizontal* gaps of disposal within and beyond the education system (see Figure 10). Young people are made disposable from one vertical institutional trajectory and horizontally transferred into another vertical trajectory through tracking within schools, segregation across schools, and incarceration in juvenile detention, jails, and prisons, disproportionately for poor Black, Latinx, and Indigenous young people.[87] These disposals are a kind of primitive accumulation, in the sense that they create new relations of separation between students as individualized producers and the means of (studying) production. The students are effectively separated from the possibility of using the resources for studying across the gaps of disposal (e.g., students in a vocational track are separated from the students, teachers, books, and technology in a college-bound track).

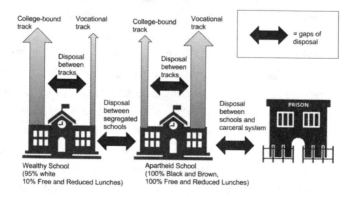

FIGURE 10. Gaps of disposal: tracking, segregation, and the schools–prisons nexus.

In the education discourse, these gaps are horizontal in the sense that a young person is seen as comparable with any other young person at the same level (whether measured by grade or age) at a different track or institution. Attending to these horizontal gaps could be the basis for raising controversies about ethical-political responsibility for the young person's relative value, or lack thereof, in their transition to the world of work. Considering such controversies could also put into question the scales of value in the education-based mode of study and liberal-capitalist mode of world-making. The dropout narrative's emphasis on the verticality of education stabilizes the imagined boundaries of seemingly self-contained units of schools, prisons, tracks, individuals, and communities.[88] This image depoliticizes and masks the effects of the horizontal gaps on young people's trajectories in the education system and working world. Young people who subscribe to these narratives feel compelled either to internalize a stigmatized identity as the rubbished dropout or to salvage their own value through dropout-prevention programs and/or returning to school and rising up its levels toward graduation.

To disrupt education's vertical imaginary, a young person could engage in the horizontalist study of a social movement, such as the long Black freedom movement, including the contemporary Movement for Black Lives. For example, in the radical studying of the Black Panther Party, they could theorize the "internal colonialism" of police occupying Black neighborhoods, thereby relating the horizontal gaps across segregated communities with a broader critique of the settler-colonial, liberal-capitalist mode of world-making.[89] Engaging in such alternative modes of study might draw a young person's attention to the gaps of segregation, tracking, policing, and incarceration, seeing these as subjects of controversy around which to organize collectively. Raising controversies about how these institutions are represented can open the possibility for imagining and making them differently. Such movement activity cuts against the dropout narrative's burying of the potentially resistant *agency* of young people during the transition between student and worker.

To frame school non-completers as dropouts is to frame them as in crisis, incapable of handling themselves on the value scale of either the student or the worker. Thus they are seen as needing management by others, such as experts in dropout-prevention programs, to transition back into either school's or work's regions of fixed assumptions. Or, if they are seen as continually subversive of liberal-capitalist norms, they are treated as a criminal and disposed of into "corrections"—that is, the incarceration system—or treated as an insane person in the psychiatric system. The dropout narrative militates against the possibility for school non-completers themselves collectively to create new alternative, subversive value practices on the basis of their imaginal trajectories, whether in social movements or in subcultures. Affirming the young people's collectively resistant agency—in association with other-than-human agencies—would contradict the liberal-capitalist norm of framing students as *dependent* in opposition to the *independent* worker. Framing young people as having resistant, collective, more-than-humanist agency would trouble that dichotomy *and* its individualizing effects. On this view, young people can be seen as having multiple, conflicting affective relations with different modes of world-making and study simultaneously—for example, torn between desires for pride associated with success within the education-based, liberal-capitalist modernist world versus desires for joy and love within a Black radical community and the blues epistemology. Such a view can help disrupt the crisis mode of narrating problems around schools and shift toward a mode of narrating an *impasse* of schools as complex terrains of political struggle between alternative modes of world-making and study.

The liberal-capitalist modernist attempts at crisis management continually fail. But those failures go unnoticed because the narratives of the dropout make people see the failures as their own individualized faults. As an antidote, by recognizing and affirming that "We are the crisis," migrants and their descendants—and anyone affected by the dropout narrative—can grapple with how their desires and movements exceed the bounds of education in liberal capitalism.

LEGACIES OF CULTURAL RACISM IN
LIBERAL AND NEOLIBERAL MULTICULTURALISMS

After the end of Project: School Dropouts in 1966, its narratives persisted in changing forms of liberal-capitalist modernity. The Ford Foundation's

Gray Areas programs influenced Johnson's War on Poverty, which took up Ford's community action approach.[90] They both diverted attention from political-economic issues, while preparing people to function within capitalism. The historical shift involved a narrowing of geographic and conceptual scope from metropolitan reform to "gray areas" rehabilitation to intervention in "the ghetto." Throughout the War on Poverty, the dropout narrative was used as part of the behavioral conception of the poverty problem. This served the political purpose of obscuring issues of structural racism. Instead of systemic transformation, the focus was on remediation of individuals and reorganization of services.

In response to criticisms of the cultural racism of the "culturally deprived" framework, promoters of the dropout narrative gradually shifted to seemingly non-cultural descriptions, such as "educationally disadvantaged," "economically disadvantaged," and "at risk."[91] Thereby, the dropout figure appeared to become disconnected from its origins in cultural racism. Yet, the narratives and institutions around this figure continued to have the same *effect* of focusing on individual-community-school-family relations and distracting from the structural racism of segregation and inequality.

The actor-network promoting the "dropout crisis" and "at-risk students" narratives now involves a "non-profit industrial complex"— including key nonprofits of Communities in Schools, America's Promise Alliance, American Graduate, and Everyone Graduates, among others.[92] They are backed with funding from corporations and the federal government. America's Promise Alliance is headed by Alma and Colin Powell. At its founding in 1997, former presidents Clinton, Bush, Carter, and Ford were present, as was Nancy Reagan.[93] Since then, George W. Bush and Barack Obama have backed the Alliance.

America's Promise Alliance was founded soon after Bill Clinton signed the 1994 Violent Crime Control and Law Enforcement Act, which vastly expanded the carceral state, leading to major increases in racially discriminatory policing and racialized mass incarceration. This was concurrent with the "culture wars," including the liberal-capitalist establishment's attack on hip-hop culture, which continued working-class African American people's blues epistemology.[94] The Clinton administration's promotion of all of these projects is not coincidental, but rather a continuation of formally anti-racist liberal-capitalist modernity. The latest phase of this mode of world-making is "neoliberal multiculturalism," which treats diversity as a valuable principle for increasing capital accumulation.[95]

Today's nonprofit industrial complex around the dropout crisis continues the logic that the Ford Foundation had pioneered through acting as a shadow state in racial liberalism. Ford simultaneously supported education programs, including the dropout project, that focused on school-community relations, while supporting the expansion and rationalizing of mass incarceration. In 1969 the Ford Foundation established the Police Foundation, which worked in the 1980s through 2000s to create and promote the community policing movement.[96] Parallel to the focus of the dropout project on school-community relations, community policing focuses on police-community relations. Both serve to reify the entities of police, school, and community while diverting attention from structural racism. This is a community-washing (like green-washing or pink-washing) of the white supremacy that persists in liberal-capitalist modernity.

The Ford Foundation's support for expansion of the pyramid of value in education was co-constitutive with their support for expanding the waste-disposal institution of the carceral state. The dropout crisis frame has created subjects desirous of higher education, thereby legitimating expansion of mass higher education, with the "Edu-deal" of students paying their way through college by taking on student debt with the assumption that their degree will guarantee employment.[97]

Part of why the co-constitutive relation of education and the carceral state remains opaque to most academics and leftists is that they tend to have subscribed to the concept that complements the dropout, the concept of the graduate, as part of their self-conception. Emotional attachments to the imaginary of the dropout and the graduate are part of an epistemology of educated ignorance that obscures the co-constitution of education and mass incarceration, and more generally, of liberal-capitalist modernity's lighter and darker sides.[98] To explore modes of world-making alternative to liberal-capitalist modernity, we need to drop our attachments to the dropout/graduate imaginary. Yet this is difficult, because this imaginary is enmeshed with the broader constellation of concepts in the education-based mode of study: an ascending, vertical life trajectory, education as a technique for crisis management, an emotional economy of credits and debts, and further binary figures of waste and value. As steps toward destabilizing our assumptions of the necessary and inevitable dominance of this mode of study, the next two chapters interrogate the historical, politically contested origins of its different elements. I show how these elements arose as part of ruling-class reactions to threats from alternative modes of study and world-making.

3

Degrees of Ascent

SCHOOL LEVELS AS PRECONDITIONS
OF CAPITALISM

The institution we know as "education" has not existed since the dawn of humanity. Rather, it developed at particular times and places, in co-constitution with particular projects for composing the world. Any historical narrative is told from some political perspective, selecting some events as more important than others and interpreting those events in particular ways. Yet, historians of education tend to obscure their politics behind a mask of objectivity while presenting the emergence of education as a necessary, progressive development.[1] By suppressing the history of education's political character, they contribute to an epistemology of educated ignorance. Conversely, they hinder the possibility for imagining alternative modes of study. Against this grain, I offer a critical genealogy of education that highlights how its emergence was bound up with struggles between conflicting modes of world-making and their associated modes of study during the rise of capitalism in Europe.

For this approach I take inspiration from Silvia Federici's historical analysis of how the politicization of sexuality and the repression of women were part of "primitive accumulation"—that is, the creation of the preconditions for capitalism. I show how these phenomena were interrelated with the rise of the institution of level-divided schools, a precursor to the education-based mode of study. In addition to this sexist politics, I contend, an interrelated aspect of these processes involved the politics of conflicting modes of study. Seeing study both formally and informally, within and beyond schools, as part of the reproduction of class relations and labor-power, I argue that the creation of a new politics of study had effects similar to misogynist laws around sexuality, that is, a gendered cross-class compromise as part of the repression of anti-feudal struggles.

New configurations of schooling, particularly the innovation of schools with multiple graded levels, along with divisions by gender—including boys and excluding girls from schools—had two effects that were key elements of primitive accumulation. These interrelated effects included, on the one hand, accumulating differentiations and divisions within the working class, and on the other, creating new relations of separation between individualized producers and the means of production and re-production.[2] As the state undermined class solidarity by decriminalizing rape and institutionalizing prostitution, a process that complemented this degrading of the value of all women's lives was through a kind of schooling that *elevated* the value of *some* men's lives, particularly those who ascended the school's levels. This mode of study was developed in explicit contrast with the communities of women in the cities, such as in beguinages, who created new modes of life, spirituality, commons, and enclosure entwined with new modes of study. Due to their challenge to patriarchal and protocapitalist relations, these "cities of ladies" were subjected to suspicions and charges of heresy.

Anything new in the world emerges from the interplay between forces for change and forces for maintaining the status quo. The birth of education is no exception. Education emerged from the messy context of struggles against the feudal system, conservative reactions that repressed and di-vided rebellious people, and people's counter-responses that combined flight, refuge, subversion, compromise, and attempts to create new modes of life and study. The emergence and development of what I call the "education-based mode of study" was in conflict with alternative modes of study, such as those that commoners and beguines embedded in their everyday lives. The whirlwind of conflicts between feudal, protocapitalist, patriarchal, statist forces and alternative, women-centered modes of life was a cauldron of experimentation for new modes of study. An implicit axis of conflict was between horizontalist and verticalist modes of study, with the former conducive to nonhierarchical modes of life and the latter conducive to hierarchical modes of life. In the chapter's first section I detail the beguines' relatively more horizontalist modes of life and study in the context of anti-feudal struggles.

In the second section I describe how a key feature of the verticalist mode of study—splitting a school into ascending grades—began with a school for boys associated with a group called the Sisters and Brothers of the Common Life, who explicitly distinguished themselves from the "heretical" beguines. This group's networks, along with their ideology of spiritual ascent, helped spread split-level schools across Europe and beyond. People experienced tensions in relation to conflicting modes of study and life, particularly between the established church and the emerging market system. In groups such as the Sisters and Brothers of the Common Life, people found support for grappling with these tensions through practices of spirituality and study. Yet their engagement with these tensions was circumscribed within certain ideological and institutional features that allowed the tensions to be managed and suppressed.

The final section of the chapter theorizes the verticalist mode of study as part of the preconditions for capitalism. Anticapitalist movements take different approaches to abolishing capitalism depending on how they define capitalism's beginnings—that is, primitive accumulation. Feminist Marxists, such as Federici, expanded the theory of primitive accumulation to include the systematic repression of women, while anticolonial Marxists, such as Glen Coulthard, have highlighted the dispossession of Indigenous peoples' land. Taking inspiration from Federici and Coulthard, I theorize the rise of the verticalist mode of study as another of capitalism's preconditions. This mode of study divides the working class, disciplines young people into individualized obedience, and creates new separations between them and their means of studying collectively across genders, ages, and abilities. I show how colonial dispossession, misogynist repression of women, and the verticalist mode of study were interconnected forms of primitive accumulation that involved various configurations of commons and enclosure. With a "more-than-humanist" approach, I highlight the key roles of non-human actors in commons and enclosure, particularly in their relations with conflicting modes of study. Through this theoretical lens, I describe how the verticalist mode of study in the schools of the Sisters and Brothers of the Common Life allowed them an escape from grappling with the impasse that they faced around the Black Plague. The imaginary of spiritual ascent up levels of schools constructs an idealized self that can escape to a realm of illuminated certainty, while the body is treated as a commons of labor-power for capitalist exploitation.

BEGUINAGES: HORIZONTALIST STUDY IN
WOMEN'S URBAN COMMONS AND ENCLOSURES

In the fourteenth century the Black Plague spread across Europe, decimating the population by more than one-third. This cataclysm destabilized hierarchies.[3] With workers becoming scarcer, their labor increased in cost, giving them power in relation to the noble and merchant ruling classes. Also, the increased abundance of land gave tenants power over their landlords as they could threaten rent strikes or a mass exodus. These conditions fomented rebellions that united peasants and urban workers, such as the revolt in Flanders from 1323 to 1328. The rebels aspired for a more egalitarian society and adopted a new, more critical attitude toward work. The ruling classes reacted by condemning idleness and persecuting vagabondage, begging, and refusal of work, with punishments that included forced labor.[4] This repression was gendered, as the ruling classes saw women's control over reproduction as a threat to socioeconomic stability.

The repression of women included charges of heresy—that is, beliefs contrary to orthodox Christian doctrine—with emphasis on the sexual aspects of heresy. This was part of what Federici calls a wider "politicization of sexuality" in the ruling classes' reactions to anti-feudal struggles.[5] So-called heretical movements often assigned high status to women and supported unorthodox sexual choices as a subversive stance against the church's attempts to control sexuality. Peasants and urban workers found common cause in these movements for supporting their resistances against the ruling classes. The latter's fear of a combined rural and urban rebellion gave them common cause in an alliance with the established church for using misogynist accusations and persecutions of heresy—with "witch hunts"—as part of a counterrevolutionary movement. The ruling classes created what Federici calls a "climate of misogyny" that "turned class antagonism into an antagonism against proletarian women"—that is, forming a cross-class compromise, a "sexual 'new deal,'" along lines of gender and sexuality.[6] A key element of this patriarchal counterrevolution was to co-opt male workers via a sexist politics in which the newly forming states decriminalized the rape of lower-class women and institutionalized prostitution with state-managed brothels. These state actions were part of a broader centralization of power, strengthening the state's capacities to manage class relations and the reproduction of laborers.

According to Federici, in feudalism, female serfs were relatively less dependent on men and socially differentiated than women would become under capitalist relations.[7] Whereas in early capitalism a gendered division of labor excluded women from the production of goods and relegated them to the reproduction of the workforce, under feudal relations women worked in both production and reproduction. The commons provided a source of power for peasant women through giving them direct access to the land. From women's cooperative work together on the commons, such as gathering wood and berries and tending animals, they organized collective defense against patriarchal and religious repression. Through women's collective studying on the commons, they controlled their own bodies and the reproduction of the workforce, such as through birth control, "mostly consisting of herbs which turned into potions or 'pessaries' (suppositories) . . . used to quicken a woman's period, provoke an abortion or create a condition of sterility."[8] They shared knowledge about these forms of contraception and passed that knowledge down from generation to generation, "giving them some autonomy with respect to child-birth"—forms of knowledge that became criminalized when the ruling classes desired women to produce more children as future workers.

The power of peasant women and their relations with men were shaped through their communities' struggles with feudal landlords, including conflicts over the commons. In thirteenth- to fifteenth-century Lower Germany (today's Belgium and the Netherlands), different areas introduced different forms of "the marks" (shorthand for *markegenootschappen*), that is, collective institutions for managing the commons, in response to a period of rapid population growth when landowners perceived common grounds as becoming scarce.[9] In some regions, such as Drenthe, the peasant farmers themselves often took the initiative for the organization of the marks, in ways that allowed them to retain power over their commons. In other regions, Overijssel and Guelderland, large landowners established the marks as institutions for governing the commons in ways conducive to their interests. In these regions, the yearly meeting for decision making about the rules of the marks was chaired by a *markrechter,* who was "normally a nobleman with extensive landholdings in the community."[10] The centralized power of the *markrechter* undercut the power women had in their communities from collectively working on the commons.

While large landowners instituted systems of marks in some areas that gave them control over the governance of the commons, in other areas they legislated enclosures of the commons that completely ejected peasants from the commons. Related, they commuted the relation of serfdom into a contractual basis with money payments that replaced labor dues owed to the large landowners, making some peasants into tenant-owners of their land while forcing others to work as wage laborers on that land.[11] This led to new divisions among the peasants, making some capitalist-landlords who exploited others as wage workers. The increasing commercialization of rural life most negatively affected women, as it decreased their access to property and income as well as their power from collectively governing and working with other women on the commons. These negative conditions, coupled with the relatively greater freedom for women in the towns and cities, led many women to migrate from rural to urban areas. They were still repressed in the towns and cities, as they could rarely buy their "city freedom," that is, "the privileges connected with city life," but urban life allowed women greater escape from subordination to men, as they gained access to new occupations and could form new communities with other women.[12]

One form of refuge that women created in the towns and cities of Lower Germany was communities of beguines. These communities ranged in size from small convents of a few women to massive court beguinages that housed from several dozen to over a thousand women.[13] Beguine communities provided institutional support for women's collective practices of companionship, mutual aid, health care, study, and relief from poverty.[14] Although urban areas provided greater autonomy for women than the rural areas did, women still faced repression, which entangled them in tensions within and outside the beguinages. Urban authorities appreciated women's economic productivity, but they saw women's public appearance as a signal of potential disorder.[15] Public spaces were gendered, with women discouraged from accessing some spaces, subjecting their behavior to discipline and constraints that men did not have to endure. Men slandered women's mode of dress and makeup for "vanity" and "excess," such as accusing them of looking like "horned beasts," and denounced them for "inorderly use of speech" and "cunning sophistry." Women were excluded from urban public life in an attempt to relegate their activities to the family.

The beguinages provided women with means for dealing with their tensions between freedom and repression. Building on Walter Simons's description of the beguines' "experiment in a restless search for new experiences," I theorize their new modes of life, spirituality, and work as entwined with a particular *mode of study*.[16] The beguines simultaneously desired to withdraw from the world into the contemplative life and to be involved with the world through charity, manual work, and teaching. Their mode of study mixed teaching and learning with their manual work, as their collective work sessions included discussion of religious texts. Some taught young girls, and "girls and women sought their guidance on a wide range of moral and ethical issues," thereby forming an alternative family among women, with girls establishing "extremely close relationships with their main mentor and other members of the beguine community." The relationship between mistress and disciple, teacher and student, "held the potential for creating strong bonds," as it "took the form of an apprenticeship based on personal example and an intense, close relationship."[17] The potential for these strong bonds between women was applauded by sympathizers but mistrusted by detractors, particularly for challenging the dominant institutions of church and family. For example, one young woman who chose the alternative family of the beguines, Beatrice of Nazareth, "attested herself that she never gave her own parents as much love as she gave these women; she, in turn, was loved no less by them."[18]

The beguines' close, strong, loving form of community inspired the ecclesiastical and secular authorities to accuse the beguines of heresy. In his study of religious dissent in the Middle Ages, R. I. Moore notes "two opposing concepts of community."[19] One kind of community is horizontally oriented, with lay members shaping it locally in the vernacular language. The other is a vertically oriented community, which is "administered from above by the higher clergy using Latin as the vehicle of communication." The conflict between these two forms of community was the source of accusations of heresy. The beguines' more horizontalist form of community threatened the ecclesiastical authorities' investment in the hierarchical institutions of the church. Although the beguines had some hierarchical relations, such as between mistress and disciples, their close, loving bonds relatively flattened these hierarchies. Also, their relations of women-to-women solidarity challenged the church's hierarchy of patriarchal relations of men over women.

The beguines endured a climate of suspicions and charges of heresy, due to their threats to patriarchal, feudal, ecclesiastical, statist, and protocapitalist relations. They subverted patriarchy through providing a refuge where women could escape from marriage, rape and other forms of sexual violence, and the "heavy yoke" of family life, refusing the labor of sexual reproduction, which included "the awful burdens of the womb, the dangers of childbirth . . . and the care of the family and household, the constant worries about the daily work."[20] They challenged the commercialization of life that the theologians had started to rationalize in the thirteenth century, embracing a life of voluntary poverty in order to "redress the injustices created by the search for greater wealth; liberated from the social obligations of property, they could devote their life to the care of the indigent."[21] The beguines' voluntary poverty presented a challenge to the church's property regime, inspiring charges of heresy.[22]

The lack of easy categorization for beguines was part of why ecclesiastical and secular authorities were motivated to investigate and punish these "extraregular" women.[23] The beguinages contrasted with nunneries, which, in accord with Pope Boniface VIII's dictate for nuns, were strictly enclosed and thereby clearly demarcated as places of withdrawal from secular life into a contemplative religious life.[24] The beguinages rejected strict enclosures and, instead, had relatively porous enclosures, which provided them with protection from the authorities, and from men in general, while allowing for their relatively freer engagement in urban life and work. Within this porous enclosure, the court beguinage often contained an inner commons, or "green," that served as a grounds and center for the beguines' communal life and labor.[25] The beguinages were sometimes established on land that had previously been used as a commons for the town.[26] In these cases, their creation of a porous enclosure was a precondition for both breaking down a patriarchal commons and creating a new, protofeminist commons—that is, to shift from governing a commons with patriarchal norms to governing with norms of woman-to-woman mentorship, love, and solidarity.

The degree of porosity of the beguinage's enclosure was itself a focus of political struggle. With increasing accusations of heresy in the early fourteenth century—particularly with the condemnation and execution of the beguine Marguerite Porete in 1310 and the Council of Vienne's subsequent denouncement of the beguines as heretics in 1311—solitary beguines were more harshly persecuted and beguinages were subjected to inquiries that led them to increase the strictness of their internal rules of enclosure.[27] The execution of Porete was a form of overt violence of primitive accumulation that was supplemented with the "softer" violence of legislation and cultural norms for increased disciplining of rebellious women.

The cultural and political climate around these conflicts was the context for experiments in new modes of life, community, spirituality, work, and study. A key axis of distinction in these experiments was between horizontalist and verticalist modes. The verticalist modes were complemented with differentiations and divisions between classes and within the peasant class and urban working class themselves. Other experimental urban projects formed in explicit contrast to the beguines, due to fear of association with their criminalized heresy. Accordingly, these other projects took on a more verticalist mode of life, community, work, and study. A key example of these experiments is the Sisters and Brothers of the Common Life.

THE EMERGENCE OF THE VERTICALIST MODE OF STUDY

In Lower Germany, the thirteenth and fourteenth centuries were a time of great upheaval.[28] Peasants fought over political rights, breaking down the feudal hierarchies, limiting the lords' abuses, and demanding the

privileges of citizenship and government offices in addition to the basic
needs of lower rents, adequate food, and improved working conditions.[29]
The ruling classes attempted to suppress these peasant revolts by dividing
the resistance movements along lines of gender, class, and rural/urban.
As women had often been leaders of rebellions, the ruling classes' countermeasures included increasingly intensified forms of patriarchal repression. Greater emphasis was placed on the gendered separation between
the so-called private and public spheres.[30] Land reform exacerbated this
patriarchal repression with the increase of large landholdings and tenant
farms, the dispossession of peasants from their land, the rise of labor
markets, and the increase of wage labor. Married women's power in the
household was undermined, as their labor was invisible from the perspective of the labor market. Conversely, unmarried women were pushed out
of their homes into the world of work, such as the labor of wool spinning.
Many peasants were forced into a state of landlessness, exacerbated due to
enclosures. Peasants' seeking life in the cities could be interpreted as not
only a submission to wage labor but also as a form of escape and refuge.

In late-fourteenth-century Lower Germany, another prominent
form of experimental spiritual movement was the Devotio Moderna, or
Modern-Day Devout. In his history of the most prominent group in this
movement, the Sisters and Brothers of the Common Life, John Van
Engen describes them as a form of converts, people in the Middle Ages
who decided to change their lives drastically, both internally through
spiritual conversion and externally through changing their social estate.[31]
The Sisters and Brothers attempted to distinguish themselves from other
converts who were stigmatized and repressed as heretics by church authorities, such as the beguines and the Free Spirits.[32] The founders of the
Modern-Day Devout, most notably Gerhard Groote, sought to distance
themselves from these other convert groups in order to avoid the ruling
classes' regulation and repression.[33]

After the Black Plague depopulated Lower Germany in the mid-
fourteenth century, the family became a crucial institution for reproducing
the population. The ruling powers saw the life of the beguines and Free
Spirits as a threat to the renewal of the population. Anti-beguine laws and
inquisitions—distinguishing "good," order-maintaining beguines from

"bad," subversive ones—were passed to counteract the danger presented by women who called themselves spiritual while refusing obedience to the church.[34] Further, the beguines enacted an implicit critique of the rich, as they made poverty a necessary step toward spiritual perfection. Groote distinguished the Modern-Day Devout from both the beguines and Free Spirits by portraying these "Others" as becoming lost in their limitless, free experiences with God and thereby avoiding discipline.[35] He also forbade the Devout from spreading these other groups' doctrines.

The Modern-Day Devout grappled with the conditions of a mixed space between peasant life and the rising market system. In the late fourteenth century, they established their first experimental communities in a territory—the Oversticht (today's Overijssel in the Netherlands)—situated geographically between two areas that exhibited a contrast between these two modes of life. On their west was Guelders, where large landholders sought to exploit their lands commercially, leasing parcels of land for short terms and employing former peasants as wage laborers.[36] On their north was Drenthe, where small-scale peasant farming and communal lands predominated due both to the low agricultural yields on sandy grounds and to resistances against feudal control. Groote officially founded the first house for a community of the Devout in 1379 in a city between these two areas, Deventer, which was a flourishing trade city due to its position on the river IJssel and on a major overland route.[37]

In these mixed spaces, the Sisters and Brothers re-created certain kinds of commons and communal life within urban territories. Their communities began as joint holding societies, organized initially in 1382 around the sharing of books and later expanded to share other forms of property. Yet these were not fully autonomous communes; rather, their societies were under private legal arrangements with town aldermen, making them subject to civil law. They lived a life that mixed the secular and the religious, finding the spiritual as the realm in which they could take on religious virtues without taking religious vows and entering the estate of religion.[38] They grappled with the tension between evading the rigid conventions of established religion and being accused of heresy for straying too far from religious norms in their worldly experiments with spirituality.

Practices of study were central for the Sisters and Brothers. Studying helped them navigate among the tensions of a mixed life and create
a new path for living spiritually, taking on responsibility for their souls
so as to find an "inner peace" and "quietude."[39] Their devotion to study
was seen in their practices of making books, keeping extensive libraries,
and allotting time every day for reading. They also supported schools for
boys in the towns through hosting students in their hostels, and eventually they ran their own schools as well. The spaces of study they created
were attractive for parents who could send their young boys to the schools
and board them in the hostels. Schoolboys were sent from all over the
surrounding regions.

Although the focus of the schools was on boys, women were consis-
tently a majority among the Sisters and Brothers of the Common Life.
Their spaces were divided into separate houses for the men, women, and
schoolboys. The women's houses were attractive places for young women
fleeing violent, patriarchal families, seeking shelter from the public life of
congested towns and from burgher, marital, or merchant expectations,
and/or desiring a devoted spiritual life.[40] These houses were separate from
the schools and focused more on work than study. This residential and
labor division by gender was a key condition that shaped the experimental
character of the Sisters and Brothers.

Despite the Sisters and Brothers' innovations in modes of living,
their leaders maintained some ordering principles from feudal modes of
life, the market system, the patriarchal family, and Christianity. These
different modes of ordering the world intersected in complex ways with
the multi-tiered class struggle between urban classes, lords (manorial and
territorial), and peasants, as well as with struggles around gender and
sexuality.[41] I contend that the intersection of these struggles and modes
of ordering was *the crucible of experimentation* out of which emerged the
theory and practice of ascending levels in schools. For analytical purposes,
I divide this crucible into theoretical and practical-institutional elements.
The Sisters and Brothers developed theories and methods of self-care for
cultivating interiority. In response to people's widespread cynicism about
religion, the Modern-Day Devout carved out a new private world, with
Groote battling other preachers to attract people hungry for experiences

of spirituality outside established religion.[42] In light of anxieties about mortality, particularly during and after the Black Plague, the Modern-Day Devout's methods of self-care allowed people to find some solace for their precarious sense of self through subscribing to an image of a bounded but malleable self. Rather than escaping or transcending the self, the Modern-Day Devout offered practices for *recrafting* the self, aiming to inspire resolve for a lifelong project of spiritual progress. Grappling with the intersection of secular and religious modes of life, they innovated a norm for self-improvement through a "spiritual ascent." This norm borrowed the imagery of a vertical hierarchy of spiritual levels from the Christian religious tradition (e.g., imagining heaven above earth above hell) and combined this hierarchy with a self that must deal with everyday problems in the world. One of the Modern-Day Devout's most popular devotional books was on "spiritual ascents" (*De ascensionibus spiritualis*). The imaginary of spiritual ascent for reconstructing an interior self was a narrative device that composed people's imaginations about the future with an image of an individualized, ascending, progressive life trajectory. This process contributed to the construction of individualized producers as part of primitive accumulation. This imaginary provided a pedagogical tool for the Modern-Day Devout and for the teachers and schoolmasters who associated with them.

The largest group of the Modern-Day Devout, the Sisters and Brothers of the Common Life, translated the Devout's theory of the ascending spiritual self into practice through a complex set of institutions for dividing and managing labor among the inhabitants of their houses, hostels, and schools. While innovating a new mode of imagining the self, their institutions also maintained feudal, patriarchal, and protocapitalist hierarchies of rich over poor, titled over untitled, men over women, and old over young. The malleable, ascending, spiritual self-image allowed for relatively greater gender and class autonomy and mobility than in the feudal and protocapitalist orders. Yet this autonomy and mobility was still circumscribed within limits that prevented fundamental challenges to the hierarchies of these orders. This institution of controlled autonomy enabled people partially to enact their desires for individual subversion, such as through women escaping from their patriarchal homes or from a grueling life of work in spinning factories, but it also served to surveil people and to co-opt their energies of potential collective resistance into forms of labor and spiritual practice that enabled their adaptation in the status quo.

This norm of controlled autonomy was embedded into the Sisters and Brothers' architecture through separate living spaces for the men, women, and schoolboys, as well as separate working spaces. Women's houses and schoolboys' hostels were also divided by class, with separate spaces for the voluntary and involuntary poor.[43] The built divisions, and the policing of these divisions by the house authorities, hindered the residents from forming cross-gender, cross-class, and cross-age relationships, which could have provided affective bases for resistance to the dominant hierarchies. The women's houses had some autonomous control, with an elected "Mother," or "Martha," of the house managing affairs, yet they were ultimately controlled by the "father-confessor" and town aldermen.[44]

Many viewed the Sisters and Brothers with suspicion. Locals distrusted their sharing of communal property, and church officials accused them of contravening church laws, especially anti-beguine legislation, leading to inquisitions of some converts.[45] The spatial divisions among the communal living arrangements were one way to deflect such suspicions. These divided spaces were connected with differences in how the residents' labor was distributed. The men were allowed two hours of reading each day, while the women were allowed only one hour and spent more time engaged in manual labor.[46] The types of manual labor were also different. The men focused more on the publicly oriented labor of copying and printing books, while the women focused on the domestic labor of spinning wool and making clothes. The women's greater amount of domestic labor was partly legitimated through contrasting it with the stigmatized activity of begging that the involuntarily poor members of the houses might have done if they were not working. The men's households also offered the refuge of communal life to the rising proletariat of young male clerics who were seeking study and jobs in the world, as an alternative to their options of paying for a university, finding a position requiring clerical skills in church, court, or town, or entering a religious order.[47]

The relations between the men, women, and schoolboys formed a protocapitalist economy in microcosm. The division of labor gave the men more free time through living off the surplus wealth accumulated from exploiting the women's surplus labor as well as from the schoolboys' lodging fees and tuition. With their extra free time, the men enjoyed the pleasures of reading, consuming their books as commodities for experiences of what they saw as "inner, spiritual peace."

Further separations within these working and studying spaces were implemented to deal with problems of administration. The men, as managers of bookmaking and wool-spinning workshops, schools, and hostels, faced problems of maintaining order, which paralleled the problem that city managers—that is, aldermen—faced with the migration of peasants into the cities. The aldermen attacked the problem of disorder through criminalizing vagabondage and begging so as to stifle resistances and to push migrants into wage labor. The Sisters and Brothers and their allied schoolmasters, such as Johan Cele, the headmaster at Zwolle (from 1378 to 1417), also experienced a massive influx into their spaces with schoolboys seeking support for their studies.[48] The large number of students, hundreds at a time in some schools, created a problem of disorder with the potential to undermine the school authorities' preferred mode of ordering. Cross-class studying threatened to build relationships subversive of class-based hierarchies. In response, the schoolmasters innovated a solution: starting with Cele's school in Zwolle, influenced through communication with Groote, the school was divided into nine grade levels. Affiliated schools copied this pattern in dozens of towns and cities, with some schools divided into seven or eight levels. Dividing schools into grades had been attempted before, such as the "catechumenal" schools grouped into four steps, but the schools of the Sisters and Brothers were the first to institute such grade levels systematically.[49]

The Sisters and Brothers' imaginary of spiritual ascent for the individualized self was coded into the school levels through numbering them from 9 (sequentially the first and "lowest") to 1 (the last and "highest"). Different subjects were taught at each level: grammar and logic in the lower classes and the basics of philosophy in the highest two classes, with variations across different schools.[50] This administrative mechanism made it easier for the teachers in each classroom to manage and surveil the students in smaller groups and at similar age and ability levels. Older boys in the first or second level acted as teachers (lectors) to the lower levels, helping the schoolmaster manage the school.

The imaginary of a spiritual ascent up the levels of the school provided the teachers and schoolmaster with an ideological mechanism for maintaining order and preventing subversive cross-class, cross-age relationships. The students' possibilities for imagining collective study and action were displaced with an individualized image of their interior self in a trajectory of improvement up the spiritual ladder. The suppression of cross-class collaboration was reinforced through the division of living spaces, with poor, "charity" boys in one building and wealthier, paying boys in another. Further, tutoring by the Brothers in the hostels provided an additional mechanism of surveillance, management, and income and allowed them to attempt to convert the schoolboys into the clerical life of the group. Another technique of disciplining the pupils was to have them wear the same garb as the Brothers.[51]

Seeing this mode of study as based on an interrelated set of divisions, by class, gender, age, labor, and study level, I theorize it as part of primitive accumulation—that is, creating the preconditions of capitalism, with new relations of separation between individualized producers and the means of production and reproduction.[52] Through this level-divided study institution, students not only undergo an individualizing ideological process but are practically separated from the collective means for the labor of study, especially the means of each other's knowledge, skills, and capacities for studying together.[53]

The innovation of splitting a school into vertical levels (or grades or classes) spread to other areas of rising capitalism across Europe and eventually the Americas. Its transmission to England likely happened through Erasmus, who had attended a school with connections to the Sisters and Brothers of the Common Life in Deventer and their boarding school at Bois-le-Duc from the late 1470s to 1482.[54] Erasmus moved to England in the early 1500s and gave John Colet, rector of St. Paul's Cathedral School of London, guidance for the reorganization of his school, probably including advice about the grade organization for the school, which took on an eight-grade plan similar to that of the Sisters and Brothers' schools.[55] Colet's school later served as a model for grammar schools throughout England. The transmission of the levels approach to America happened by way of John Calvin, who had been an assistant of Johann Sturm from 1539 to 1541 at his school in Strasbourg, which was modeled after the Sisters and Brothers' schools. Calvin imitated Sturm in the school he founded in Geneva in 1559; he split the school into seven grade levels and placed ten pupils under a tutor in each. The English Puritans then adopted the levels institution from Calvin and carried it to America along with their use of education for their "errand into the wilderness."[56] Puritans used the latter narrative to justify their founding of settler colonies while dispossessing Indigenous peoples of their land and using education to attempt to convert them to Christianity, among other methods of eliminating their modes of study and world-making.

The following chapter examines how the verticalist mode of study became associated with an ideology of education as an increasingly powerful tool for governing the modernist/colonial world. But first, the next section theorizes how the verticalist mode of study was a key part of the emergence of capitalist relations, interrelated with misogyny and settler colonialism.

THE VERTICALIST MODE OF STUDY AS A PRECONDITION FOR CAPITALISM: A MORE-THAN-HUMANIST APPROACH

Karl Marx's history of "primitive accumulation" provides a useful starting point for describing the emergence of capitalism.[57] Rather than feigning positivist neutrality, Marx takes an openly political perspective, committed to the working-class, anticapitalist side of struggles. Taking a side is inevitable, as there is no possible position outside politics. Yet treating concepts as tools for deployment in struggles requires short-circuiting study of the complexity of controversies in these struggles. One such controversy is over how the emergences of capitalism and education were interrelated. Not only does Marx neglect this controversy, but his theory relies on explanatory abstractions that deaden inquiry into it. Instead of offering a language that enables open-ended, descriptive study of the

complex connections between capitalism and education, his use of dichotomous, modernist concepts—tradition versus modernity, and society
versus nature—serve as shortcuts around deeper inquiry.[58] Marx implies
that a communist society would require an alternative *kind* of education
in contrast with that of capitalist society, but he does not consider the
possibility of a mode of study that would be an alternative *to* education.

Marx's modernist framings keep him stuck within the education
romance. For example, in the third volume of *Capital* he envisions a communist world as a "realm of freedom" with "socialized man . . . rationally
regulating their interchange with Nature, bringing it under their common
control."[59] The nature/society dichotomy frames an imagined, stabilized
division of the world into two boxes. Combining this seemingly uncontroversial dichotomy with other descriptions allows people to presuppose
as already sufficiently described—that is, as explained—much of what
they are supposed to be describing. The limits of modernist concepts
on the Marxist imagination are seen in their narratives about commons
and enclosure: they tend to use a melodramatic storytelling mode about
the history of capitalism, a mode of narration that they share with liberal
capitalists.

Histories of capitalism from a pro-capitalist perspective tend to provide a melodramatic narrative, with heroic promoters of enclosure and
"improved agriculture" against villainous defenders of the commons.[60]
Prominent examples run from John Locke's defense of private property
to William Forster Lloyd and Garrett Hardin's "tragedy of the commons"
arguments and contemporary defenders of property rights in neoliberal
development, such as Hernando de Soto.[61] These narratives derive their
normative power from deploying modernist/colonial dichotomies, such
as calling the commoners "traditional, backward, primitive, and closer
to nature" in contrast with the enclosers as promoting an "improved,
modern, progressive, socialized agriculture."

Typical anticapitalist narratives portray a melodrama as well, but they
invert the roles: villainous promoters of enclosure against the defenders
of the commons as both victims and potential heroes. Traditional Marxist
views of primitive accumulation frame it as a historically bound, necessary, and progressive development. They frame the enclosure of the

commons as a key part of this primitive accumulation process. Marx saw the violence of enclosure, or what becomes "primitive accumulation" in the fifteenth century, as taking two intertwined forms. The first is the violence of expropriation, that is, ripping producers away from the means of production, particularly the land. Feminist Marxists have expanded this view of primitive accumulation to include the process of creating relations of separation between producers and the means of *re*production as well, such as Federici's theorizing of the witch hunts and broader climate of misogyny as ways of separating women from their commons- and land-based communal power.[62]

Marx theorized a second form of the violence of enclosure with the "bloody legislation," that is, legal acts and penal regimes that dealt with the newly property-less "free workers" by criminalizing and controlling their attempts to survive as vagabonds, robbers, and beggars, thereby forcing them into productive work in the new factories as part of a controlled and contained "working class."[63] Anticapitalist narratives often combine this melodrama of enclosure versus commons with the narrative form of a jeremiad, calling for a return to the past practice or ideal of the commons.[64] The melodramatic and jeremiadic elements of their narrative lend normative weight to their arguments. The simplifying narrative genres enable a formulaic romanticizing of the commons and stigmatizing of enclosure. This can lead to wishful thinking about left social movements' revolutionary potentials.

As an antidote, recent attempts to de-romanticize the commons have shown how there are *conflicting* types of commons and how some types are actually conducive to primitive accumulation and the emergence of capitalism.[65] Historian Allen Greer rejects the colonialist ideology that frames commons in the Americas in terms of a "universal open commons." Instead, in his more nuanced theory of commons, in the Old World, the commons "might be thought of as both a place—the village pasture—and as a set of access rights, such as gleaning and stubble grazing," which corresponds to an "inner commons," "located in the tillage zone of a given community."[66] Greer distinguishes this from an "outer commons," "the collectively owned resources in the surrounding area beyond the cropland." Based on many historical studies, we can now see that, although Indigenous peoples did not use a language of "commons," varieties of common property were practiced by Indigenous peoples all over the Americas.[67] There was a wide variety of these "Indigenous commons," interrelated with specific features of the Indigenous collectivities with their own "land-use rules" across the Americas.[68] When Spanish, English, and French colonists arrived, they were confronting a pre-owned continent. Part of this confrontation involved their clearing, plowing, and enclosing of farms, but it also involved creating "colonial commons," of both the "inner" and "outer" varieties.

Contrary to the usual narrative of colonization as enclosure, the expansive tendencies of the settlers' outer commons threatened the Indigenous commons. Greer gives many examples of these confrontations.[69] In countless cases across the Americas, roaming domesticated animals in the colonial outer commons often destroyed the land-based conditions for Indigenous peoples to maintain their commons. The colonists followed their own rules for governing the commons and only rarely respected the Indigenous peoples' rules, and usually only when it suited their purposes.[70] The expansion of the colonial outer commons, coupled with the colonists' violence, diseases, and accumulative desires, paved the way for colonial enclosure and dispossession of Indigenous peoples' lands.

The capitalist, colonial commons continues today in many forms. George Caffentzis and Silvia Federici describe how the World Bank uses the language of "commons" to promote "softer forms of privatization," such as by "posing as the protector of the 'global commons,'" to pacify resistance through legitimating the market as "the most rational instrument of conservation," while opening up ecosystems for commercial exploitation.[71] Appeals to the commons have also been used to remedy the destructive effects of neoliberalism, such as in UK prime minister David Cameron's Big Society program, which aimed to compensate for cuts in social services through recruiting unpaid volunteers for activities such as day care, libraries, clinics, and elderly care "to cheapen the cost of reproduction and even accelerate the lay-offs of public employees."[72] Another form of capitalist commons is when people use commons to produce goods for profits on the global market, such as farmers using

Alpine meadows commons for their dairy cows, providing milk for the Swiss dairy industry.[73]

Building on the recognition of conflicting types of commons, I contend that anticapitalists should also take the converse move of destigmatizing enclosure. Anticapitalists have often equated enclosure with primitive accumulation, while also framing commons as antithetical to primitive accumulation and, by extension, to capitalism as well.[74] Yet this is historically inaccurate, because enclosures existed for centuries before the rise of capitalism in Europe.[75] Further, there have been many cases of enclosure with effects *counter* to primitive accumulation, and, conversely, forms of commons that were *conducive* to it. One example of this is the history noted above of colonists' "outer commons" that were destructive of the Indigenous peoples' commons. A second example is from the anti-feudal struggles in the late Middle Ages: the peasants in the Drenthe region of thirteenth- to fifteenth-century Lower Germany partially enclosed their own lands to outsiders in order to exclude large landowners, thereby resisting the landowners' preferred mode of governing the commons with marks.[76] A third example is the court beguinages, where women took refuge and lived a mixed life in a compound that was often created through partially enclosing commons on the outskirts of a town, while within the compound the beguines shared an inner commons.[77]

For a deeper understanding of the links between the emergences of education and capitalism, we need to go beyond accounts that frame commons and enclosure as mutually exclusive. This dichotomy lends a normative boost to anticapitalist authors' arguments but forecloses deeper studying of the controversies involved in these struggles. An underlying problem with most of their approaches to commons and enclosure is their use of modernist/colonial assumptions, particularly the dichotomies of social versus natural, space versus time, and value versus waste.[78] These dichotomies have been deployed to legitimate the project of modernity/coloniality, such as through labeling Indigenous peoples as "closer to nature" in contrast with European peoples as "developed societies." Further, with the dichotomy of value versus waste, figures of modernity are framed as productive of value, while figures of tradition, the colonized

Others, are framed as incapable of producing value from their land and resources, and hence as wasteful.

For a more nuanced theory of primitive accumulation, I conceptualize commons and enclosure in a way that avoids modernist/colonial dichotomies. I define "commons" as modes of associating, or creating connections between, some people and resources.[79] Conversely, I define "enclosure" as modes of disassociating, or breaking connections between, some people and resources. In both commons and enclosure here, the entities of "people" and "resources" could have various extents of overlap or distinction—that is, the resources might be associated within, across, and beyond the constructed boundaries of the people themselves. In both commons and enclosure, people practice some norms of valuation and disposal for regulating their connections with, or separations from, the resources. These normative practices are related to the group's mode of study. The norms are learned and changed *through* studying, and conversely, the norms create conditions *for* studying. Further, the mode of study shapes the group's own definitions of the boundaries and identities of people and resources.

With these general concepts of commons and enclosure, we can define "primitive accumulation"—the creation of the preconditions of capitalism—as involving particular kinds of *both* commons *and* enclosure. This view allows for developing a more complex theory of primitive accumulation, particularly for theorizing its co-constitutive relations with a particular mode of study, the verticalist mode, and also with a particular mode of epistemology, the zero-point epistemology. The zero-point relation to knowledge constructs a subject-position—whether God, the state, the expert, or the self—from which a zero-point perspective can be deployed.[80] Such a perspective purports to take a comprehensive view of the world from which to give explanations—that is, descriptions of phenomena that include an additional description of them as true and complete.[81] For stabilizing belief in this position, its subject must be understood as politically neutral—that is, as immunized from political controversies around its historical and contemporary relations with particular bodies and places. The verticalist mode of study is conducive to maintaining this apolitical view of the subject. With the Sisters and

Brothers of the Common Life's innovative institution of ascending levels or grades of study in schools and their ideology of spiritual ascent, the verticalist mode entails the imaginary of rising up, out of the darkness, for a clearer, more comprehensive, more explanatory view of the world. This imaginary privileges the sensory faculty of vision over other senses.

Primitive accumulation is constituted through these modes of epistemology and study. It entails overt and covert forms of violence that can effect a new relation of separation between producers and means of production. Producers and means of production are not pre-given in such a process. Instead, their boundaries, surfaces, and identities are themselves constructed through this process. Examples of the violence of this process include erecting fences, legislating and carrying out punishments and imprisonments, repressing women with a culture of misogyny, and creating artificial scarcity of the means for life—food, clothing, housing, and so forth—that forces people to become wage laborers (producers) in order to earn money for buying commodified versions of those necessities.

Primitive accumulation also entails discourses that legitimate this violence and shape people's subjectivities in ways that make them accept it as legitimate. These narratives compose people's understandings of themselves as individualized selves and of their relations with things as "objects" or "means of production" separated from themselves. These framings include modernist/colonial dichotomies that box the world into explanatory abstractions—for example, "Education brings people closer to Society and further from Nature." Such explanations short-circuit people's studying of the world. *If* people subscribe to these framings, they create new conditions that are conducive to further primitive accumulation, because they stabilize belief in the "self" that is the main subject in the zero-point epistemology and the verticalist mode of study.

The Sisters and Brothers of the Common Life's ascending levels of schools and their imaginary of spiritual ascent provide a means of constructing beliefs in a bounded, individualized self. In chapter 2, I described a more recent, intensified manifestation of this phenomenon with the narrative of the school dropout problem. This narrative incites an emotional economy in relation to imagined motions up or down education's vertical imaginary: imagining a rise up toward becoming a graduate produces pride and desire, while imagining a drop down toward becoming a dropout produces shame, fear, and anxiety. Through metonymic slides, these figures are associated with other figures and images (e.g., obedient, valuable worker versus criminal, wasteful delinquent). By subscribing to the imaginaries associated with this emotional economy, people stabilize their beliefs in the surfaces of an individualized self.

To break out of these modes of thinking, I borrow insight from modes of life, epistemology, and study that are radically opposed to those of capitalism, such as the working-class, African American blues episte-mology (see chapter 2) and Indigenous modes of life associated with a place-and-body political epistemology and a horizontalist mode of study.[82] I take inspiration from Glen Coulthard's synthesis of Indigenous and feminist-Marxist political theory. While noting the wide variance among Indigenous modes of life, Coulthard theorizes the "place-based practices and associated forms of knowledge" across North American Indigenous peoples as the basis for "grounded normativity"—that is, "the modalities of Indigenous land-connected practices and longstanding experiential knowledge that inform and structure our ethical engagements with the world and our relationships with human and nonhuman others over time."[83] Coulthard interprets the mode of life of his own Indigenous community, the Yellowknives Dene, as including an understanding of land-based ethical relations between humans and non-humans that transgresses the modernist/colonial dichotomies of nature versus society and value versus waste.[84] On this understanding, Coulthard argues against calls for "a blanket 'return of the commons.'"[85] Instead, we should ask, Whose commons? In the Canadian settler state, the commons were stolen from Indigenous peoples, "*the First Peoples of this Land,*" and they not only still belong to them but "also deeply inform and sustain Indigenous modes of thought and behavior that harbor profound insights into the mainte-nance of relationships within and between human beings and the natural world built on principles of reciprocity, nonexploitation and respectful coexistence." Such reciprocal relations are "the grounded normativity" that guides these Indigenous communities' "critique of colonialism and capitalism."[86]

Coulthard's combined Indigenous political theory and body-and-place political epistemology resonates with "more-than-humanist" political theories that highlight the agency of non-human actors.[87] Against the tendency of modernist/colonial narratives to ignore non-human agency, I take a more-than-humanist approach to describe how non-human actors participate in the normative practices that shape configurations of commons and enclosure. When a human actor affirms or negates a connection that facilitates commons or enclosure, non-humans act in ways that can be counter to and/or facilitative of the human's action. For example, the colonists' domesticated animals overgrazed the vegetation in the colonial outer commons in ways that broke down the Indigenous peoples' conditions for maintaining their commons (or "grounded normativities," in Coulthard's terms), while preparing conditions for colonial-capitalist forms of enclosures—that is, facilitating a configuration of commons and enclosure for primitive accumulation. Further, this approach highlights how actors seen as human are composed of assemblages of non-human actors. Trillions of bacteria self-organize within and across the assumed boundaries of a human body, playing key roles in digestion, immunity, and the production of feelings of pleasure, hunger, desire, fear, shame, pride, and so forth.[88] These bacterial-human affects play important mediating roles in practices of valuation and disposal in configurations of commons and enclosure.

With this more-than-humanist approach, I theorize how non-human actors played key roles in the rise of the verticalist mode of study. The Sisters and Brothers of the Common Life and their associated schools experienced traumas of the Black Death in multiple outbreaks during the late fourteenth and early fifteenth centuries in Lower Germany, including in the town of Zwolle, the location of Johan Cele's school.[89] Two of the key theorists of the Sisters and Brothers' ideas died from the plague: Groote, their founder, and Gerard Zerbolt, the author of their widely circulated text *The Spiritual Ascent*.[90] The origin of the disease in humans, *Yersinia pestis*, a kind of bacteria carried by fleas on rats, was not diagnosed as such until the 1890s, after the development of bacteriology. Instead of describing the non-human actors involved in this disease, it was originally narrated as a "black sickness" (*peste noire*), attributing magical, evil, dark origins to the disease. These narratives deployed moralized dichotomies—black

4

Educational Counterrevolutions

MANAGEMENT THROUGH AFFECTIVE
CREDITS AND DEBTS

Why did the term "education" arise in 1530s England? What political, economic, and cultural forces facilitated its emergence? Why did it stick around? The only historical analysis that makes note of the specific emergence of the term "education" is in the essay "In Lieu of Education" by Ivan Illich, a critical theorist of education and a promoter of alternative modes of study with the Deschooling movement. "We often forget the word 'education' is of recent coinage," Illich notes. "In the English language the word 'education' first appeared in 1530."[1] In this chapter I take the baton from Illich for a critical genealogy of education to explore how and why the term "education" emerged and gained broad acceptance.

The anti-feudal struggles of people's rebellions were a first strike against the ruling powers. Processes of primitive accumulation, including institutions of education, were a counterrevolutionary reaction. In the first part of this chapter, I argue that the term "education" emerged and increasingly circulated in 1530s England because those who used the term saw it as part of a narrative solution to their crisis of governance. First, I situate the spread of the verticalist mode of study across Europe with Martin Luther in the political-historical context of the tumults of peasant rebellions, the Reformation, and the Counter-Reformation. A famous student of the Sisters and Brothers of the Common Life, Erasmus, probably brought the innovation of split levels of schools to England in the early 1500s, yet the term "education" did not emerge in English to describe this practice until thirty years later. A key change in conditions enabled the term to circulate. During King Henry VIII's reign in the 1530s, his regime faced a crisis of legitimacy in response to people's rebellions. His advisers saw the term "education" as a narrative solution to their crisis. The rebels criticized the "low-born" origins of the king's advisers in an attempt to delegitimize them. The advisers needed a new political imaginary that could replace the legitimizing function of the older, relational, feudal hierarchies. Their solution included the narration of "education" with a constellation of binary, individualized figures, such as traitor versus loyal subject, which came to replace the relational hierarchies of feudalism. Education offered a narrative solution to explain how an individual could transform from one side of the binary to the other. This contributed to primitive accumulation through constructing an imaginary of individualized producers in new hierarchical binaries.

The second part of the chapter examines how, amid the tumults of 1600s England, the practice and ideology of education was shaped into a tool of governance for the modernist/colonial world-making project. The English Civil War and the subsequent Glorious Revolution were expressions of parliamentary reformers' challenges to absolute monarchy. At the same time, openings were made for pushing even more radical reforms than what the parliamentary reformers desired. The reformers' espousal of philosophies of liberalism and humanism opened up a dilemma. On the one hand, they proclaimed ideals of universal equality, liberty, and rights to inclusion in government based on a social contract. On the other hand, they desired stability of the hierarchies (of class, gender, and race) that they were personally invested in maintaining. Their liberal ideals were ideological weapons for convincing the poor to support the gentry, merchants, and protocapitalists in their struggles against the absolute monarchy. Yet, they also aimed to legitimate the everyday exploitation of the poor through wage labor. These ideological functions of legitimating cross-class alliances were responses to the ultimate *dependency* of the ruling classes on the desires and labor of the poor. This dependency existed in feudal relations but became more intensified with the rise to dominance of capitalist, colonial relations. Liberal, humanist philosophers offered practical-theoretical solutions to their dilemma, including proposals for education.

In the royalists' and reformers' theories of education, they had both conflicts and continuities. I show this through examining two of the key theorists of the modern individual and state, Thomas Hobbes and John

Locke. Situating them in relation to the three-way class struggle between nobility, peasants, and the urban burghers, we can see how Hobbes and Locke wrote their different theories of education to serve different political projects. Hobbes's view continues the royalist line of elite-controlled education, while Locke picks up the parliamentary reformers' expansive approach to education and develops new techniques for raising sons of both the nobility and the rising bourgeoisie. While Locke maintains the framework of education as an ascending life trajectory for individuals, he innovates a new educational approach. With his theory of the self as not essential but constructed through conscious experience, he argues that education is needed for creating the boundaries of the self. The capitalist class motivations of this rising liberal project are intimately connected with colonialism and patriarchy. Locke's theory of education binds these political projects together, as he contrasts the educable self with the reified Others of the colonized, the poor, and women. He offers a provisional solution to the liberal dilemma through a pedagogy of managing the self's formation in a household-based affective economy of credits and debts—with affects of fear, love, shame, esteem, and anxiety. This "mode of accounting" gives teachers educational tools for suppressing possible collaborations across class, gender, age, and race that could be subversive of the dominant hierarchies.[2] This pedagogy contributes to primitive accumulation through further stabilizing the boundaries of the self of individualized producers. Over a century later, with the rise of mass education, Locke's educational mode of accounting will be transplanted from the household to schools with the pedagogical technique of graded exams.

THE ORIGINS OF "EDUCATION" IN ENGLAND'S REBELLIONS AND REFORMATION

The Sisters and Brothers of the Common Life (discussed in chapter 3) did not refer to the levels of their late-fourteenth- to mid-fifteenth-century schools as "education" or "schooling" (in Dutch, "onderwijs" or "schooling"). Only with later developments did the terms "education" and "schooling" arise to refer to such institutions of study with ascending levels. These concepts did not become terms in any language until the late fifteenth century. The first recorded use of the term "education" in English was in 1527, used with the meaning of "bringing up a child."[3] The first major written work to focus on the term was Thomas Elyot's *Boke of the Governour*, first published in 1531. Elyot uses the word "education" seven times in his treatise, defining it as a means for raising the male children of noblemen or gentlemen into governors who will create and maintain "right order" in the "public weal."[4] John Major notes that Elyot uses many other new words, such as "chaos," "democracy," and "society," possibly for the first time in print.[5] In the second edition, from 1537, in response to charges of obscurity, Elyot reduced the number of new words, replacing some of the Latin derivatives with "words derived from Old English or words already established in the vernacular."[6] Yet he kept the uses of "education" in this new edition, suggesting that the term had gained significant enough circulation during the 1530s to avoid being considered an obscure term. Why did "education" resonate while other terms became obsolete?

I contend that an ideology around "education" emerged as a reaction to the "first strikes" of rebellious peoples. The latter's alternative modes of study and world-making conflicted with the world-making projects associated with the verticalist mode of study. The initial episodes in the emergence of explicit narratives of "education" were in the context of peasant rebellions in England and Germany in the early to mid-sixteenth century with the Reformation and Counter-Reformation. In the three-way class struggle among the peasantry, the urban burghers, and the nobility, these rebellions led to feudal reactions of repression of women and "heretics" and the dispossession of peasants of their land, pushing them into wage labor for tenant farmers or migrating into the cities to work for the burghers. Yet, the urban burgher class also attempted to ally with the peasant class against the nobility and their allied church authorities. They attempted to ideologically incorporate the peasantry into their protocapitalist project through new programs of religion and education.

German peasant revolts were shaking the foundations of the feudal order in the early sixteenth century. Luther's doctrines added fuel to this fire, as he argued that people have the freedom to make their own terms with God without the mediation of the church. Although peasant leaders had argued this before, Luther's support from the burghers of the cities gave him vast resources to help spread his doctrine widely and with greater legitimacy in many communities. The Protestant Reformation was symbiotic with the rise of what Benedict Anderson calls "print-capitalism," as the invention and spread of the printing press enabled a faster and broader spread of Luther's ideas, with his works representing "no less than one third of *all* German-language books sold between 1518 and 1525."[7] Luther's doctrines provided the spark for revolt, breaking the dam of ecclesiastical justifications for hierarchies of lay authority and property relations.[8] The flames of revolt grew beyond Luther's intentions and control, leading peasants to demand full Christian equality, with leaders formulating their demands with justifications drawn from their copies of vernacular Bibles. The peasant rebels came to these conclusions and made their plans for rebellion based on their own study practices, separate from any established schools.[9] They did not call their collective studying "education." The rise of literacy and circulation of printed tracts in the vernacular, such as the radical writings of Thomas Müntzer, were aided by the development and spread of printing presses.[10] With the prospect of a general rebellion in the air, the wealthier burghers became concerned, especially during the peasant wars of 1525. In response to warnings from his burgher backers, Luther turned from inciting action "to preaching the need for consolidation of government, the church, and education."[11] To quell the revolt, he urged obedience to the civil power.

In order to enlist the civil authorities of the towns in this counter-revolutionary movement, Luther presented them with educational plans and pleaded for their implementation.[12] He argued for the secular powers to finance and administer his new system of education, which was needed both for training knowledgeable clergy and making people literate so that they could understand the religious services and learn their obligations from the clergy. Luther's plans for educational organization shared a key commonality with the schools of the Sisters and Brothers of the Common Life: splitting the schools into multiple classes and arranging them in an ordered sequence of ascending levels. Luther had studied for a year (1497–98) with the Brothers in Magdeburg and was fascinated with their teachings, especially, according to historian Albert Hyma, their belief "not only in the fall of man but also in the rise of man," as epitomized in the Brethren writer Gerard Zerbolt's masterpiece, *The Spiritual Ascent* (described in chapter 3).[13] A famous institution of this vertical imagery in a Lutheran school was seen with Johann Sturm organizing his school in Strasbourg into ten levels or classes with a planned order of teaching.[14] Lutheran schools contributed to the outcome of the peasant wars, pushing them in ways that supported the powers of the burgher class, while dampening their revolutionary potential and recuperating them into the protocapitalist project. Luther said the training of youth in schools was needed "for the welfare and *stability* of all our institutions, temporal and spiritual alike."[15] The powers of the church and the lay nobility were broken down, and princely rule was established over the cities as parts of small states with Lutheranism recognized as the official religion. Revolutionary victory for the peasants was denied, as the ecclesiastical lands went to the princes and town patricians rather than being divided equally among the peasants.

The ruling classes in England were well aware of the German peasant rebellions.[16] Fearing such wars in their own country, they trod lightly in relation to the more passive resistances from their peasantry, particularly against taxation. Throughout the early sixteenth century there were sporadic outbreaks of violence against tax collectors. In 1525, with the king seeking money for a military venture against France, these disparate struggles coalesced into nationwide passive resistance and various risings against taxation.[17] Cardinal Wolsey sent commissioners to the countryside to collect this money, called the Amicable Grant, but people were vastly resistant, as they were poor and lacked enthusiasm for a continental conquest. Many refused to pay, and in some places, such as Suffolk, there were risings of thousands of people. Some of the organizers of these risings were arrested and brought to the king, but he recognized the danger and, with political savvy, pardoned the ringleaders and abandoned the Amicable Grant.

After these resistances, Cardinal Wolsey was sensitive to their danger as well as to the reliance of the kingship on a partnership with the taxpaying classes. Compounded with this, the nobility feared the influence of

Luther's writings, which had crossed the English Channel. In 1521, Wolsey presided over a ritual burning of Luther's works, and throughout the 1520s people who read and distributed them were accused of heresy.[18] These experiences form the background to Wolsey's foray into new projects of schools for producing obedience among the masses. Combining humanist learning with traditional learning, Wolsey aimed to maintain the church against Lutheran heresy, traditions of the unorthodox spiritual sect of Lollards, and threats of rebellion from increased literacy and reading of the Bible and other books in the English vernacular, such as Tyndale's English version of the New Testament published in 1526.[19] Around this time, in 1527, the word "education" first arises in written English texts.[20]

Wolsey modeled his schools on John Colet's school at St. Paul's, having a division into eight forms.[21] Colet had himself been greatly influenced by Erasmus, who may have given him the idea for splitting the school into levels, on the model of the Sisters and Brothers of the Common Life's schools that Erasmus had experienced as a young student.[22] This "ascending levels" type of organizational model was an essential feature of the mode of study that would eventually be called "education." The levels served as a flexible tool for managing a large number of students in a way that disciplined students into obedience to the dominant mode of order. This tool is flexible in the sense that the character of the educationally produced order is open to different configurations, depending on the aims of the school managers and the content of their lessons. While Colet, in collaboration with Erasmus, designed their school at St. Paul's with the aim of providing learning for laymen broadly, Wolsey had a more controlled aim with his schools: to counteract the rebellious effects of widespread literacy. According to a later commentator, Wolsey's intention was that "as printing could not be put down, it were best to set up learning against learning and, by introducing able persons to dispute, suspend the laity betwixt fear and controversy, as this, at the worst, would yet make them attentive to their superiors and teachers."[23] This aim animated the Counter-Reformation and would guide more conservative education programs in reaction to further rebellions.

During Henry VIII's reign in the 1530s, his regime faced a widespread crisis of legitimacy. With the Henrician Reformation breaking from the

Roman Catholic Church, people were torn between obedience to the king and to their religious beliefs.[24] Theologians reflected this "crisis of obedience" through debates about "whether the fourth commandment included honoring and obeying secular authorities."[25] In addition to people's religious motivations for disobedience, many felt anger and disrespect for the king due to the way that he had broken from the Roman Catholic Church and had dealt with those who dissented from this move. Henry VIII had split from Rome because Pope Clement VII refused to grant him a divorce from his wife, Catherine, who was not producing a male heir. Going around the pope in 1533, Henry had the Archbishop of Canterbury, Thomas Cranmer, declare the marriage invalid. The divorce was very unpopular, and his new wife, Anne Boleyn, was popularly slandered. Those who publicly objected to the divorce and new marriage were subjected to trials and punishments, including fines, imprisonment, and even executions. In 1534 the Parliament passed the Act of Supremacy, which required the king's subjects to take an oath swearing that Henry, not the pope, was the supreme authority of the Church of England. In 1535, two well-respected figures, Sir Thomas More and Cardinal John Fisher, were executed for refusing to take the oath. Their executions caused further dissension, as people were shocked at the loss of "the most profound men of learning in the realm."[26] Further anger was raised by the execution of monks, such as the Carthusians, who refused to take the oath of supremacy. In 1536 the king passed a subsidy tax and seized the property of monks and other religious houses throughout the country, dissolving monasteries, nunneries, and abbeys if they had a net income of less than £200 per year.[27]

Simultaneously with all of these delegitimizing factors, Henry's regime could no longer turn to their old source of divinely sanctioned legitimacy, the Roman Catholic Church. Instead, the king's regime, led by Thomas Cromwell and Thomas Cranmer, sought new ways to create legitimacy for the regime and to suppress challenges. They interwove ideological and repressive approaches. Cromwell's main ideological approach took advantage of the new technology of the printing press to circulate letters around the country with orders to officials who were supposed to enforce and disseminate them in their local community.[28] These letters included new legal statutes as well as propaganda elaborating on the theory of non-resistance.[29] Cromwell also closely monitored and controlled the printing presses in order to suppress counter-propaganda. To enforce the orders and statutes proclaimed in Cromwell's letters, the regime incited fear in readers and listeners with threats of punishment for non-obedience. Laws against treason, vagabondage, and other criminalized acts were backed up with an informal policing system and courts, which meted out judgments of guilt or innocence.[30] Punishments for those found guilty included fines, imprisonment, corporal punishment, the galley, and executions. These were forms of the extra-economic violence of primitive accumulation, that is, the creation of capitalism's preconditions.[31] Cromwell intended that people's fear of disgrace for arrest, and especially of undergoing these punishments, would suppress their thoughts of disobedience, rebellion, and vocal critique.

But rebellion is contagious. Narratives from rebellious people themselves could counteract this suppression of subversive thoughts, making people receptive to critiques that could spread the rebellion further. Henry's regime faced another crisis in 1536 with the outbreak of two major rebellions, first with the Lincolnshire Rising and later with the Pilgrimage of Grace.[32] The rebels raised a stinging critique of the regime with their calling out the "low birth" of the king's counselors, a critique directed mostly at Cromwell but also applied to others, such as Richard Morison.[33] This critique exacerbated the crisis of legitimacy for the king's regime, for two related reasons. First, this critique drew an internal distinction within the king's regime between the "high born" king and his "low born" counselors. This division disconnects the counselors from their source of authority in the king and dispels the appearance of unity and coherence, which is symbolized in the image of the body politic often used to legitimate the regime's actions.[34] Second, this critique sought to delegitimate the counselors themselves, denigrating their qualifications as articulators of laws and policy measures for the commonwealth. Drawing critical attention to the counselors as "low born" prevented the counselors from drawing on the feudal hierarchy of nobility and gentry over commoners for a source of legitimacy for their words.

In order to respond to this critique in a way that could suppress it,

Cromwell's network deployed a range of countermeasures, including narratives of "education." Situating the rise of "education" within its political context, the overall approach of these countermeasures was to create a new political imaginary that could replace the legitimacy-producing function of the old feudal imaginary's hierarchies. This new imaginary entailed a new constellation of binary oppositions—with "education" as a means of transformation between them—that could provide legitimacy for the king's regime while narratively responding to the critique of the counselors' low-born status. To distract attention from the regime's own crisis of legitimacy, Cromwell and his network narrated a crisis for the commonwealth in terms of a problem of disorder or anarchy. Appealing to an audience of the gentry for this narrative, Cromwell's propagandist, Morison, elicited the gentry's fear of the threat to their wealth and property from the multitude, conjuring images of disorder in an imagined situation "when every man will rule."[35] Narrating the commonwealth's crisis in terms of disorder set up a prescribed solution of means for restoring and maintaining order.

The new political imaginary entailed a new way of conceiving the means for creating order in relations between people, land, and property. A key aspect of this imaginary was the beginning of what would become a distinction between state and society, as well as a distinction between society and nature. The term "the state" was not in circulation in the 1530s, but when it did begin to circulate in the 1590s the state and its associated institutions were framed as the primary means for creating and maintaining order among both society and nature.[36]

I draw inspiration for this analysis from Timothy Mitchell's theory of the "state effect." Mitchell describes the historical construction of an apparently *external* distinction between abstractions of society and state, framed as separate from each other in a "two-dimensional" relation.[37] I build on Mitchell's insights here for a historical analysis of how an appearance of an external distinction was constructed while suppressing recognition of the distinction's *internally produced* character. I show how a key part of this technique has been through the coupling of "education" with a constellation of dichotomous, individualized figures. I gleaned a clue to this theoretical discovery when I noticed that key writers in Cromwell's network—Elyot, Starkey, and Morison—all used the relatively new words of "education" and "society" while also centrally using terms that were precursors for "the state," such as "commonweal," "public weal," "commonwealth," and "respublika."

In the context of the Henrician Reformation and the popular rebellions of the 1530s, I inquire into how these writers articulated these new concepts together through the mediators of new binary figures that increasingly replaced the relational hierarchies of feudalism. Under feudalism, people were in hierarchical relations with each other, but these relations also entailed explicitly recognized obligations that went both ways. Although serfs and commoners were submissive to the lords and nobles, they also expected reciprocity, not of submission but of obligations such as protection.[38] The interdependent character of these relations was symbolized in the imagery of the Great Chain of Being.

King Henry VIII's regime needed to respond to challenges from the rebels. They found part of their narrative solution in replacing the legitimacy-producing function of the feudal hierarchies with a new political imaginary, which entailed new hierarchies. Unlike the relational feudal hierarchies, these new hierarchies included a constellation of binary figures and associated qualities. This new imaginary allowed for the ruling powers to maintain their preferred mode of ordering the world while also allowing for a limited amount of class mobility—that is, for some controlled mobility of individuals across the hierarchies. This imaginary decoupled class status from the feudal interdependent obligations, as well as from the rigidity of those feudal hierarchies. Some of the figures in this imaginary were new, while some were older but increasingly deployed. The binary figures include the witch (vs. the obedient woman), the vagabond (vs. the hardworking person), the traitor (vs. the loyal person), and the barbarian (vs. the civil person), among others. They were associated in this imaginary with certain binary attributes, especially darkness/blackness versus lightness/whiteness, idle versus hardworking, waste versus value, natural versus social, human versus animal, and masculine versus feminine. The devalued, stigmatized figures in the binaries were associated in various ways with the negative attributes. Some of these dichotomous attributes were newly constructed, while others drew upon older traditions, such as contrasts of darkness and light from Christian symbolism in which blackness was associated with death, mourning, sin, and evil.[39] With imperialism, colonialism, and slavery, this earlier Christian association of blackness was transferred to Native Americans, Indians, Africans, and other colonized peoples.

Even before English involvement in enslaving colonized people and profiting from the slave trade, ideas of blackness/darkness and other negative attributes became associated with other stigmatized figures within England. The new political imaginary for framing these figures combined the traditional Christian symbolism with humanist ideas that drew upon classical Greek thought. This is seen especially with the humanist counselors in King Henry VIII's regime drawing upon the philosophy of Plato in their theories of education. The figures framed as "educated" provided the positive, valued, light sides of the binaries, in contrast with the negative, wasteful, dark figure. The figure of the "educated" was constructed partly through articulating oppositional, non-dependent relations with these Othered figures.

The construction of "the witch" throughout sixteenth-century England was a way for men to repress and suppress women who dissented and rebelled.[40] During the regime of King Henry VIII, this repression of rebellious women increased. This is seen with narratives around Elizabeth Barton, the Nun of Kent, between 1529 and 1534. The government accused Barton of treason for her prophesying, but their main problem was "the whole idea that a young woman in the countryside could receive the same level of divine commission as the king himself."[41] The threat of the movement behind Barton motivated the government to execute her. The government's persecution of rebellious women is also seen in the participation of one of the key early promoters of the idea of education, Thomas Starkey, in the witch trials of 1538 in London.[42]

The construction of "the vagabond" as a figure of disrepute ramped up in the 1530s with King Henry VIII's passage of Vagabond Acts in 1531 and 1535.[43] These acts were partly a repressive response to the increased number of landless people who were roaming the countryside after being pushed off their land through enclosures. The construction of the vagabond as an Other of the educated person is seen in the writings of

Cromwell's favorite propagandist, Richard Morison. In *A Remedy for Sedition*, circulated in response to the "seditious" acts of the rebels in Lincolnshire and the Pilgrimage of Grace, Morison articulates a connection between "idle" people and "evil education."[44]

Another figure narrated as an Other in the 1530s was "the traitor." The first attempt, since 1352, to draft a new law of treason was made in 1530.[45] This was one year before Elyot's first published use of the word "education." In contrast with framing "education" as a way to bring up children of the gentry and nobility in the *service of* the commonwealth, the "traitor" was constructed as a figure *injurious to* the commonwealth. Cromwell sent circular letters around the country that called on people to inform on their neighbors for traitorous activity. Throughout the 1530s he increasingly expanded the scope of the laws of treason. In 1533, Cromwell found that he was unable to try the Nun of Kent for treason under the existing law, as her seditious activities did not count as treason.[46] In response, Cromwell's 1534 treason statute brought hostile propaganda within the scope of the treason law. With the 1536 treason act, words alone—and failure to take the oath of succession—became sufficient grounds for treason.[47]

These threats of punishment for counter-propaganda were the repressive counterpart to Cromwell's positive program of maintaining a hold on public opinion with his own propaganda. Fear of repression for disloyalty allowed Cromwell's regime to hide the internally generated character of the distinctions in his promoted imaginary. The treason laws were coupled with trials and a diffuse proto-policing mechanism of neighbors reporting to the government on each other for treason, encouraged by Cromwell's circulars.[48] Cromwell did not attempt to organize a formal police force or a network of spies; instead, the Crown depended upon the voluntary actions of the gentry, as Cromwell had little influence on the lower classes. He relied on the gentry informing on people in their capacities as private individuals, "both for the initial discovery of offences, the passing of information to the centre, and executive action against suspects and offenders."[49] The trials had an individualizing effect of judging a person guilty or innocent, with careful attention devoted in trials to establishing guilt for a responsible self.[50] The charge of treason

implied disloyalty to an object with a territorial definition, a commonwealth with governance of all people and land within "the realm." Thus,
the treason laws, proto-policing, and trials had effects of simultaneously
constructing ideas of "individuals" and a kind of proto-state as a "commonwealth" attached to territorial boundaries. The rebels in Lincolnshire
and the Pilgrimage of Grace also claimed to be defending an ideal of a
"commonwealth."[51]

In this political imaginary of binary figures, the regime faced the challenge of explaining how people could change from one side of a binary to
the other. Education served the function of portraying a possible pathway
of transformation. Distinctions between good and evil education were
developed in the writings of key theorists and propagandists—Elyot,
Starkey, and Morison—in Cromwell's regimes through the 1530s. They
drew their conceptions of education from humanist and classical philosophy, especially Plato, as well as from their experiences in the ascending
levels of schooling in Cardinal Wolsey's schools. Through "evil (or ill)
education," one could become a "bad" kind of figure, no matter one's
class position. For example, in *A Remedy for Sedition*, Morison argued
that the "evil education" of nobles is "the ruin" of a commonwealth and
that the servants will imitate their masters, becoming vagabonds.[52] This
gave Cromwell's regime a way of delegitimating the voices of the "high
born" among the rebels. Through "good education," one could become a
governor, no matter what one's initial class position. For example, against
the rebels' claim "that none rule but noblemen born," Morison argued
that "true nobility is never but where virtue is," and "they must best be
esteemed that have most gifts of the mind, that is, they that do excel in
wisdom, justice, temperancy, and such other virtues."[53] To bring up people
to have such "gifts of the mind," Morison called for education in the form
of a "good institution" of the mind, "handled and ordered as it should
be," such that the mind is "so taught that there be no rebellion within
ourselves."[54] This narrative gave Cromwell and others among the king's
counselors a means to deflect the rebels' critiques of their "low-born"
status. Thereby, they used education narratives as a tool to support their
own legitimacy as counselors for the king, in order to defend their own
credentials for narratively resolving the king's broader crisis of legitimacy.

THE ENGLISH CIVIL WAR AND CONFLICTING MODES OF STUDY

After the political emergence of the "education" imaginary in response
to the rebellions of the 1530s, another tumultuous period—the English
Civil War (or English Revolution) of 1642 to 1651—saw a deepening of
the complexity of narratives around education. Advocates of both sides in
the Civil War, the royalists and the parliamentarians, deployed competing ideologies of education. Yet both sought to control the "disorderly"
population through using education as a mechanism for disciplining the
"unconstant rabble" and guaranteeing the stability of the state. According to Ann McGruer's history of this period, education reformers in
1640s England—most prominently John Dury, Samuel Hartlib, Johann
Comenius, John Milton, Marchamont Nedham, John Hall, and William
Petty—were concerned to control the dangers of wider literacy.[55] They
aimed to make the populace's literacy an asset rather than a danger to the
state. Part of their goal was to use education to maintain religious unity,
which they saw as connected with state stability. Although the different
reformers articulated their programs for education in different ways,
they all aimed for a state-dominated stability and order. Milton and Dury
argued for an education program that would provide the monarch with an
educated populace that could defend the nation against military threats
and provide national leaders.[56] Comenius devised an education program
that focused on a right ordering of knowledge and education, seeing the
aim of education as constructing "an happy ladder leading us to God."[57]

A crucial element of these reformers' narratives of education was
how they framed negative situations and figures in contrast with what
they sought to form through education. They portrayed the instability of
the Civil War as a result of God's punishment, and they recommended
education as a remedy to prevent this fate in the future.[58] Nedham constructed an opposition between "the rabble" as uneducated, in contrast
with "the people" as educated.[59] He highlighted the danger of the rabble
becoming *mis*educated, leading to youthful rebellion, which he analo-
gized with a bowel disorder.[60] In opposition to the royalists, who feared
any kind of extension of education to the broader populace and aimed to
restrict education to the upper classes, the reformers prescribed a kind

of education for all people but attuned to their different "aptitudes." Hall argued that rather than restricting the printing press, it should be used in a managed way to educate the people "about politics, about their entitlements, duties, and responsibilities as citizens."[61] The reformers' education program was intended to fit education to children's different capacities so as to help them take their proper place in society. The reformers sought a limited kind of equality of education, such that everyone in the nation would be able to attain a basic set of skills through education.[62] Within this basic level of equality, they prescribed separations of schools by class and gender, modifying the educational content across these divisions with different aims for each type. Separate schools were prescribed for "the gentry," educated to become leaders, and for "the vulgar," assigned to workhouses to control the poor, keeping them in their place, while making them useful and productive for the nation.[63] Young girls of the gentry class were seen as "young gentlewomen" and assigned to separate schools with a different aim of their education: to become "modest, discrete, and industrious house-keepers."[64]

With the Restoration of Charles II in 1660, his regime squashed the hopes of the education reformers, as he reasserted social class rather than aptitude as the door to education.[65] The royalists saw the regime-destabilizing dangers of the printing press and widespread literacy as insurmountable and thus legislated the restriction of education programs and free presses so as to limit the dissemination of subversive information. The alternative solution, which the education reformers promoted, was to provide the populace, through education, with the capacities to interpret and evaluate this potentially subversive information in ways that would be consistent with maintaining state stability.[66] Both of these options sought to suppress a third option: recognizing and affirming that the populace already had their own means to interpret and evaluate information in ways that would be subversive to the state while constructing their own alternative modes of studying and world-making. Such a third alternative, an affirmation of study in and for rebellion, was seen concurrently with, but marginal to, the English Civil War, in the radical undercurrents of the Diggers and of the rebellious women who were repressed in the witch hunts.

Hobbes and Education in the Context of Anti-feudal Struggles

The royalists and reformers had both conflicts and continuities in their approaches to education. They converged in their support for a modernist/ colonial world-making project and in their opposition to radical alternatives. To clarify the political-theoretical implications of this convergence, I compare the educational writings of two of the key political theorists of the royalists and reformers, Thomas Hobbes and John Locke, respectively.

Hobbes and Locke wrote their theories of education in the tumultuous context of struggles around late feudalism and early capitalism. As I described in chapter 3, education emerged as part of primitive accumulation—that is, the creation of the preconditions for capitalist relations, which also involved the violence of expulsion of farmers from the land through enclosures, colonial dispossession and enslavement of Indigenous peoples, military suppression of peasant rebellions, and the degradation of women, seen most brutally with the execution of thousands of so-called witches. In opposition to the dominant view that capitalism evolved from feudalism, all of these forms of violence were part of capitalism's beginnings, as what Silvia Federici calls "the counter-revolution that destroyed the possibilities that had emerged from the anti-feudal struggle" of the European medieval proletariat—small peasants, artisans, and day laborers—who had "put the feudal system into crisis."[67]

Hobbes was responding to the political terrain created around the anti-feudal struggle. During and after the Reformation, religious pluralism stimulated the creation of competing education programs through what historian Lawrence Stone calls "the rivalry of the various Christian churches and sects for the control of men's minds" and "the loyalties of the poor."[68] In addition to religious conflicts, local grievances motivated many poor people to join the side of Parliament against the royalists, particularly when King Charles awarded contracts for drainage of the Fens that affected the livelihoods of thousands of poor people.[69] Before the English Civil War erupted, Hobbes had fled to Paris in 1640 due to his worries about political persecution. He remained in Paris throughout the conflicts (until 1651), meeting many royalists there who had also fled. In response to the disorder of these times, Hobbes hoped to help the ruling, noble class shore up their capacities to maintain their preferred mode of order. Writing *Leviathan* during this time, he aimed to prevent further rebellions and unrest. The passionate terrain of these struggles is key: he calls for education to instill poor people with fear of the state of nature, and with fear and love of the sovereign and the civil laws.[70]

Hobbes offers his theory of the social contract as a means to justify the maintenance of the monarchial status quo. The binding force of the social contract between the sovereign power and individuals is supposed to be based on the *reasonableness* of individuals' choices to enter the contract. In Hobbes's theory, a crucial problem arises when considering how reason can have any binding force on those who are seen as lacking capacities to reason.[71] This problem comes to a head with the question of how to justify a child's filial obligations, and conversely, parental dominion, especially since even the normative, reasoning adult man had once been an unreasoning child. Hobbes explores three possible solutions: the parents' greater power over the child, the child's gratitude to the parents, and the child's consent.[72] But, he ultimately finds each of these to be incomplete and unsatisfactory. Instead, Hobbes presumes that the basis of such obligation is a belief that it is in the child's best interests. Yet, he begs the question of who gets to define what is in someone's best interests.

Rather than continuing to grapple with these questions, Hobbes suppresses them through dogmatically prescribing that people are to be *educated* as to what their best interests are. He gives the state and its universities the charge of training educators with the correct doctrines that they can then spread to the rest of the populace. In *Leviathan,* Hobbes theorizes the role of education and the universities for maintaining a peaceful polity. Motivated by fear of repeating the upheavals of the English Civil War, Hobbes joined many of his contemporaries in blaming "impure" education for causing the tumults.[73] The education boom in the late sixteenth century had the unintended effect that the increase of literacy helped spread revolutionary ideas through practices of studying separate from education institutions, such as "intensive bible-reading, extreme religious enthusiasm, a flood of pamphleteering, and the emergence of radical ideas about equality and democracy."[74] Rebels, such as the Diggers, took advantage of people's new literate capacities. Their autonomous practices of study were sometimes called "education," but they were not part of education in the schools and universities of the ruling classes.[75]

Having diagnosed the existing approach to education as the cause of the upheavals, Hobbes prescribes a cure through a better kind of education. His elite-controlled ideal of education promotes a kind of "trickle-down" theory of knowledge. The "divines in the pulpit" derive their knowledge from the universities and the "schools of law" at the top of the social pyramid, and then act as "fountains" of knowledge to "sprinkle" it upon the populace below.[76] For the content of this "pure" doctrine, Hobbes implies that the universities themselves need to be taught and that his own doctrines in the *Leviathan* provide the proper lessons.[77] The sovereign's duty is to make sure his subjects are taught doctrines that are conducive to the maintenance of peace and order: not to desire change of government, not to be obedient to any of their fellow subjects against the sovereign, not to argue or dispute the sovereign's power, to honor their parents, to avoid doing violence to their neighbors, and to be sincere in doing all of this.[78] The purpose of this education is to instill poor people with *fear* of both the sovereign's punishments and the state of nature in the absence of a sovereign, and with *love* of the peace (absence of conflict) that the sovereign and civil laws create.[79]

Hobbes diagnoses an obstacle to such education in the problem of "indocibility" or "difficulty of being taught."[80] This occurs when people's minds vary from an ideal of their being like "white paper" for easy imprinting, and instead are like "a paper already scribbled over" with "prejudices." As a solution to this problem, Hobbes argues that the sovereign can prescribe the proper educational content, which teachers are legally obligated to teach. The philosopher Teresa Bejan notes that Hobbes "distinguished between different forms of teaching appropriate to different sections of the population."[81] The elite can enjoy learning in universities through teaching as step-by-step demonstration for "begetting in another the same conceptions we have in ourselves."[82] For "the vulgar," Hobbes prescribes popular instruction via the pulpit's "fountain" of knowledge—with means of persuasion, preaching, and pithy summaries (a civil catechism)—seeing "education of the people as a kind of sacrament of remembrance" and aiming to develop a "love of obedience."[83] This division of education into different types for different classes is a key way that both Hobbes and Locke deal with the complexity of studying the world. Such divisions short-circuit the possibility of collectively studying the messiness of political controversies. Compared with Hobbes, Locke offers an even more effective approach for using education to prepare young people for governance and to suppress their rebellious impulses.

Managing the Child-to-Adult Transition with Locke's Affective Mode of Accounting

Like Hobbes, Locke was directly involved in service to certain factions of the ruling class. But Locke was aligned more with the growing gentry than the nobility. Locke himself was part of the gentry. The son of a country lawyer, he rose in social position through his Oxford education, eventually becoming the personal physician of Lord Anthony Ashley Cooper in 1667. Locke also worked in colonial administrative positions that served the gentry's interests in plundering Indigenous American and African peoples' land and labor through colonialism and slavery.[84] Locke gained financially from investing in these colonial projects.[85]

Locke picks up Hobbes's basic problem for social contract theorists: how to explain the binding force of reason for those persons who are seen as lacking the capacities for reason. He follows Hobbes in seeking to solve this problem through the realm of education. While Hobbes offloads responsibility for education to the state and religious authorities, Locke empowers parents, especially gentry fathers, to resolve this educational problem in their own homes, and he equips them with new practical techniques and ideologies for doing so. Locke constructs education as what Michel Foucault will call a "technology of the self," which serves the purposes of individualizing, privatizing, and depoliticizing the problem of managing the contradictions of the modernist/colonial world order.[86] The key, interconnected elements making up Locke's educational innovations include a malleable but bounded self, a model of development for this self with a period of ascending transition from childhood to adulthood, and a pedagogical mode of accounting with affective credits and debts for collaboratively shaping the self.

Breaking from earlier views of the self as an essential, spiritual entity, Locke re-imagines the self. In contrast both with Descartes's view of the self as a mind separated from the body and Hobbes's view of the self as reduced to a machine-like body, Locke cuts a path between them with his theory of a malleable yet precariously bounded self. According to political theorist Chad Lavin, Locke presumes individual sovereignty while "subordinating the world to the self's organizing principle."[87] This is seen most clearly in Locke's theory of labor: through mixing one's labor with the world, the self is extended into the world and, conversely, part of the world is made into one's property.[88] Locke theorizes this self in distinction from the world around it and with an ideal of *sovereign* control over itself and its boundaries. This view of the self provides ideological support for the creation of individualized producers in primitive accumulation.

Hobbes had based the sovereignty of the self in a non-dualistic view of an organically unified "thinking-body." By contrast, Locke seeks a basis for the sovereign self in a principle distinct from the body: the "identity of consciousness."[89] Yet, the physical, living body continually refuses Locke's supposed discrete identity of a consciousness—through the body's boundary-crossing actions, such as bleeding, crying, sex, and digestion. In response, Locke prescribes education as a technique to discipline people into internalizing governance over these bodily disruptions of the bounded self.

For forming this self, Locke prescribes a model of affectively managed education. This model's imaginary includes an ascending transition between two phases of life, childhood and adulthood, associated with many other evaluative dichotomies. Locke narrates the subject of education—a European, heterosexual, gentry male—as undergoing multiple transformations: a "rising up," not only from childhood to adulthood but also from a heteronomy of desires and appetites to self-governing, rational autonomy, from immaturity to maturity, from dependence to independence, from emotional softness (associated with femininity) to emotional hardness, from incivility to civility, from idleness to industriousness, and from being uneducated to becoming educated.[90]

I use the concept of "modernity/coloniality" to direct attention to the colonizing processes that underlie forms of so-called modernity.[91]

Boosters of modernity narrate "colonial differences," which construct distinctions between the colonized and the colonizers. The most obvious colonial differences are those directly related to people's bodies and cultures, such as white versus non-white, European versus Indian or African, and civilized versus savage. Other colonial differences are more subtle, such as social versus natural, mind versus environment, and time versus space. In his writings on education, Locke deploys colonial differences to construct both techniques for expanding the colonial, capitalist project and legitimations for hiding this project's violent aspects. These colonial differences act simultaneously as *capitalist* differences, in the sense that they contribute to narratives for legitimating the rise of capitalism.[92] This follows Federici's insight that "primitive accumulation was not only an accumulation and concentration of exploitable workers and capital but also an accumulation of differences and divisions within the working class," including hierarchies of gender, race, and age.[93] Building on Federici's argument, I offer a theory of how differences articulated in relation to education were intertwined with these other differences.

To see how these differences operate in Locke's theory of education, I begin, not with his main subjects, but with those whom he excludes and marginalizes. Through deploying divisions of gender, class, age, and race in his narratives, Locke sets up a bounded scope for both the educator and the educated. The work of education happens on a self that is male, gentry, young, and European. Those who do not fit this bounded subject-form—whether as female, poor, old, Indian, or African—are made into the co-constitutive Others of education. By *abstracting* the subject of education from the subject's relations with these Others, Locke sets up a new practical-theoretical terrain for managing the subject's educational formation.

Almost all of Locke's subjects of education are boy pupils.[94] He makes distinctions of girls and boys explicit a few times as background for describing proper methods for the education of sons. For example, he describes boys as having relatively less concern about "beauty."[95] One point where Locke refers to daughters without implying a contrast is in his prescription to use violent beatings for instilling obedience in cases of "obstinacy or rebellion."[96] The link between Locke's promotion of patriarchal domination of children through education and of women through sexual norms is seen in the parallel Locke draws between the emotional economies that he prescribes for both: "Shame has in children the same place as modesty in women, which cannot be kept, and often transgressed against."[97] Conversely, Locke associates femininity with particular emotions that he seeks to suppress through education, such as sadness, obstinacy, and insolence.[98]

Locke is clear that his doctrine of education is not for poor children but for "young gentlemen."[99] He does have another text that discusses the teaching of poor children, "An Essay on the Poor Law," but he never refers to this teaching as "education." Instead, he calls it "work" in "working schools," which is part of his wider proposal for discipline and punishment against vagabondage, debauchery, drinking, and begging.[100] To combat these vices, Locke recommends more serious execution of the existing laws, and he proposes new laws with especially harsh punishments for begging, including banishment, hard labor, incarceration in houses of correction, cutting off ears, or transportation to plantations, with the punishment varying depending on the severity of the crime and the identity of the criminal.[101] These are the "bloody laws" that were part of the state-enforced violence of primitive accumulation, laws executed against people who were pushed off of their land through enclosure. The ruling class's creation of class divisions in the peasantry and criminalizing of peasant mobility give important context for Locke's class-divided modes of study. On the one hand, for poor children (both girls and boys) he promotes legally mandated "working schools" that discipline "begging drones" and "idle vagabonds." He recommends that the "working schools" double as wool-spinning factories that both increase capital for their owners and discipline the poor.[102] On the other hand, for the gentry's sons he prescribes "education" in the form of a child-centered pedagogy of emotional management.

In abstaining from use of the word "education" in his text on the "working schools" while using the word heavily throughout *Some Thoughts concerning Education*, Locke distinguishes between one mode of study intended for the poor and another for the gentry. He gives the title of "education" only to the gentry's mode of study. At the same time, he does include the poor in his text on education, as the abjected, dangerous Other to education's subjects. The "mean servants" are represented as a threat to the educator's emotional management of the student. The servants can offer the child acts of care and esteem that can counteract the educator's affective weapons of disgrace and shame when punishing the student.[103]

Locke also uses Indigenous Americans and Africans as abject figures. In his essay on "Study," Locke writes: "perhaps without books we should be as ignorant as the Indians, whose minds are as ill-clad as their bodies."[104] In "An Essay on the Poor Law" he refers to "Indians" in a morality tale about the "noble savage" for prescribing the norm of "civility."[105] In the *Two Treatises* he denigrates the Native Americans' agricultural capacities in contrast with European methods of agricultural "improvement."[106] In "The Fundamental Constitutions of Carolina" he gives Europeans "absolute power" over all enslaved Africans.[107]

Locke's educational method aims to manage and shape the behavior of children in their ascending transition to adulthood. He calls for forming children with dispositions to desire and value the favored side of the dichotomous attributes that he associates with the dominant social divisions. They are to develop positive affective relations with the dispositions of self-governing, self-regulating, autonomous, civil, mature, independent, emotionally "hard" adults. A large part of education for Locke is teaching children the "proper" behaviors of self-control in response to physical stimuli.[108] A key technique Locke prescribes for this purpose is to manipulate the children's affective relations with other people in their lives.

Locke's new pedagogical technique has depoliticizing effects. Locke shifts the focus of education from the political relations between groups of individuals and the sovereign, as it was in Hobbes, to individuals' relatively depoliticized relations to their idea of a self and their emotional interactions with other persons. In Hobbes's prescription of what philosopher Megan Boler calls a "collective, collaborative construction" of fear through education, he makes clear the harmony of this fear with the political purposes of the ruling class: to reduce conflict and stabilize the state.[109] Locke shifts how the emotions around education are constructed, in a way that obscures the political purposes of these emotions. In contrast with Hobbes's national scale with preachers instructing from every pulpit, Locke narrows the scale of political oppositions to a household-focused economy of credits and debts.

With the malleable self abstracted from the political relations of gender, class, race, and coloniality, on this "pure" terrain of subjectivity, Locke promotes an economy with a currency of affects. The objects of these emotions circulate within the self, across the constructed boundaries of the self, and between the self and persons immediately in one's life, including parents, tutors, servants, siblings, and community members.[110] The affects are centered within and around the precariously bounded self: disgrace, shame, esteem, respect, credit, anxiety ("uneasiness"), fear, love, friendship, and trust.

Although Locke uses only the language of credit and not that of debt, I interpret the negative emotions he prescribes as implying a kind of affective, ethical debt that counterbalances the positive emotions that he associates with credit. Locke frames an economy with a currency of affects in the form of credits imagined and felt as love, friendship, trust, respect, and esteem, in contrast with debts imagined and felt as sorrow, guilt, disgrace, and shame, as well as anxiety about these relations.[111] I refer to these relations as what Miranda Joseph calls a "mode of accounting"—or a "technique for constituting and attributing credits and debts"—through which the self is constructed as self-regulating of these accounts.[112] With Sarah Ahmed's theory of "emotional economies," I see boundaries and surfaces of the self (and of the "we" to which the "I" belongs) as not pre-given but as constructed in such emotional economies *through* the circulation of the objects of emotions.[113] Rather than theorizing the circulating and constructive character of such emotions, Locke describes these emotions as if they are contained "inside" the self. For example, he says: "If you can *get into* children a love of credit, and an apprehension of shame and disgrace, you have *put into* them the true principle, which will constantly work, and incline them to the right" (emphases added).[114] Thereby, he frames the self as if it has boundaries between inside and outside that preexist the circulation of emotions.

Locke's imaginary of the malleable self and method of education serves to construct that self's ascending transition to autonomous adulthood. On the basis of this imaginary, eventually a science and industry of experts would arise around education, "a science of personality formation."[115] The affective credit/debt economy around the malleable self gives educators a more definite scope for their expertise and instills the subjects of education with dispositions for a mode of accounting that makes them more pliant. In addition to the imagined construction of the self's boundaries through the circulating emotional economy of credit/debt, Locke's narrowed scope also comes from the ideologically and geographically *bounded* relations of this economy. On the one hand, this economy is bounded ideologically with divisions of child and adult, men and women, savage and civilized, rich and poor, and white and racialized Others. On the other hand, it is bounded geographically with the household or town or whatever area defines the community of reputational credit/debt relations. The malleability and boundedness of the self are actually not opposed. Locke's affective credit/debt economy increases the educator's ability to stabilize the imagined boundedness of the self through inciting students' continual anxiety about the affective relations of those in their community to their self's bounded appearance.

The imaginary of the self's boundaries draws on a dichotomy of mind and environment, which is a colonial difference associated with the social versus natural dichotomy. Locke's concern to construct a bounded self depends on stabilizing this distinction of mind and environment against phenomena that continually destabilize it.[116] For example, Locke has a long section in *Some Thoughts concerning Education* on how to handle bowel movement problems—dealing with the self-boundary destabilizing phenomena of what Lavin calls the "digestive self" through attempting to suppress and control it.[117] Locke also uses analogies of controlling "Nature," such as comparing a child to an unruly garden, to prescribe discipline through education.[118]

Locke's imaginary of an affective credit/debt economy offers educators the conceptual means for continually reconfiguring the bounded self's imagined relations of internal and external in ways conducive for maintaining order.[119] Locke prescribes a differential deployment of affective relationships over the developmental stages of their pupils' lives, providing a reinterpretation of the imaginary of ascending levels of education. This entails a gradation of approaches across two distinct periods of emotional association between the student and the parent, tutors, siblings, and servants. In the early stage, educators are to act as "lords, their absolute governors" with relations of "rule" over the student, so as to engender "fear and awe" in them, for "the first power over their minds."[120] In "riper years" they are to act as "friends" with relations of "love and reverence" in order to "hold" that power. Along with affects of shame, esteem, and anxiety, these relations constitute Locke's household-based emotional economy of credit/debt. Techniques of surveillance enhance this approach and are the precursors of educational practices of graded exams.

At the same time that Locke promoted these curated emotional experiences, he prescribed the suppression of emotions that limit the child's capacities to govern themselves and to be governed. He called for discouraging "sorrow," "insolence," or "obstinacy," expressed bodily through crying.[121] Like bowel movements, crying is a bodily action that destabilizes the imagined bounds of the self. The boundaries Locke aims to construct for these selves have a controlled *porosity*: they allow passage for objects of emotions conducive to forming obedient, self-governing selves, while they deny passage to the objects of emotions that indicate capacities to be ungovernable. "Idleness" is to be discouraged in favor of love of work, and anger that "offends others" is to be discouraged in favor of "civility."[122]

To increase the felt intensity of these affective, educational experiences, Locke prescribes coupling them with threatened and actual material punishments and inducements, including beatings and deprivation or allowance of commodities. To manage this educational economy effectively, Locke promotes certain divisions within the household—of the student in relation to the tutor, siblings, and servants—that aim to prevent affective collaborations that would be subversive to Locke's intended form of collaboration between educator and student.[123] When children are "discountenanced by their parents for any fault," they can "find usually a refuge and relief in the caresses [of servants]."[124] The boundaries of the self are at risk of "contagion" through such contact, so children are to be kept from "conversation" with the "meaner servants."[125] Locke recognizes that cross-class, cross-age, cross-gender, cross-race solidarities threaten the established order.[126]

Ultimately, like Hobbes, Locke begs the question for the grounding of reason as a binding force for filial duties. The cracks in Locke's facade of a seamlessly reasoned, liberal educational program are seen when he makes exceptions to allow violence: his prescription of beatings in the case of "obstinacy and rebellion." This exceptional violence is co-constituted with Locke's stigmatizing and marginalizing of education's abject Others, who are themselves treated with normalized violence.

Locke's affective debt/credit economy for managing the ascending educational transition from childhood to adulthood eventually became institutionalized in the practices of graded exams and courses that are central to education today. Grades first emerged at Yale University in the 1780s, as a disciplinary technique in the context of an increasingly unruly and rebellious student population.[127] Institutionalized modes of violence continue as the often hidden underside of education. In response to the struggles of women, the poor, and people of color to try to gain control over resources for study, the ruling classes have expanded education institutions to capture, co-opt, and manage their struggles. With such expansions, education experts have constructed new techniques for managing the childhood-to-adulthood trajectory so as to more effectively prevent subversive "contaminations" across socio-geographic divisions. These divisions continue in gendered racial and economic segregations between and within schools and across levels of "lower" and "higher" education. New ideologies for legitimating educational control have included the figures of the adolescent, the delinquent, and the dropout. Building on previous figures, such as the witch, the criminal, the barbarian, and the vagabond, they provide imagined forms around which the affective relations of education can coalesce. The contrast between the "educated self" and the "uneducated Other," as well as the ascending educational imaginary, continue and crystallize with the graduate/dropout dichotomy (the focus of chapter 2).

Despite the increasingly global hegemony of education, it is not the only possible mode of study. By presenting histories of how different elements of the education-based mode of study emerged contingently through ruling powers' reactions to threats to their dominance, I hope to have broadened our imaginative horizons. The next chapter examines a more recent movement for alternative modes of study in association with world-making projects alternative to modernity/coloniality.

5

Experimental College

A FREE UNIVERSITY FOR ALTERNATIVE
MODES OF STUDY

with Erin Dyke

When the administration of Macalester College, a liberal arts institution in St. Paul, Minnesota, pushed to end "need-blind" admissions in 2005, dozens of students responded with protests, calling this policy change "affirmative action for rich people." The administration initially framed their policy of "need-aware" admissions as a "financial necessity," but continued protests forced them to shift their rhetoric to a "balance of priorities" between "access and quality," while framing "quality" in terms of a higher ranking in *US News and World Report*. The protesters questioned the legitimacy of such rankings and argued that, instead of a tradeoff, "access equals quality."[1] Despite broad support across campus, the protesters were unable to stop the policy change. Yet, rather than seeing this as the end of their struggle, they took their failure as a spur for reflecting on the struggle in a semester-long process. Through their collective study, they found that the inequity they were fighting at Macalester was not unique but part of broader trends across higher education in the United States: increasing racial and economic inequalities in access to, and success within, colleges and universities, while those institutions compete for rankings that have little relation to their impacts on local communities.[2]

During this time of reflection, the participants came to desire a radical alternative to Macalester: an institution that could serve as both a critical contrast and a base for studying and organizing that would continue their resistance movement. They found a model for such an alternative in the Experimental College at Oberlin College and were inspired to start their own Experimental College of the Twin Cities (EXCO) as a social-justice-oriented infrastructure for supporting free classes that anyone can take or teach. One year later, a second collective branch of their project emerged at the massive public university in the Twin Cities, the University of Minnesota (U of M), out of three overlapping struggles: an attempt to save a program for racial and economic equity called General College, a graduate student unionization campaign, and a campus workers' union strike. Despite resounding failures in each effort, the organizers sought to continue their relationships and their movements. In a "People's Conference" for reflecting on the failure of the strike in fall 2007, the participants heard a presentation from an EXCO organizer, inspiring them to found a new chapter of it. Within two years, a third chapter was created by EXCO course participants in the South Minneapolis Latinx community, who put on free classes in Spanish.

From 2006 to 2017, EXCO hosted more than five hundred courses with thousands of participants. The EXCO organizers provided support for facilitators of courses through finding spaces, raising funds to give facilitators honoraria and supplies, publicizing the courses, and hosting pedagogy workshops. At least three main types of studying occur in EXCO classes, recognizing that these are almost always intertwined in any given class. First, in EXCO classes such as computer programming and bike or auto mechanics, the participants and facilitators co-produce knowledge and skills that they find useful for a job or improvements in their lives. Second, participants can produce more intangible benefits—such as relationships, creativity, and self-confidence—whether through a knitting circle, dance class, or reading group. Third, participants can transform the world (and themselves) through a class that contributes to a collective, prepares for the creation of such a group, or puts on a project or performance, such as in the Bike Feminism class, which created a feminist bike collective called Dames on Frames; the Dakota Decolonization: Solidarity Education for Allies classes, which led to the creation of a collective called Unsettling Minnesota; the Fermentation classes, out of which emerged a food-bartering network; and the Art Shanty class, which built an ice shanty with an art installation around the theme of participatory cartography.[3]

EXCO's principle of free classes destabilizes the motivations for attending and participating in normal university classes of "getting one's money's worth" and of earning grades or credentials. Participants are, then, free—in the sense of liberated—to produce their own motivations on the basis of their own lived experiences, desires, and needs. Through an EXCO class, the participants also enjoy a positive sense of becoming free: gaining capacities for self-organizing their own projects of collective study. Through their class discussions, the participants can redefine their singular and common desires for learning skills and knowledge as collectively validated needs and as bases for designing their class's collaborative study activities.[4]

EXCO of the Twin Cities blazed a unique path for radical study projects. What distinguished EXCO from most of the fifty or so free universities and free schools in North America that were coterminous with it is that it emerged out of struggles within and against normal education institutions. From continuing to engage with those struggles while creating an alternative, EXCO's organizers developed a particular kind of political project that, if strengthened and spread, could become a powerful infrastructure for supporting modes of study alternative to education. Yet, they have faced many challenges. Writing from our (Eli's and Erin's) perspectives as former EXCO organizers, we offer selected narratives and critical analyses of the challenges EXCO has faced, leading toward our conclusion with a proposal of strategic guidance for study projects that are embedded with movements for making worlds alternative to modernity/coloniality.[5]

Taking the lead from EXCO's formative struggles, a driving motivation for many EXCO organizers over the years has been the opportunity to create an alternative university that would, among other things, avoid reproducing the modes of teaching and learning, and the demographic composition, of higher education institutions in the Twin Cities. Instead of the predominantly white, middle- and upper-class knowledges and bodies that were valued at local universities and colleges, we would create EXCO as a working-class institution centered on ways of knowing and learning that resonated with people's everyday lives and histories, especially people who existed only on the margins, if at all, within higher education. Despite our experiments to envision and create a critical university utopia, we often failed, with organizers and class facilitators being mostly white and college-educated.

We focus our analysis here on EXCO's first six years (2005–11) in order to highlight what we see as a major shift in its organizing practices. EXCO began through practices of collective, messy studying in and through organizing and building "a/effective relationships" of creative resistance to higher education.[6] This continual, collective studying in the impasse enacted a mode of study alternative to that of education, as well as an alternative to crisis narratives about impasses in the politics of education (see chapter 1). However, this messy studying of questions and controversies—around access to/exclusion from higher education or around whom EXCO should be for—often became a source of discomfort. As an escape from this discomfort, some organizers (including ourselves) sometimes fell back on subscriptions to an epistemology of educated ignorance and to technocratic modes of crisis management. Our analysis highlights the various ways in which organizers tended to short-circuit, or take shortcuts around, these messy, collective inquiries.

Our reflections and analyses of EXCO's early years in this chapter are acts of care and love for the many people, over the years, with whom we have built relationships, agonized over values and vision questions, biked and bussed all over the Twin Cities to put up flyers, studied in EXCO classes, and cooked countless community meals. Our intellectual work is deeply situated within our experiences as longtime organizers, class facilitators, and class participants. In our lives as academics, it is often easy to avoid acknowledging the ways in which the questions we engage are constructed in and through our bodies, places, desires, and webs of relationships. The university often claims itself as the zero-point, ivory tower, or some heavenly location from which we "academics" have the potential to discover and produce knowledge about the communities "below," and we are rarely required to reveal our location, our intentions, or our desires for doing so.[7]

Writing this chapter became, for us, an opportunity to question the kinds of simplified and celebratory histories we (EXCO organizers) often told ourselves about how EXCO came to be. Instead of recirculating triumphal or teleological narratives that would smooth over the tensions that shaped EXCO in practice, we dug into EXCO's archive, excavating seemingly lost conversations and disagreements, in order to paint a more insightful picture. We conducted formal interviews with fifteen past and present organizers as well as numerous informal interviews with current organizers, and collected and analyzed nearly nine years' worth of meeting notes, proposals, and other documents.

The following more detailed retellings and analytical interludes attempt to reveal the labor and relationships of organizers as they unfolded over time. While stories or analyses of radical, autonomous projects tend to deemphasize these everyday, affective modes of relating and organizing, they are critically important for understanding how such projects can be sustained and can move closer to fulfilling their visions. Given our political commitments to the project, we are writing this analysis of challenges that EXCO organizers have faced in order to offer guidance for grappling with these challenges in practice.[8] We construct particular stories about EXCO that we hope can inspire and guide the creation of more projects for fostering movement-embedded, alternative modes of study.

In telling stories of EXCO's origins, we find a kind of indeterminacy about when and where the project begins. In the first part of the chapter, we give historical background of EXCO's influences and predecessors in other kinds of experimental study projects. In the second part, a retelling of EXCO's emergence, we highlight how EXCO's growth and change cannot be easily ascribed to linear narratives of intentionality-action or clean arcs of progress/growth and failure/decline, but were embedded within the place- and body-political relationships and study of those who were attracted into its project. In the third part we narrate how, in EXCO's expansion, organizers grappled with tensions from trying to hold together both elements of EXCO's mission: its engagement with university struggles and its creation of a radical alternative. Attempts to deal with these controversies through structural transformation ended up reproducing some of the technocratic, patriarchal features of the education system within EXCO's own approach. By falling back on an epistemology of educated ignorance and crisis management, the organizers short-circuited the process of continual studying of EXCO's tensions. Our co-written chapter and this whole book are minor attempts to continue EXCO's alternative mode of study, organizing, and relating.

EXCO'S PREDECESSORS IN ALTERNATIVE STUDY PROJECTS

EXCO's organizers were motivated by principles that stuck with us from our reflections on our project's origins in struggles. We refined these principles through learning about other radical university-focused movements and struggles over resources for conflicting modes of study. Alternative study projects can unsettle many of the modernist/colonial, capitalist assumptions that are associated with the education-based mode of study. They have been organized outside and across the boundaries of the dominant education institutions—*with and for* movements of the communities that are marginalized and excluded from those institutions and that, to varying extents, are enacting alternative modes of study. These alternative study approaches include popular education, experimental colleges, free schools, anarchist education, and deschooling.

"Popular education" refers to a diverse body of theory and practice. Developed by practitioners such as Paulo Freire as well as institutions, notably the Highlander School in Tennessee, popular education begins with the recognition that all people already have knowledge and power, and thus creates practices for people to transform their knowledge and power into consciousness and action.[9] Expanded by many, such as Augusto Boal, into a series of pedagogical practices and "games," popular education is for movement-based self-education.[10] It draws upon the support and infrastructure of people and institutions who, as "facilitators," "circle keepers," or "jokers," create transformative space-times for people to figure out how to make their movements more effective, build leadership and capacity, and live out the relationships that they desire.

Although popular education approaches take on the question of struggling with and for marginal communities, beyond the dominant institutions of teaching and learning, they often retain some assumptions from the education-based mode of study. Popular educators often present themselves as necessary mediators for progressive social change. Hiding behind the masks of care, love, and solidarity, popular educators "legitimize their intervention in the lives of others in order to conscienticize them." Thereby, they hide "the disabling nature of service professions, like education," which is "based on the assumption or presupposition of a lack, a deficiency, a need, that the professional service can best satisfy."[11] Yet popular education approaches could overcome these vestiges of the education-based mode of study, particularly if they can be combined with struggles within and against education institutions that highlight the limits of those institutions while practicing alternatives to them.[12]

Alternative institutions include "free schools." Under this category we include a general set of countercultural institutions of teaching and learning that exhibit, in different ways, attempts to challenge, and create alternatives to, the education-based mode of study. These include free schools, free universities, and experimental colleges, which have overlaps and mutual borrowings with the long tradition of anarchist study projects. During the 1960s, students around the United States established experimental colleges and free universities to appropriate the resources of their normal universities for expanding types of learning experiences and access to education.

In comparison to free universities, experimental colleges (ECs) were more explicitly designed to appropriate resources from the normal universities while attempting to change those universities. The first EC was created by students at San Francisco State College (SF State) in 1966. This EC supported student-organized courses, including the first Black studies courses at SF State. The EC was an experiment in the *undercommons*, stealing resources—including spaces, money, teachers, credits, and technologies—for studying *in* but not *of* the normal university. The EC facilitated courses with revolutionary content and fostered modes of study in these courses that were alternative to the normal mode of study at SF State. Through their collaborations with the Black Students Union, the EC helped build one of the most revolutionary movements in the history of U.S. universities: the Third World students' strike, which shut down SF State for five months in 1968–69 and led to the creation of a School of Ethnic Studies and a Black Studies Department. Yet the strike also resulted in the end of the EC at San Francisco State in the spring of 1969. Based on analysis of archival materials and interviews with organizers of the EC, Eli found that the EC organizers' potential for supporting revolutionary study was limited by their romanticizing of education, which was co-constituted with their subscription to modernist/colonial imaginaries.[13] In 1971, at the height of the counterculture movement, there were at least 110 experimental colleges and free universities in existence, but their relatively unstructured organization limited their resilience and they began to die out *en masse* along with the decline of the wider movement, dwindling to four or so remaining today.[14]

Connected with this movement were free schools that withdrew children from the K–12 public schools, which were seen as part of the "technocracy" that "seeks to discipline and limit experience to make it conform to the routines of the assembly line, the bureaucracy, and procedures dictated by the machine and the clock."[15] In contrast, many of the free schools—numbering between four hundred and eight hundred from 1967 to 1973—sought to create "personalistic enclaves in which every child, every teacher, was free to think, feel, dream, and engage in interactions according to their own authentic needs and passions."[16] However, there was a tension within the free school movement's praxis. On the one hand, some organizers, such as Jonathan Kozol, emphasized the political critique of schooling and remained engaged with social-justice-focused projects for more urban, racially and economically marginalized young people. On the other hand, other organizers, such as John Holt, emphasized the individual student's development of "existential wholeness."[17] With the decline of the wider countercultural movement after the end of U.S. involvement in the Vietnam War in 1973, the free school and free university movements also dissipated. Their unraveling was accelerated by the tensions within the movement turning into a split between three camps around three different kinds of collective study projects: "organic" community-based schools, public alternative schools, and homeschooling.[18]

In considering the factors that led to this fracturing of the movement, a key problem with the countercultural, often rural free schools was their complicity with a kind of individualization that unwittingly supported racial inequality and segregation. Kozol criticized them for "running away," abandoning their "obligation to stay here and fight these battles in the cities where there is the greatest need," an obligation made stronger as "the passive, tranquil, and protected lives white people lead depend on strongly armed police, well-demarcated ghettos."[19] Further, Kathleen McConnell argues that the free schools—through their deferring to individuals' "natural" impulses to self-realization and their rejecting of the impositions of schooling—were complicit with overtly racist opponents of desegregation, as both devalued the kinds of institutional changes deemed necessary to bring about desegregation.[20]

Yet, Kozol's overtly political free schools also contributed to the fractioning of the movement. Despite his push against the white supremacist aspects of the education-based regime of study through his call for permanent struggle with the public schools, Kozol was uncritical of a push for inclusion within that regime, such as with his emphasis on the "importance of learning skills for beating exams, getting into college, etc."[21] Related to this valuing of inclusion within the status quo, he rejected the counterculture's visions of alternative economies and alternative modes of study too quickly (e.g., he said that his preferred free schools are "outside the white man's counter culture"). Part of the converse side to his lacking a vision of a "beyond" is that he seemed to take the separation and pyramidal relationship between lower and higher education as a given, rather than considering ways that the boundaries between lower and higher education could be broken down and reconfigured (as we see with some contemporary experiments in free universities, addressed below).[22]

Overlapping with the free schools and free universities, a broader approach to alternative study projects is anarchist education. This movement is based around anti-authoritarian studying encounters for the sharing of skills and knowledge. Anarchist education is both a means to create a utopian society and a model of it in microcosm, what Judith Suissa calls "an experiment in non-hierarchical, communal forms of human interaction where, crucially, alongside a rigorous critique of existing capitalist society, the interpersonal relationships which constitute educational interaction are based on the normative role assigned to the human qualities of benevolence, mutual aid, and social cooperation."[23] Historical examples include the Escuela Moderna (founded by Francisco Ferrer in Barcelona, 1904–7) and its American successor, the Ferrer School (New York City and Stelton, New Jersey, 1911–53).[24] These have some overlap with the

U.S. free school movement of the "long 1960s," for which anarchist educator Paul Goodman was a major influence. Many of their principles continue today in the roughly thirty free schools (often spelled "skools") reemerging in the 1990s and 2000s around the United States, as well as globally.[25] Similarly to the countercultural free schools of the "long 1960s," the contemporary anarchist free skools—while having a relatively more explicit anti-racist, anticapitalist politics—tend to disengage from struggles with the dominant education institutions and to become self-marginalized in mostly white, activist countercultures.

Closely related to anarchist education are some contemporary free universities that arise from movements within normal universities, attempt to create autonomous learning spaces within and outside of their campuses, and struggle on their margins to expropriate resources and transform them. Examples include Meine Akademie in Berlin, Really Open University in Leeds, UK, Free University of New York, the Metropolitan Free University of Rome, and the focus of this chapter, Experimental College of the Twin Cities.[26] More than the free skools, these autonomous university projects bring together struggles of being *within* and *against* the dominant universities and *with* and *for* the studying and organizing of those who have been excluded. Their participants often grapple with the tensions across these approaches.

A fourth kind of alternative study project, deschooling and unschooling, emerged in intimate relation with the free school movement of the "long 1960s." Its main theorist, Ivan Illich, rejected compulsory education, because, according to Prakash and Esteva, he saw how it "creates structural injustice; teaching people to blame themselves for failing to reach its mirage of equality and success."[27] In its place, he promoted deschooling: "the current search for new educational *funnels* must be reversed into the search for their institutional inverse: educational *webs* which heighten the opportunity for each one to transform each moment of his living into one of learning, sharing, and caring."[28] Many educational reformers misinterpreted Illich, leading them to try to create alternative forms of schooling, such as alternative public schools and homeschooling. Illich criticized these alternatives because they "cover up the fact that the project of education is fundamentally flawed and indecent"[29]—flawed because it figures learning as taking place "under the assumption of scarcity in the means which produce it."[30] He feared that "the disestablishment of the educational church would lead to a fanatical revival of many forms of degraded, all-encompassing education, making the world into a universal classroom, a global schoolhouse." Yet these misinterpretations were partly based on his own mistake—one that he later acknowledged and recanted—which was that he "called for the disestablishment of schools for the sake of improving education." The more important question became: "Why do so many people—even ardent critics of schooling—become addicted to education, as to a drug?"[31]

Illich's critique of education overlaps with our critique of the education-based mode of study. We contend that the latter concept provides a more nuanced frame of analysis. Interrelated with the tradition of deschooling, some institutions and movements have continued its rejection of schooling while also creating autonomous initiatives for collective study that go beyond the education-based regime. These include the work of John Holt, Gustavo Esteva, Madhu Suri Prakash, and Matt Hern, among others. These approaches—similar to and overlapping with free schools and anarchist education—have remained marginal to the dominant education institutions and thus have hardly realized their revolutionary potential on any broad scale.

We see EXCO as partly a synthesis of these different, overlapping types of projects—popular education, free schools and universities, experimental colleges, anarchist education, and deschooling—but we also recognize that combining the principles from these projects creates several interrelated tensions in practice. In contrast with experimental colleges' and anarchist free skools' tendencies to situate themselves, respectively, either within the terrain of established institutions or outside that terrain, EXCO positioned itself—similarly to some popular education projects—on and across those boundaries. Learning from other experimental colleges, EXCO had a resource-using relationship with universities of the education-based regime (via student groups that allowed access to grant money and class spaces). At the same time, it adopted the anarchist free skools' critique of these universities for their key roles in the perpetuation of white-supremacist, colonial, heteropatriarchal capitalism. Further, it took up the spirit of popular education to translate that critique into a project for connecting radical movements with an infrastructure for alternative modes of study.

Yet EXCO went beyond most popular education projects as well by seeking to focus the imperative for radical change onto schools and universities themselves. This extension of EXCO's critique onto the established education institutions is one that its organizers made explicit in narrating its historical origins in university struggles. However, we contend that EXCO organizers (including ourselves) had never articulated this critique in a clear and coherent enough way for guiding our organizing practices. Thus, we see our project here, in conversation with other EXCO organizers, as shifting EXCO's self-description toward such a better understanding. Using the concept of "modes of study," we call for differentiating between institutions of study—schools and universities, including the dominant ones and alternative ones such as EXCO—on the basis of the extents to which they enact the education-based mode of study and/or alternative modes. The neglect of EXCO organizers to make such distinctions can be seen in a story of what happened when we were faced with the Minnesota state government's threat that, if we did not remove the word "college" from our name, EXCO would be fined an exorbitantly high amount of money. Instead of holding strong to our name and fighting the state to retain it, we capitulated and replaced "college" with "community education." At the time, we did not have a nuanced understanding of the political implications of these different names.

Recognizing that the education-based mode of study is inextricably bound up with the project of modernity/coloniality, EXCO could have created an infrastructure for alternative modes of study that are embedded with radical, decolonial movements. Simultaneously, this infrastructure could create means, not only for exodus from the dominant institutions, but also for transforming these institutions and redirecting their resources into projects for creating alternative communal futures. In crossing the boundaries between education institutions and community-embedded study, EXCO faced a further web of tensions around avoiding recuperation of its relationships within the dominant institutions, both on the level of its broader organization and on a more micropolitical level within its courses, as facilitators and participants brought into EXCO's study situations the dispositions and expectations that they had acquired in education institutions and the broader modernist/colonialist world.

Faced with these tensions, the easier path for organizers of projects like EXCO to follow would be to fall on one side or another of these tensions by limiting the scope of their ambitions to the well-developed blueprints of its four main predecessors. Such a limited project, however, is not the only possibility. Instead, we argue that organizers of autonomous study projects could push themselves to create something new that attempts to realize all of the desires for their project—the different ideals associated with the imaginal trajectories of their predecessors—simultaneously. In doing so, they can take inspiration from the Black Campus Movement, which sought to create a completely new university, the Black University, with their decolonial, abolitionist relations to the established universities.[32] Yet, embarking on this uncertain path—making the ground by walking—left EXCO organizers in the precarious position of lacking the blueprints for achieving some kind of sustainability and resilience. They faced the temptation of falling back on the stability of the dominant forms of institutions and subjectivities. In EXCO, the organizers had to develop practices of continual experimentation with, and transformation of, their institutional forms, while simultaneously maintaining a core stability through affective, trusting, place-and-community-grounded relationships, co-constituted with practices of collective study.

EXCO'S EMERGENCE: INTERTWINED STUDY, ORGANIZING, AND RELATING

After the struggles to save Macalester's "need-blind" admission policy, what at first seemed like a failure became an opportunity for study, inspiring the creation of a radically new project. Miriam, one of EXCO's early organizers, saw a silver lining in their failure to prevent Macalester's "need-aware" admission policy: "It cultivated a lot of conversation around access to education." Through these discussions, the participants cultivated desires for creating something new that could realize their ideals. Miriam shared her motivations for this constructive turn:

There was a handful of us who were interested in continuing the work of thinking about access to education at Macalester and, it wasn't me, but someone else had heard of the Experimental College as something that had been done before. I was interested in the fact that it was constructive as opposed to reactive. Some of the ideas that we started to talk about were that it shared Mac's resources with the rest of the community; it was a chance for us to get to know the community better.[33]

Although most of the initial EXCO organizers were involved in the struggle to save need-blind admissions, others became connected with EXCO in different ways. Callie was a sophomore at Macalester when her friend and housemate, Miriam, connected her with the project. Before it became EXCO, Callie participated in visioning discussions that led to its birth. She saw it as "a way for people involved in the end of the need-blind aid struggle to put their energy into something else. Over the years, it's become a bigger thing." On a personal level, she saw EXCO "as a way of exploring education more deeply." On a collective level, through many visioning sessions, they defined its goals of "challenging the lack of access" and of "trying to get people to think critically about higher education." Callie saw EXCO creating spaces for "participatory education," in which "everyone would have a voice."[34]

The story of the beginning of the second EXCO chapter, at the U of M, is not a linear narrative of protesters learning from a Macalester EXCO missionary. Rather, some of the U of M organizers and Macalester organizers had already built relationships with each other through other activities, such as the struggle to save the General College at the U of M, which was a program with supplemental instruction and advising to facilitate the transition to college for many working-class people of color. One of the eventual EXCO organizers at the U of M, Arnoldas, had participated in the General College defense along with some of the EXCO-Macalester organizers. He also learned about EXCO through reading a zine, *Dames on Frames*, which members of an EXCO class on "Bike Feminism" had created.[35] He then took an EXCO class called "Anarchist Anthropology," in which he became friends with some of the EXCO-Macalester organizers.

A few years after becoming involved in EXCO, Arnoldas moved back to his home country of Lithuania, where he helped found a project similar to EXCO, the Lithuania Free University. When he tells people about why EXCO was successful, he "often emphasizes the importance of people developing certain relationships over time," such as doing things together after the class, where "it's not always the result or end product that is so visible," but "relationships happen . . . that create a web or network of people doing things together." Arnoldas's own involvement in EXCO started through a complex web of connections: meeting an EXCO organizer, David, through the "Anarchist Anthropology" class, then bringing David to the post-strike "People's Conference" to talk about EXCO, which inspired the creation of a new EXCO chapter at the U of M. Arnoldas's relationship with David and his desire for studying anarchism converged with another political trajectory in his life: his solidarity with the U of M campus workers' strike, including his participation in a four-day hunger strike with an encampment in the middle of campus.

More than six years after the failure of this strike to achieve the workers' demands, Arnoldas reflected that one of their main motivations for creating a new chapter of EXCO was "continuing to have a certain space where either confrontation or critique or a different kind of engagement with the U could happen." Reflecting on their "feeling of failure," they wanted to address the seemingly intractable problem that "not only the U administration is the oppressor but also a certain disengagement of all the other actors that were constituting the U." For example, when on hunger strike, they heard "occasional comments from passersby such as 'these workers are a labor aristocracy. We are in an even more precarious position.'" They felt it was important to create "a critical space" for engaging strategic questions inspired by these experiences. Similarly, another EXCO organizer, Lucia, described the need for this critical space based on her experiences organizing in support of the clerical workers:

> And thinking about who the university is for is what made me think about starting EXCO because I wondered, if the university isn't for the people who work here, is it even for anybody who doesn't work here? So, who is the university for?[36]

In their quest to build an alternative- and counter-university, for Arnoldas, Lucia, and many others in EXCO, anxieties surfaced over the question, "Who should EXCO be for?"

During EXCO's first two years, centered around student groups at Macalester and the U of M, its organizers created an infrastructure for continuing the study practices and insurgent relationships that had formed through reflection on the failures of university-focused struggles. Organizers not only created spaces for such studying in classes but also made space-time in their own meetings for study of the messy tensions that striated their mission—especially the tensions around struggling "against and beyond": between ideals of radically changing the existing higher education institutions and creating alternatives to them. These tensions were present in EXCO's beginning, but organizers discussed them in increasingly serious ways in relation to EXCO's organizational structure, building to a crescendo in 2009. Their collective study was both motivated by and gave rise to concerns over *how* they would keep EXCO from becoming just another exclusionary university. These discussions dove into complex controversies over how to understand "community" and "education," which interwove with tensions over values and principles (e.g., should EXCO be politically neutral?) and organizational questions (e.g., how should EXCO define its structure in relation to the universities and various communities?).

From EXCO's beginning at Macalester, its organizers had expressed desires to diversify the demographics of who was organizing, facilitating, and participating in classes. Organizers saw a contradiction between their ideal of expanding access to higher education and their reality of mostly white, mostly class- and education-privileged participants in the project. With their growth to a second organizing chapter based out of the U of M, this contradiction sharpened. The doubling of the organizers merely replicated another university-centered collective and failed to significantly diversify EXCO's demographics. Organizers' anxieties about this tension were heightened in 2008. In a meeting of the U of M chapter, David talked about their need for "a plan for how to make a more diverse group of participants and organizers."[37] At a visioning session, organizers articulated multiple tensions within our definition of how "education should be: Free . . . A process of community resource mapping, and as such, build upon and strengthen existing communities and movements . . . A good in itself . . . A way of bringing people together for social equality and justice." Amy, an organizer and a grad student at the U of M, set out a tension: "How much do we want EXCO to be attached to the university and how much do we want it to be attached to communities outside the university?" Arnoldas also spoke about this tension and argued for an approach of "one foot in, one foot out," calling "to keep ties to the historical origins of our chapters, Mac with exclusion and U of M with labor," and "to do the community work, but also to simultaneously challenge the structure of the university." One of us, Eli, as a participant in this visioning session, noted, "We need to problematize the distinctions and boundaries between university and community."[38]

The organizers' discussion of these tensions was prompted by questions about how to define EXCO's shared values and vision. Yet they faced so many controversies about these questions that they could not agree upon an organizational structure. In response to a proposal to form autonomous chapters and class-creating collectives around different issues, Miriam raised the questions of "how we communicate our relationship to social movements" and of how social-movement-oriented classes could "break down fragmentation" between movements. She argued that "the more important issue is setting the tone for teachers about what we're looking for . . . not so much about disapproving classes, but about being proactive about what we're approving." A central question was how chapters should define their autonomy while having a citywide core that shared common resources and values. Some attempted to skirt around this discussion. For example, Dan from Macalester argued for extreme autonomy of the chapters—that "each chapter is free to decide" on its political approach. By contrast, others argued for continuing to engage these tensions in collective study, such as with Arnoldas's plea that "whether we work more apart or closer, we need a time where we can autonomously communicate with each other." He acknowledged that this "communication contributes to this feeling of ambiguity that is frustrating," and yet he insisted we should "try to work out a way to have both communality and autonomy." The group as a whole sided with this plea for continued study.

With their organization remaining informal and improvisational, throughout the summer of 2008 some organizers embarked on experiments envisioning EXCO's relations to different communities and universities. They built relationships with communities that were marginalized from higher education. They talked with workers at nonprofit institutions in the Twin Cities, including Project for Pride in Living, the U of M's Community Service–Learning Center, and the Waite House Community Center. The Waite House focused on serving a primarily Latinx community in South Minneapolis. Relationships with people in this community, mediated through the Waite House and its staff, eventually blossomed into a major innovation in EXCO's organization: a new chapter called Academia Comunitaria.

After an EXCO class on media representations and independent media was scheduled in Spanish at the Waite House, participants in the class asked for more classes.[39] Enthusiastic about this development, the Waite House director approached EXCO organizers to fill in their Saturday programming with EXCO classes. Several productive tensions soon emerged. First, while EXCO offered an outlet for the community center to create the types of politicized programming that it otherwise would not have been able to create, the legal restrictions on the space in relation to childcare and food made the organizing unexpectedly expensive and bureaucratic. Moreover, by starting immediately, they did not develop the base of relationships and community involvement—particularly as organizers—from the breadth of the population they were trying to serve. Productively, this meant that the organizers refused to stand in for the community and its desires, but it also resulted in two sets of classes that, while impressive, were not thriving as much as the director hoped. What resulted was the closing of open Saturdays for classes as well as the withdrawal of the Waite House's two paid staff organizers. This could have been a disaster for the project. What saved it was twofold. First, the community center had compiled the phone numbers of past participants, which EXCO was given when the collaboration ended. Second, a set of innovations emerged from the process: volunteer infrastructure for providing free childcare (which became the Twin Cities Childcare Collective), public presentations at food shelf distribution days, and a seasonal reflection dinner where past course participants, organizers, facilitators, and their friends and family were invited to come together to talk about what they had to share, what they wanted to learn, and what they envisioned for EXCO. Academia Comunitaria emerged out of these discussions, becoming EXCO's third organizing chapter. By the spring of 2011, a quarter of EXCO's courses were in Spanish.

The expansion of EXCO to three chapters increased its organizers' capacity to host classes—building up to over seventy courses in the spring of 2011. Yet, their shift in operations also forced the organizers to confront anew the messy controversies about their vision, values, and organizational structure. They revisited these discussions in May 2009, as Academia Comunitaria was getting started, debating whether EXCO's organization should be a network of autonomous collaborating chapters, a collective of collectives, or a single organization.[40] Despite having intense, elaborate discussions of these tensions, they could not reach a consensus. They sent the question to a committee for coming up with a proposal, but the committee did not follow through with its charge. Thus, the questions about EXCO's organizational form remained open. At another visioning session a year later, some organizers felt that their capacities were over-loaded with work from their expansive mission.

Analytical Interlude 1: Studying against and beyond Fixed Identities

Drawing together threads from the narrative above, we believe that the most important aspect of EXCO organizers' approach was their messy mixing up of organizing with studying and relationship building. In response to the complex mess of the world, EXCO organizers created space-times—in classes, meetings, and other events—for grappling with their controversial questions around how to engage with the world.[41] In their ongoing discussions about EXCO's values, visions, and organizational structure, despite failing to come to a settled, unified agreement on them, EXCO organizers still developed makeshift understandings that guided their fluid, informal approach.

Reflecting on these messy practices of studying, organizing, and relating, we theorize what organizers found important about them. The foundational moment for EXCO organizers involved, simultaneously, a yes and a no. They said yes to the joyful experiences of studying and relationship building that higher education institutions (sometimes) offered, and they said no to the limits on that studying, in terms of its limited access, quality, and associated modes of world-making. After dealing with the tensions between this yes and no through their attempts to reform the institutions, and reflecting on the failures of these attempts, they regrouped to form new practices for grappling with their tensions. These practices of study coalesced into the relatively more settled, formal institution of EXCO. Yet, through continually studying these tensions, they forestalled any fixing of EXCO's institutional form.[42] Organizers had unwittingly innovated a way to avoid reproducing one of the main functions of education institutions: the pressuring of students to subscribe to the fixed identities and life trajectories of the liberal-capitalist status quo—for example, becoming a graduate, pursuing a career, making a heteronormative family, becoming a voting, law-abiding citizen in a liberal democracy, and so forth.[43] Rather than inscribing students with desires for "unified, coherent, bounded selves," EXCO's messy studying, organizing, and relating corresponds with practices of grappling with ambivalent relations to education and troubling any conception of a bounded self.[44] Thereby, EXCO's practices counteract the intertwined processes of education and capitalist primitive accumulation—that is, by constituting collective subjects with relationships that transgress the bounds of individuated producers and undo the separations of these producers from their means of studying.[45]

An expression of these ambivalent relations is seen in the tensions within EXCO organizers' understandings of their motivations for EXCO—for example, between loving experiences of studying and hating the alienation in normal education. At EXCO's best, the organizers made it into a project for creating space-times in which they could play/work with these tensions, in meetings and classes. For a more micropolitical analysis of these tensions, we engaged in research through facilitating an EXCO course on "Radical Pedagogy."[46] Through reflecting on this course and interviewing participants in the course, we investigated how subtle modes of thinking—expectations and dispositions that we acquire through the education-based mode of study—infiltrate activities of aspirationally radical study and pedagogy. In a project that attempts to constitute an alternative mode of study—in which there are no grades, tests, credits, wage labor, tuition, or bureaucracy—we experimented with the different possible modes of association between, on the one hand, various aspirationally radical conditions of space-time, place, and pedagogy, and on the other hand, the habits and expectations that participants bring into the situation. Grappling with these tensions in the course as a kind of "playful work," we analyzed how assumptions of modernity/coloniality created obstacles that we experienced in our class and, more broadly, in projects for alternative modes of study.[47]

Organizationally, EXCO organizers' desire to grapple with their ambivalent relations to education and the self was seen in their discussions of overlaps between roles of organizers, facilitators, and participants. Also, this was seen in their discussions of relations between universities and communities, and of their ambivalent and transgressive memberships within/across/against/beyond the normalized borders of these groups. The messy intertwining of the organizers' affective relationships in and through studying in EXCO classes and organizing was the basis for the organizers, particularly the new ones from Latinx South Minneapolis, to decide to form Academia Comunitaria. Thereby, the organizers did not "resolve" their ambivalent relations to education into some new, coherent unity, but rather they opened up new channels for communicating about these tensions with each other. The relationships and discussions across the chapters cut across the usual segregations between people who experienced their ambivalent relations to education in significantly different ways: the Academia Comunitaria organizers/facilitators/participants, many with undocumented status that excluded them from higher education, and members of the university-based chapters with privileges in terms of race, citizenship, class, language, and education. The no of Academia participants enacted implicitly through their experiences of crossing colonial borders and evading police, and their many yeses—desiring study to maintain their communities and cultures and to learn new skills and knowledges—offered new tensions for EXCO organizers. They had to re-envision their project in ways that could expand their messy studying, organizing, and relating around these new tensions. At the same time, they needed to increase their capacities for engaging with such messiness, against the norm of escaping from the anxieties of ambivalent selves into the deceptively comforting liberal-capitalist fantasy of unified selves.

The new Academia chapter offered the EXCO organizers a new terrain for studying the tensions around creating an alternative study project. At the same time, their shift in focus to Academia coincided with a diversion of their studying focus *away* from the tensions that had initially inspired their formation of EXCO: the tensions between a yes and a no in relation to normal universities—that is, between creating a propositional alternative *beyond* the university (*with and for* those excluded from it) and struggles *within and against* the university. With the creation of Academia, organizers focused more on the "beyond" side of this tension. In reviewing our meeting notes, EXCO organizers seem to have continually deferred study of the question of how to define the oppositional focus of their project. It seemed easier, and more comfortable, to explore the mess of creating new alternatives than to attempt to clarify the opposing political forces in the terrain of struggle around education institutions. Only through later reflection and co-research have we (Erin and Eli) begun to theorize this political opposition more precisely with our concepts of "modes of study" and "modes of world-making." By theorizing the education-based mode of study and the modernist/colonial mode of world-making in opposition to alternative modes of study and world-making, we offer a theoretical avenue for continuing study of the tensions *within, against, and beyond* universities.

One key way that EXCO organizers could have continued to study this tension within their own organizing is around the idea of diversity. In their calls to diversify the demographics of EXCO, they (and we) seem to have lacked the theoretical tools to distinguish between different kinds of diversity associated with different political projects. Drawing now on Jodi Melamed's work, we can distinguish between the ideals of diversity associated with the project of liberal-capitalist modernity, such as liberal multiculturalism and neoliberal multiculturalism, and the alternative ideals of a radical multiculturalism associated with radical movements, such as the Black Power movement.[48] The latter challenged liberal-capitalist modernity and its associated projects of white supremacy and settler-colonialism. Rather than merely calling for diversity in general, such distinctions could help EXCO organizers avoid tokenistic practices of inclusion that would reinforce liberal-capitalist norms.

THE SHIFT TO COMMUNITY-LED CHAPTERS: SLIPPAGES, SHORT-CIRCUITINGS, AND AVERSIONS TO MESS

Expanding EXCO to three chapters enabled organizers to host, publicize, and support many more classes. Yet, with this expansion came critical questions around whether and how EXCO could maintain integrity to its principles. The increase of classes resonated with one half of EXCO's constitutive mission: to create an alternative institution for study. Yet, it had no clear connection with the other half: to transform the dominant education institutions. In 2010, organizers theorized this split as a tension in their imagined possibilities for EXCO's future. Based on our reading of meeting notes, we see this tension playing out practically in the form of three narratives. One was that, in the U of M chapter, organizers attempted to reconnect their EXCO organizing with struggles at the U of M.[49] The second was attempts to create community-led chapters, taking a model from Academia Comunitaria and trying to replicate it with other communities. The third was discussions of structural transformation of EXCO's organization.

In the spring of 2010 the organizers in the U of M chapter observed that their group was at an impasse. They noted that "there are only a few organizers who are students at the U; we need at least 5 to re-register as a student group."[50] In addition to this pragmatic concern, they focused on re-grounding the chapter in its "rooted history in the struggles at the U," aiming "to get more participation, build coalitions, and take part in struggles from within the University." As an idea for how "to get people involved and participating," David suggested that "we have a concrete goal, like working for course credit." The pursuit of this goal, among others, became the U of M organizers' focus throughout that summer and fall. At another meeting they articulated a multi-pronged strategy: students would earn credit at the university for taking classes through

EXCO, and the content of these classes would engage the participants in organizing at the university, such as classes on "speed-up, access, and organization at the U in the last 50 years," on "radical history at the U," and on "visions for a new university."[51] Getting credit was seen as a way to give people "more time to do the organizing they want to do and also as a way of having more organizers," while being "self-reflective . . . about involving different people from across the U."

The principle that inspired some organizers for this project was the idea of "inflating the credit," borrowed from a social center in Rome called ESC.[52] The organizers recognized that "the really hard part is the credit part," particularly through building relationships with faculty at the U of M who could give students credit, such as through an independent study course or service learning. To address this challenge, they devoted several meetings to planning a reflection dinner with professors and others who might be interested in receiving credit and organizing projects.[53] They framed this project in relation to a wider aim of "building a movement for free education and a democratic university at the U of M."[54] In planning for the reflection dinner, one of the guidelines was to "talk up the point that we're experimenting; we're running it ourselves, so it's going to be a little messy."[55]

The reflection dinner resulted in a rich discussion with several undergraduate and graduate students. Despite having months of planning and outreach, however, no faculty came to the meeting. Over the years, a few students figured out ways to gain credits for involvement in EXCO as either facilitators or organizers, but EXCO had not implemented a program to "inflate the credit." Yet, the discussions at the reflection dinner did lead to another project: a "Disorientation Gathering" at the U of M, which took place on the October 7, 2010, National Day of Action in Defense of Education, and during Ethnic Studies Week. Inspired by disorientation guides that student groups at other universities had made to counter their administrations' "student orientations," the Gathering sought to "disorient" people through "unsettling dominant understandings of the U and its history" as well as to "re-orient" through "helping situate current organizing in relation to a broader history of struggles at the U."[56] Ideally, the Gathering was also supposed to channel "some of these new relationships and collective energies into creating new classes through EXCO."

The Gathering failed to meet its main goal but had unintended benefits. Around forty attendees participated in a "popular education"–style activity, discussed their ideas for issues around struggles at the U of M that they would like to study, and heard speakers on contemporary and historical movements.[57] Although the Gathering did not result in any new EXCO classes, it did contribute to building relationships that coalesced into the most powerful project around education organizing at the U of M that year: the "Whose University?" movement, which was a massive collaboration of over a dozen student groups focused on struggles at the U of M around access, maintaining cultural space for students of color, and saving the ethnic studies departments in the face of budget cuts.[58]

Although much discussion at U of M chapter meetings focused on reconnecting EXCO with struggles at the university, organizers devoted just as much, if not more, energy to creating new community-led chapters on the model of Academia Comunitaria. We tried to see overlaps between these two narratives—for example, to "think about the U of M chapter as a communities-based chapter itself with goals to be involved in struggles with the wider U community and surrounding communities like Cedar-Riverside."[59] Yet, in practice, they had little overlap.

At the peak of EXCO's organizing strength in the fall of 2010, the U of M chapter decided to split its energies into two directions: one relating to struggles at the U of M and the other creating a new EXCO chapter grounded in "the South Minneapolis radical/anarchist community."[60] Looking back, the timing of this decision seems strange, coming immediately after the Disorientation Gathering, an event to which organizers had devoted three months of planning. Perhaps we felt disappointed, as that event had not lived up to our expectations of serving as an incubator for EXCO classes around U of M struggles. The rationale that the organizers gave for creating this second chapter was that we had "two bases of relationships," one at the U of M and the other in the DIY/anarchist community, and that some in the group, those who were not students, were not well connected or invested with the U of M struggles. At least some organizers said that we should prioritize building the U of M chapter and its organizing base, because of its constituent mission in those struggles, and to make the anarchist chapter a second priority. However, over the next few months the organizers veered away from their focus on the U of M and moved toward a focus on the new anarchist chapter, which became known as the South Side Free Skool (SSFS).[61] Part of their reasoning for this move was framing the SSFS according to the model of community-led chapters, seeing it as having a more clearly definable community in comparison with the U of M. Reflecting critically now, this observation obscured the communities of students of color at the U of M, such as those who had organized the "Whose University?" event.

Another reason given for expanding to community-based chapters beyond the U of M was that organizers wanted to break out of EXCO's centering of higher education institutions. They wanted to stop reinforcing these institutions' position at the top of the education pyramid. The creation of the SSFS chapter as well as two other attempts to create community-based chapters in particular neighborhoods allowed for expanding EXCO's mission to include engagement in struggles around education more broadly, in the realm of P–12 education, an area that is often treated in more feminized ways. Many Macalester EXCO organizers were gearing up for graduation and felt that since their institutional membership was nearing its end, they wanted to create a community-based chapter in which they and others could be involved long-term. Jason explained that he was also tiring of the "not-so-sexy" work of logistics and emailing facilitators and wanted to engage in "relationship-based activism that's about changing hearts and structures."[62] He said he felt the most energized in EXCO when he was doing neighborhood-based organizing. The Macalester organizers tried to reach out to community residents and leaders in Hamline-Midway, a diverse working-class neighborhood nearby Macalester, to find potential class spaces and facilitators. Similarly, some U of M organizers built what initially seemed like a solid base of organizers within Cedar-Riverside, a neighborhood bordering the U of M whose residents were mainly East African refugees. Yet in both of these projects, decreasing organizer capacity and challenges of adapting to the complex politics and desires of neighborhood residents led to their eventual collapse. Neither neighborhood easily fit into Academia's model of a community-based chapter.

The third simultaneous narrative in play was a kind of metanarrative in relation to the other two. The organizers attempted to figure out how to maintain and strengthen their capacities to organize together in light of challenges brought on from EXCO's new directions, while continuing to provide support for courses each semester. Their approach took two main forms. One approach was to expand and intensify the messy process of relating, studying, and organizing in the reflection and visioning meetings. The other approach, proposed in such meetings, attempted a structural transformation of EXCO's organization.

At a citywide organizer retreat in November 2010, the organizers articulated their different experiences with EXCO's challenges. Jason, a Macalester organizer, noted that "citywide [meetings] are not convenient for both chapters [Macalester and Academia]" and that student organizers have difficulties making time for citywide meetings, especially when they are located far from their homes.[63] Andrew M. emphasized the challenges of becoming involved and fitting in as a new organizer: "despite hearing that there is so much to potentially be done, but we don't have the organizer energy or capacity, I'm unclear about who is doing what and what's not getting done." Ayanna echoed this concern: "People might not get equal access to organizing." Christian, an Academia organizer, emphasized the strain on their capacities in the Academia chapter: "It's only three or four people doing everything, and mostly just two people doing it by phone and email. There's a lot of ignorance about Latin@ culture. It's hard to invite people into EXCO—people are looking for resources, trying to work and deal with needs, not enjoying life." Rita raised her concerns "around balancing energy levels—I want to give more and to also take care of myself, and not ask too much of others." Erin and others echoed this burnout concern and also pointed to the need for better communication among organizers.

In response, they suggested more or less formal approaches to these problems. The more formal approach was to argue for new organizational roles: "inter-chapter liaisons," "treasurer," "secretaries," and "go-to persons" (i.e., bottom-liners of the working groups). In the most extreme version, some organizers built on the concern with fund-raising problems to push toward creating a nonprofit 501(c)(3) organization. The other, more informal tendency was to create more opportunities for communication. This was seen, for example, in Kelly L.'s call for more "cross-chapter participation, and citywide communication," and in Erin's noting that "citywide meetings are a good space, but there is not enough time. Could they be more often and more regular?"[64] These formal and informal tendencies overlapped, and some organizers pushed for both: for example, Kelly L. called for "inter-chapter liaisons" and Erin said, "We could use more clearly defined roles." Yet certain organizers, particularly a few cisgender males (including one of us, Eli), pushed more heavily than others for a more formalizing approach, which eventually prevailed.

The tension between these two approaches was expressed repeatedly at meetings. In a discussion at a U of M chapter meeting, everybody said they felt "low energy."[65] This was problematic, because we had just implemented new organizing roles that required each of us to devote *more* energy. Despite talking so much about the organizing structure, organizers' bodies and affective relationships were not energized sustainably enough to give life to that structure. Going into 2011, the organizers ran out of steam and could not continue to hold together all three of their narratives at once. Since the plan for structural transformation was biased toward the parts of EXCO's mission that were replicable (community-led chapters), when the plan became relatively solidified, that part of the mission won out: deemphasizing struggles at the U of M and focusing on creating new chapters while continuing the usual business of EXCO's operations. Faith in the new structure and a replicable model allowed organizers to take shortcuts around the challenge of studying EXCO's controversies. Yet, its tensions continued to bubble to the surface.

Analytical Interlude 2: Structural Transformation as an Escape from EXCO's Impasse

Reflecting now on EXCO's transition from the height of its capacity in 2010 to its reorganization in 2011, we make a diagnosis similar to the one we made about EXCO's earlier period. Again, the aspects of EXCO we

can look back on and affirm emerged in and through the organizers' process of organizing, studying, and relationship building, while its failures
occurred from attempts to take shortcuts around, or short-circuitings of,
this messy process. These shortcuts and short-circuitings were multiple
and interconnected: shifting to "earning credits" as a goal of study practices, relying on top-down expertise, and settling on particular roles for
organizers. Each of these shifts reproduced elements of the education-
based mode of study and the liberal-capitalist, modernist/colonial mode of
world-making. Thereby, these shifts served as escapes from the disorder
of messy studying, organizing, and relating into a mode of ordering associated with the dominant modes of study and world-making.

First, the proposed shift to a strategy of "inflating the credit"—giving
credits for EXCO organizing or for taking or facilitating EXCO classes—
would have introduced an external motivation for involvement in EXCO.
In other words, it would have short-circuited the need for EXCO participants to engage in studying, organizing, and relationship building with
other participants as the source for creating and maintaining their motivations for involvement. This would have partly reproduced an element
of the education-based mode of study, namely, its affective economy of
credits and debts (with emotions of pride, shame, fear, and anxiety—
elaborated in chapter 4). This would cut against EXCO's principle of
having no grades, exams, credits, or financial debt, which disentangled
studying from education's "mode of accounting." Yet earning credits can
still be important for gaining work in order to survive within the capitalist
system. So, this strategy raises questions of how to organize "in but not of"
the dominant institutions while also struggling "against and beyond" them.

Second, the formal organization tendency rose to dominance through
a structural proposal that was written from the perspective of top-down,
patriarchal, technocratic expertise. Although EXCO organizers were
facing problems in realizing EXCO's mission as a whole—that is, in both
its oppositional and propositional parts—the proposal highlighted the
successes of only one form of the propositional part, the community-led
chapters model, and sought to "transform all of EXCO on this model."[66]
The proposal took on a kind of zero-point epistemology, that is, seeing the
world from a "God's-eye" perspective above rather than from perspectives

grounded in people's particular embodied, place-located experiences.[67] Such an approach also relies on the modernist view of the world as split into a binary of the realm of representations—which experts produce correct knowledge of—and the realm of the represented.[68] This desire for the certain settled knowledge of expertise was seen in the proposal and in discussions promoting it. Concerns about the current organization were expressed as "a tendency to get stuck in uncertainties" and "confusing communication dynamics." In contrast, the proposed new organizational form (of community-based chapters and citywide organizing teams with go-to persons) was to make "chapter functioning that is much more simple."[69] Organizers used abstract phrases to signify this desire for certainty in their relationships, such as "a critical mass," "a solid place," and "structure."

Third, and related to the expertise-driven proposal, was a move to implement *roles* in the organization, including the citywide secretaries, treasurer, and the go-to persons. Organizers were expected to develop expert knowledge of how to perform their role. The euphemism "go-to persons" *intentionally* masked the technocratic aspects of the role—that is, we also considered calling them "managers" or "coordinators." Thereby we reproduced a key element of the education-based mode of study from the higher education institutions with which EXCO's mission had been in antagonistic relation (i.e., expert administrators who rule over hierarchies of persons and knowledge). Taking on such fixed identities served to deaden EXCO's messy, playful experimentation. More-settled roles in the organizational structure hardened the distinctions between organizers and facilitators and participants. Also, the community-led chapters model engendered more settled identities of particular "communities" and a tendency for university community chapters to take on a "privileged allies" identity in relation to "oppressed" communities (rather than as accomplices in a shared struggle for mutual liberation, willing to "pick up a hammer" against the institutions, including universities, in which our privileges were formed).[70]

The organizers were promoting a new emotional economy in relation to studying. The circulation of the objects of emotions, such as comfort and anxiety, produced and stabilized understandings of the boundaries of their group formations of individuals and collectives, which include the various groups involved in EXCO: the EXCO organization as a whole, the EXCO chapters, the communities, the universities, the classes, and even the "selves" of EXCO organizers, facilitators, and class participants. On the latter point, the self is a group formation in the sense that any conception of a human body as a unified, bounded group is formed through subscribing to particular conceptions, such as "self," "individual," "subject," "consciousness," boundaries of "inside" and "outside," and conceptions of the "surfaces" of the body (such as from perceiving blush "on" one's skin when one feels shame).[71]

These stabilized definitions of the self and other groups circulate in harmony with formations of the self produced and stabilized by the emotional economy of credits and debts in the education-based mode of study. By contrast, the messier ordering (and disordering) processes of EXCO's studying, organizing, and relating had allowed for continual destabilizing of any group formations of the self—for continually in-process conceptions of self as well as of the EXCO organization, community, university, and other group formations. By treating our conceptions of such groups as themselves objects of critical study—as questions to be explored collectively in the impasse—we had maintained a state of unpreparedness for governance within any particular order.

In previous visioning sessions, organizers grappled collectively with their disagreements and debates on political, ontological, and epistemological controversies (especially the questions of what EXCO's political values are, how should those be implemented through organizing, and what are the best ways of framing and knowing such values). Such collective studying occurred on the basis of their affective relationships and, simultaneously, transformed their relationships. These discussions drew on their body-and-place particular epistemologies and emotionally grounded motivations for commitment to the EXCO project. With the top-down structural proposal, what were seen as intertwined political, ontological, and epistemological disagreements between organizers over EXCO's composition—that is, the questions of what values are or should be in its constitution and how they should be interpreted—became reframed as technical problems of distorted communication (on a collective level) and uncertainty (on an individual level) over a pre-settled, correct knowledge of an already-agreed-upon set of values and visions.

Looking back through the meeting notes, we see gendered trends. Female-identified organizers tended to push for holding the reflection and retreat meetings as events supportive of playful, messy studying, organizing, and relating. Cisgender male organizers pushed more for meetings focused on structural transformation, centered on "business," and perceived as means for devising solutions to problems of inefficiency. This gendered division of labor reproduced patriarchal norms that associate femininity with emotional, reproductive labor and masculinity with supposedly emotion-free rationality and "getting business done." This observation resonates with David Graeber's critique of expert-led bureaucracy as a "lopsided structure of imagination" with unequal divisions of emotional and imaginative labor that maintain the intertwined structural violences of racism, sexism, and capitalism, among others.[72] A related trend of how such patriarchal norms infiltrated EXCO organizing practices is seen in how female organizers (especially Kelly L.) tended to contribute the bulk of the reproductive labor of translating and interpreting English-Spanish at the citywide meetings. Likewise, the Childcare Collective was female-led, and mostly women offered their caring labor through it.

These contributions of organizers who were not cisgender men— renewing relationships in retreats, translating, and childcare—were all essential ways of fostering and maintaining affective relationships across segregations of race, class, citizenship, age, language, and so forth. These micropolitical practices could be seen as creating potential points of synergy with a more macropolitical institutional shift that EXCO organizers attempted with community-led chapters. Against the pyramidal education system's norm of feminized P–12 education and masculinized higher education, EXCO's shift toward a community-led model was partly motivated by a desire to decenter the universities. Unfortunately, the organizers did not clearly articulate this motivation, and other motivations dominated that were more about pragmatically avoiding, rather than studying, the challenges of EXCO's complex political controversies, both within and beyond its organizing group.

CONCLUSION: INFRASTRUCTURES FOR ALTERNATIVE, DECOLONIAL MODES OF STUDY AFTER EXCO

Sadly, EXCO is now defunct. In the time between our initial writing of this chapter (summer 2014) and our revision of it for inclusion in this book (summer 2017), the EXCO organizing core dwindled until the remaining organizers felt unable to keep the project running. As neither of us was an organizer of EXCO during its last three years, we do not feel qualified to offer an analysis of its period of denouement. Instead, we offer some reflections based on our above analysis of EXCO's early and middle periods. Some problems that we diagnosed during those periods *might* have contributed to EXCO's eventual disintegration.

We see a key turning point for EXCO in its organizers' relative shift from political-ontological and political-epistemological discussions to technocratic, expert-led problem solving. The organizers allowed themselves to make this shift by subscribing to certain abstractions as guiding ideals in their model: "community-owned education" in a "diverse, community-based institution" with "community-led chapters." These abstractions were seen as representing an agreed-upon, core set of values, in contrast with how, in EXCO's early years, these values were continuously up for debate, disagreement, and study. Subscribing to abstractions of *university, education,* and *community* gave shortcuts around difficult discussions of controversies over EXCO's political values and visions. Organizers' romanticizing of community was seen in their assumption of a coherent "South Minneapolis DIY/radical/anarchist community" around which to organize the new South Side Free Skool chapter (though some critical questions were raised about its internal differences).[73] Likewise, in talking about Academia Comunitaria they often reified the idea of a "South Minneapolis Latin@ community."[74] Their romanticizing of both education and community was seen in their name change to Experimental Community Education of the Twin Cities, in response to the threat of being fined by the Minnesota state government for having "college" in the name. Also, the Spanish translation that we decided on (Educación Comunitaria Experimental de las Ciudades Gemelas) contains an interesting reinterpretation of "community" as "communitarian," which shows a tension in our understanding.[75] Alternative possibilities for a name were suggested that would have avoided formalizing the "community education" model, including "Experimental Collège of the Twin Cities," "EXCO of the Twin Cities," and using an Indigenous word for "school."[76]

Taking up the last Indigenous possibility could have been an incitement for EXCO organizers to explore possible accompliceships with Indigenous people's movements. Indigenous modes of study, in association with projects of decolonization and Indigenous resurgence, present alternatives to the education-based mode of study. EXCO, as a non-Indigenous free university, has acted in some minor ways as a decolonial accomplice by bridging between Indigenous movements and people positioned in normal universities, especially by expropriating funds, classroom space-times, and labor from the latter institutions.[77] EXCO has done this in support of courses such as "Dakota Decolonization: Solidarity Education for Allies" and "Unsettling Minnesota." In collaboration with local Indigenous activists, a group of non-Indigenous settlers formed with the purpose of "unsettling themselves," that is, learning to undo their internalized colonial dispositions, while supporting local Indigenous resurgence movements.[78] The courses were tied with practical goals in organizing for decolonization as well, including fund-raising for The Land Project (Oyate Nipi Kte in the Dakota language). A participant described The Land Project as "the first step in real, material reparations for Dakota people . . . an attempt to allow them to return to some of their traditional ways," including "wild ricing, sugar bushing."[79] In the Dakota people's worldview, wild rice plants and maple sugar bushes are agents that can be likened to actors in networked associations with people, land, stories, and affective relations.[80] Through telling stories that articulate vital, affective relations of kinship between the plants and the Dakota people, they give meaning to their conceptions of themselves, their communities, and their land. The Indigenous, specifically Dakota, mode of study exhibited here contrasts sharply with the education-based mode of study, which relies upon the modernist/colonial dichotomies between nature (plants, animals, land) and society (made up of humans) wherein only the latter are seen as agents of studying and meaning-making.

To build on the decolonial effects of these EXCO classes, EXCO organizers could have taken on more critical awareness of their own positionality as settler-descendants. Such self-awareness would be a precondition for them to take on ethical-political responsibility for unforgetting, and making reparations for, the historical and ongoing violent structures of settler colonialism. EXCO, and other free universities for alternative modes of study, could situate themselves as aspirational settler-accomplices with Indigenous movements. This could entail projects of leveraging spaces and resources to create enclaves of study-in-resistance, where participants could collectively compose anticolonial and anticapitalist projects. Such study-in-struggle could include relationship building across different Indigenous peoples, such as between the Dakota people and the migrants participating in Academia Comunitaria who have roots with Indigenous communities in Central and South America.

Instead of settling on abstractions of university, community, and education, radical study projects should make more and better opportunities for the messy processes of studying, organizing, and relationship building. The move toward a more efficient organizational structure with expert management roles enabled EXCO organizers to avoid the discomfiting challenges of relating with people at the U of M and in surrounding neighborhoods who embodied different positions. This also reinforced our romanticization of education—we avoided dealing with how participating in EXCO was seen by some communities as a luxury activity. People in Academia Comunitaria, and in the fleeting Cedar-Riverside and Hamline-Midway chapters were often more focused on surviving, finding resources, trying to work, and dealing with basic needs.

During our revising of this chapter, we have communicated with current EXCO organizers about what we learned from the interviews and EXCO's history. We tried to incite a collective return to the messy, unsettled questions around EXCO's values and its relationship to struggles within and against education institutions. With increasing organizer turnover and frustration with feeling bogged down in the semesterly business of putting on classes, many current organizers felt that they could not continue to do work for EXCO without knowing or discussing why or for whom they were laboring. In the summer of 2014, organizers decided to step back from "business" and hold a series of intensive visioning potlucks. Through sharing meals and meeting in different organizers' homes, EXCO organizers were prioritizing affective relationship building and studying. Yet, some raised concerns that once the summer ended, we would still have to get back to "work." Given that organizing EXCO and other radical study projects is our third shift, how do we make space-times for the messy work/play of studying, organizing, and relating versus seeing these as separate activities where study and relationship building are often feminized and given short shrift to the more masculinist "action" of organizing? This question should not be seen as solvable but as an ongoing problematic that, kept at the fore, can enable radical study and education projects to carve out space-times to continuously revisit and reimagine our transformative, political aspirations and build more effective, and affectively resonant, movements.

The co-writing that Erin and I took on in this chapter, and which I took on in this book as a whole, is continuous with the collective alternative mode of study that we began with our involvement in EXCO. We hope that others will take the baton from us to experiment with the possibilities of what an anti- and alter-university can do. When we refuse to take shortcuts—whether with crisis narratives or the romance of education—around the infinite complexity of studying, organizing, and relating, new horizons and new worlds open up. When we unlearn our epistemology of educated ignorance, the impossible becomes imaginable. The conclusion that follows opens further critical inquiries as avenues toward dismantling this epistemology.

Toward an Abolition University

This book was written for those who have snapped at the university. For those who refuse to "move on" from the impasse of the university's entwinement with racial capitalism, settler colonialism, and heteropatriarchy. For those who have organized in movements—such as the Movement for Black Lives who called for tearing down their campuses' monuments to white supremacy, the women who said #MeToo to call out academic men with histories of sexual abuse, and the students who occupied campus buildings with the call of "We are the crisis"—highlighting the political conflicts that striate the university. Against moral and analytical approaches to the impasse with "crisis" narratives that simplify away these political controversies, this book has offered theoretical tools to help penetrate these movements' vectors more deeply into the hearts of universities.

This book has argued that education is just one of many possible modes of study. Rather than assuming the necessity of the education-based mode of study, I showed its historical contingency, revealing how it emerged in intimate association with the capitalist, modernist/colonial mode of world-making and in opposition to alternative modes of study and world-making. I gave critical genealogies of elements of the education-based mode of study: the "dropout," the vertically ascending imaginary, techniques of governance for managing disorder, and an emotional economy of credits and debts. I highlighted contemporary examples of alternative modes of study, particularly EXCO of the Twin Cities, with its "undercommons" relations with dominant universities, stealing their means of study for alternative modes of world-making.

Assumptions about the necessity of the education-based mode of study are part of an epistemology of educated ignorance. They suppress thought of controversies that might destabilize the institutions of education and threaten one's own position in relation to those institutions. I contend that, for movements on the terrain of universities, it is strategically important to tackle the elements of this epistemology as an *interconnected* constellation of concepts and narratives, rather than treating them as isolated phenomena. Articulating such a pattern can guide movement participants for organizing politically, fanatically, strategically, with clear oppositions and propositions, *against* a particular mode of study and world-making, *for* alternative modes of study and world-making. When we understand how the epistemology of educated ignorance works as a pattern of narratives that legitimates the education-based mode of study and world-making and that obscures alternatives, we gain better capacities for navigating the tensions of being *in* this dominant mode but not *of* it while simultaneously struggling collectively *against* and *beyond* it.

In giving the critical genealogies in chapters 2, 3, and 4, I tackled only a few key elements of the education-based mode of study. These are important ones, but not necessarily the *most* important. More such critical genealogies—critical histories of the present that respond to contemporary concerns—are needed in further research. In calling for this broader research agenda, I am building on the work of many others: for example, Erica Meiners's critical genealogies of zero-tolerance policies and special education, William Watkins on segregated education, Damien Sojoyner on policing in schools, Nancy Lesko on the cultural construction of adolescence, and Jeanie Oakes on tracking.[1] Further critical genealogies should be conducted on other elements of the education-based mode of study, such as mass education with graded exams, the grade curve, compulsory schooling, and the figure of the truant, among many others.

To make these critical genealogies relevant for the concerns of present movements, they should not aim for a politically neutral, "objective" history; rather, they should detail the political conditions out of which their objects of study emerged. Particularly, they should investigate how these elements of the education-based mode of study emerged from conflicts with alternative modes of study and world-making. Thus they should simultaneously include histories of the alternative modes of study and world-making in reaction to which these elements were constructed.

Most of the elements of the epistemology of educated ignorance that I have set out here are focused on institutions of education at the K–12 levels. Yet, I also theorize an interrelated epistemology of *academic* ignorance. The latter is not only a subset of the epistemology of educated ignorance, focusing on narratives about "higher" education institutions; these epistemologies also build on and amplify each other. In chapter 1, I described one part of this epistemology of academic ignorance—the approach to the university's impasse with moral and analytical frames—as a "crisis" narrated with genres of melodrama, jeremiad, and consumer guide, all of which obscure the political questions of conflicts between alternative modes of world-making and study.

Returning to the phenomenon of snapping in and at the university, I ask, Why doesn't *everyone* who experiences exploitation and oppression snap? I hypothesize that our anger at the university is continually mollified by the epistemology of academic ignorance. We fall back on romanticized views of higher education, where some ideal—the academic vocation, the public university, academic freedom, tenure, the liberal arts, slow scholarship, and so forth—is framed as in crisis and in need of defense. As an antidote, we need to engage in more thorough critical genealogies of *all* of the elements of this epistemology. Seeing this book as the beginning of a broader, collaborative research project, I call for further genealogies of these romanticized ideals about higher education.[2] Showing how these ideals emerged as moralizing crisis responses to struggles can help unsettle our subscriptions to these narratives and expand our horizons to alternative modes of study and world-making. As a step toward this project, I set out here some suggested lines of inquiry for critical genealogies of each romanticized ideal.

A foundational ideal is the academic vocation, seen as a calling set above the other forms of labor on campuses. In the shadow of the elevated academic vocation, other forms of campus labor are obscured. This ideal is related with a hierarchical division of labor on campuses between intellectual, academic labor and manual, service labor. To conduct a critical genealogy of this ideal would require examining its deployment in the context of the early American universities in which non-academic, service labor was performed by enslaved African and Native American peoples. This inquiry could build on histories of early universities' entwinement with slavery, such as Craig Wilder's *Ebony and Ivy*, as well as many universities' recent attempts to reckon with their troubled pasts.[3] Yet, going beyond these histories, such a critical genealogy would explore and highlight the alternative modes of study and world-making that enslaved campus workers were engaging in, such as in their maroon networks to aid in their flights to freedom.[4] This genealogy would investigate how such alternative modes of study threatened the white-supremacist, settler-colonial, capitalist mode of world-making, and how narratives of the academic vocation served as reactions to these threats.

Ideals of the public university have emerged at different times, in contexts of different political struggles. A critical genealogy of the earlier public land-grant university ideal would examine its origins in the context of settler-colonial, capitalist expansion in the nineteenth century. The land that was "granted" to these public universities had been stolen from Indigenous peoples. The settlers were not given this land; they took it from Indigenous peoples by force, and they tried to eliminate the peoples on it by genocide and assimilation. Yet, the Indigenous peoples resisted, thereby constituting a threat to the settler-colonial, capitalist mode of world-making. Building on the work of Indigenous historians and settler-colonial studies scholars, a critical genealogy of the public land-grant ideal would investigate how narratives around this ideal obscured the violence of settler-colonial dispossession and counteracted the threatening alternatives of the Indigenous modes of study and world-making.[5]

The ideals of tenure and academic freedom emerged in the United States during the early-twentieth-century Red Scares around World War I. A critical genealogy of these ideals could build on Clyde Barrow's history of this period of struggles between academic unions and the capitalist state.[6] To defend themselves from business and government leaders' interference with universities, academics had organized the American Association of University Professors (AAUP) in 1914 and the first academic unions, with the American Federation of Teachers, in 1919. During the Red Scare, the capitalist state deployed threats, firings, and blacklistings against leftist professors. At the height of this repression, in 1916, the AAUP rejected unionization in favor of a different kind of protection for threatened academics: the institutions of tenure and a limited form of academic freedom.[7] In this "divided governance," academics relinquished to administrators their power over the political-economic functioning of the university, while retaining academic freedom in the sphere of knowledge production, with power over their departmental, classroom, and disciplinary communities.[8] A critical genealogy would build on this history by revealing how the academic labor movements were engaged in alternative modes of study and world-making, such as in the Intercollegiate Socialist Society, and how the corporate and government forces reacted to these alternatives as threatening to their capitalist, statist mode of world-making. It would also highlight how these alternative modes of study were bound up with organizing and relationship building across classes, races, genders, and sectors of workers within and beyond the universities.

A second form of the public university ideal emerged in the 1950s and 1960s with the democratized mass university. This ideal emerged along with the GI Bill's vast expansion of higher education access, the growth of community colleges, and new narratives (from "manpower development" to "human capital") to justify increased funding for higher education. A critical genealogy of this ideal would examine how, in the Cold War context, Third World Liberation and Black freedom movements appropriated universities' resources for their insurgent studying. Building on histories of these struggles, such as those by Rod Ferguson and Nick Mitchell, it would investigate how, in response to these movements' demands for expanding admissions and curricula—such as with the creation of ethnic studies departments—administrators reacted by raising tuition, increasing campus policing, hiring more contingent faculty, and using liberal and neoliberal discourses of "multicultural diversity."[9] This inquiry would highlight how the movements enacted alternative modes of study—such as Black studies in the Experimental College at San Francisco State—that were threatening to the modernist/colonial mode of world-making.[10]

More-recent elements of the epistemology of academic ignorance should also be subjected to critical genealogies. One is the idea of the university as an "economic incubator" around which a city's economy revolves. This includes the ideas of the university as a job creator and as a center of urban revitalization. These narratives tend to obscure the universities' contributions to gentrification, their exploitation of campus workers, and their tax-exempt status. Histories by Davarian Baldwin, Sharon Haar, and LaDale Winling have detailed universities' involvement in battles over urban space.[11] A critical genealogy could build on these histories with inquiry into the conflicting modes of study and world-making involved in urban struggles over space and resources. In movements against university-driven gentrification and for campus workers' unionization, how have the participants engaged in modes of study alternative to the education-based mode, and how have universities sought to suppress and recuperate these threats to their mode of world-making?

Further critical genealogies could focus on other elements of the epistemology of academic ignorance, such as the liberal arts, collegiality, continuing education, innovation, slow scholarship, online learning, the global university, interdisciplinarity, rankings of universities, service learning, and digital humanities, among many others. Spilling the histories behind these reified ideals could destabilize our subscriptions to them, weakening the dam that holds back our flood of anger from experiences of university-related exploitations and oppressions. Going beyond critical university studies, such histories could guide our collective creation of not only abolitionist university studies but also an *abolition university*, one that aligns itself with modes of study in abolitionist movements within, against, and beyond the university as we know it.[12]

FOR AN ABOLITION UNIVERSITY

Popular narratives portray society as made up of "good" and "bad" people. Figures of the citizen, the worker, and the graduate are contrasted with the deviant, the criminal, and the dropout. For the safety of good people, we are supposed to put bad people in separate places. When young, those stigmatized as bad kids—as potential delinquents, failures, dropouts— are sent to lower-tracked courses, detention, or juvenile hall. If they continue "down" this criminalized life path, they are sent to jails and prisons. By contrast, those deemed good through the categorizing and sorting of the education-based mode of study are admitted to the place where good people rise: "up" through the school grades and into higher education.[13]

Prisons and universities complement each other as two sides of the same coin. They are institutions for producing obedient, governable subjects—shaped in a mode of accounting with incarceration for "debts to society" and education for "credits." Abolitionist movements should seek to abolish the whole coin. From a decolonial, abolitionist perspective, this coin is the intersecting regimes of white-supremacist, settler-colonial, heteropatriarchal capitalism. Abolitionists have organized against institutions associated with the "bad" side of the dichotomy of good/bad persons—including prisons, corporal punishment in schools, the school-to-prison pipeline, the death penalty, and the police—as well as against the "redemptive" intermediaries of the military and work. Yet abolitionists also need to engage in resistance in institutions, such as higher education, that are associated with the "good" side of the coin.

This book's theory of conflicting modes of study contributes to abolitionist perspectives on the school-to-prison pipeline. Going beyond an approach that, as Erica Meiners notes, "simply posits schooling as the antidote to carceral expansion, without linking the two structures," and theorizing, instead, the "school-to-prison nexus," these abolitionist perspectives articulate "linkages between schools and jails" as "less a pipeline, more a persistent nexus or a web of intertwined, punitive threads."[14] Some studies focus their analysis on the nexus between pre-K–12 schools and prisons, seeing schools as part of the prison-industrial complex (PIC), while other studies have expanded this analysis to include higher education institutions, such as by analyzing how teacher training and criminology programs are part of the PIC.[15] I affirm these studies of the school-to-prison nexus, but I also build on them in a critically constructive way. They share an unexamined assumption: that some form of education is a necessarily good thing. This assumption limits the potential for more effective abolitionist movements on the terrain of universities. By contrast, I put education itself into question. With my theory of conflicting modes of study, I offer tools for expanding and deepening the critique of the school-to-prison nexus by shifting to a focus on what I call *the education-carcerality nexus*. I contend that we need a deeper analysis of the co-constitutive relations between the education-based mode of study and processes of criminalization, policing, and incarceration. Such an analysis could guide a more nuanced and thorough abolitionist approach to the terrains of struggle in schools and universities.

Education can be a key to open the locks for some prisoners to escape a life of incarceration. But the locks remain in place, leaving cells to be filled with more prisoners. The lock and key justify each other's existence, as the education-based mode of study and incarceration are co-constituted in settler-colonial, liberal-capitalist modernity. Academia locks away the means for study, sequestering them for private use either by those students who pay tuition for access or by those who have ascended the heights of the education-based mode of study to earn access as professors. Prisons lock up people, further separating them from the means for study. We lock up our private property, including our books, computers, and bodies secured in our houses and offices. We have our property patrolled by police and security guards in order to prevent theft by so-called criminals, while those who are tainted with criminality get locked up in jails and prisons. All these locks and keys, walls and fences, feelings of insecurity and tools of securitization, are bound up with each other through the institutions of liberal-capitalist modernity. An abolition university would take aim at this whole system. As we break down the prison walls, we must simultaneously destroy academia's locks on the means for studying and engage in subversive modes of study. We can collectively refuse the locks and keys of this system's privatized and securitized means of studying. Instead, with alternative modes of study, we can build new worlds within, against, and beyond this world.

Acknowledgments

This book would have been impossible without my many interlocutors and supporters. The roots of this book are with the people in my life, in the joys of their love, solidarity, friendship, care, and integrity. I dedicate this book to the memories of Adam Briesemeister, Andy Dickinson, and Joel Olson, three friends who died too soon. This book continues their commitments to ground radical thought in practices of building new worlds in the shell of the old.

For feedback on drafts of this book's chapters, I am grateful to Elisabeth R. Anker, Nicole Barnes, Chris Buck, James Chappel, Ashley Farmer, Farrow, Monica Huerta, Anatoli Ignatov, Miranda Joseph, Jenny Kelly, Marisol LeBron, Erica Meiners, Gabe Rosenberg, Harris Solomon, Eli Thorkelson, and Matt Whitt. I am especially thankful to Erin Dyke, Elizabeth R. Johnson, Isaac Kamola, Zach Schwartz-Weinstein, and Fern Thompsett for giving me feedback on chapters as well as for coauthoring articles with me. Along with my other coauthors, David Boehnke, Keno Evol, Elsa Noterman, and Sophie Strosberg, our collaborations were the groundwork for the ideas that I developed in this book. Likewise, I am grateful to Bruce Braun for coauthoring with me while also serving on my dissertation committee. I thank the rest of my dissertation committee as well—Bud Duvall, Nancy Luxon, Richa Nagar, and Joan Tronto—for giving me crucial guidance, support, and constructive critique.

I have had the honor of teaching and studying with hundreds of students who have shown me the limits of the education-based mode of study and the possibilities for enacting alternatives in the cracks of the university. Many further interlocutors have fundamentally shaped my thoughts in this book, including Scott Abernathy, Morgan Adamson, Christian Anderson, Amanda Armstrong, Arnoldas, Liz Ault, Yesenia Barragan, Patricia Bass, Lauren Berlant, Abbie Boggs, Mark Bray, Kevin Bruyneel, George Caffentzis, Teri Caraway, Charmaine Chua, George Ciccariello-Maher, Andy Cornell, Glen Coulthard, Mary Dietz, Andrew Dilts, Lisa Disch, James Farr, Silvia Federici, Craig Fortier, Steph Gans, Laura Goldblatt, Jesse Goldstein, Samantha Gomez, Sandy Grande, Max Haiven, Rita Hardie, Michael Hardt, Stefano Harney, Robert Haworth, Mark Hoffman, Nate Holdren, Amanda Huron, Joy James, Justine Johnson, Malav Kanuga, Jonneke Koomen, Steve Lorenz,

Brian Lovato, Wahneema Lubiano, Liz Mason-Deese, Meghan McDowell, Steve McFarland, China Medel, David Meek, Andrew Meeker, Sandro Mezzadra, Nick Mitchell, Chris Moore, Fred Moten, Kevin Murphy, Ray Noll, Anthony Pahnke, Dimitris Papadopoulos, Sean Parson, Mark Paschal, Amy Pason, Lucia Pawlowski, Carlos Perez, Amanda Priebe, Vijay Raghavan, José Romero, Jason Ruiz, Carolina Sarmiento, Bill Scheuerman, Stevphen Shukaitis, Audra Simpson, Leanne Betasamosake Simpson, Althea Sircar, Araby Smyth, David Spataro, Tim Stallmann, Joe Stapleton, Allison Swaim, Kim TallBear, David Theurer, Steven Thrasher, Hồng-Ân Trương, Kathi Weeks, and Jasmine Yarish, among many others.

I am indebted to my friends and comrades for teaching me how to intertwine our organizing, studying, and relationship building, particularly with AFSCME, Experimental College of the Twin Cities, Minnehaha Free Space, the IWW, the Twin Cities Anarchist Bookfair, Graduate Student Workers United, the Committee on Revolutionizing the AcaDemy, *Abolition: A Journal of Insurgent Politics,* Undercommoning, Inside-Outside Alliance, and NC Women's Prison Book Project.

I am grateful to my editor at the University of Minnesota Press, Jason Weidemann, for his encouragement, guidance, and patience throughout this project, and to two anonymous reviewers for crucial feedback on chapter drafts. I thank Gabriel Levin for his careful editorial assistance, Jonathan Lawrence and Mike Stoffel for their work in copyediting, Rachel Moeller for her guidance in the production and design process, Brad Norr for his design of the book's cover, and Siobhan McKiernan for her expert composition of the index.

Thanks to PM Press for permission to reprint a revised version of chapter 5. I thank Lucas Buresch for his guidance with the Ford Foundation archives. I thank Lisa Poteet and Jon Puckett for their good humor in maintaining our office in International Comparative Studies.

I owe deepest gratitude to my mom, Lisa Lloyd, and my dad and stepmom, Randy and Ramona Meyerhoff, and to my parents-in-law, Srinivasan Namakkal and Carol Sarraillon, for their eternal love and support.

Finally, I could not have completed this project without my partner, Jecca Namakkal. Sharing the joys and pains of graduate school and the precarious academic life beyond—reading, cooking, traveling, laughing, making a life, and now raising our daughter, Usha, together—her love has transformed me in ways I could never have imagined.

Notes

INTRODUCTION

1. Sara Ahmed, "Resignation Is a Feminist Issue," *feministkilljoys,* August 27, 2016, https://feministkilljoys.com/2016/08/27/resignation-is-a-feminist-issue/.
2. In this excerpt, Ahmed links to her initial blog post in which she announced her resignation: Sara Ahmed, "Resignation," *feministkilljoys,* May 30, 2016, https://feministkilljoys.com/2016/05/30/resignation/. For her elaboration of the idea of a "feminist snap," see her book *Living a Feminist Life* (Durham: Duke University Press, 2017).
3. Menafee quoted in "Yale Dishwasher Broke Window Depicting Slaves: 'No One Has to Be Exposed to That Anymore,'" *NPR: Weekend Edition,* July 17, 2016. Emphasis added.
4. The gag provision only pertains to the act itself and the administrative response. Menafee has subsequently spoken publicly at rallies in favor of changing the name of Calhoun College. Daniela Brighenti and David Yaffe-Bellany, "Yale Gags Rehired Cafeteria Worker," *New Haven Independent,* July 26, 2016.
5. I draw the concept of "ways of world-making" from Nelson Goodman, *Ways of Worldmaking* (Indianapolis: Hackett, 1978).
6. Walter Mignolo, *The Darker Side of Western Modernity: Global Futures, Decolonial Options* (Durham: Duke University Press, 2011), 80.
7. According to Mitchell Dean, what Michel Foucault calls a "critical history of the present" is "concerned with that which is taken-for-granted, assumed to be given, or natural within contemporary social existence, a givenness or naturalness questioned in the course of contemporary struggles." Dean, *Critical and Effective Histories: Foucault's Methods and Historical Sociology* (New York: Routledge, 1994), 35.
8. Stefano Harney and Fred Moten, *The Undercommons: Fugitive Planning and Black Study* (New York: Minor Compositions, 2013).

9. "Exclusive: Meet Yale Dishwasher Corey Menafee, Who Smashed Racist Stained-Glass Window," *Democracy Now*, July 15, 2016.

10. Daniela Brighenti, Qi Xu, and David Yaffe-Bellany, "Worker Smashes 'Racist' Panel, Loses Job," *New Haven Independent*, July 11, 2016.

11. Menafee quoted in "Yale Dishwasher Broke Window."

12. For Ahmed's explanation of her resignation, see Ahmed, "Resignation Is a Feminist Issue."

13. Sara Ahmed, "Affective Economies," *Social Text* 22, no. 2 (2004): 117–39; Sara Ahmed, *The Cultural Politics of Emotion*, 2nd ed. (Edinburgh: Edinburgh University Press, 2014).

14. Ahmed, *Cultural Politics of Emotion*, 24.

15. Menafee quoted in "Yale Dishwasher Broke Window."

16. Ahmed notes that sensations of pain are connected with memories: "How the feelings feel in the first place may be tied to a past history of readings, in the sense that the process of *recognition* (of this feeling, or that feeling) is bound up with what we *already know*" (*Cultural Politics of Emotion*, 25).

17. Lindsey Bever, "A Yale Dishwasher Broke a 'Racist' Windowpane: Now, He's Fighting to Reclaim His Job," *Washington Post*, July 19, 2016.

18. Brighenti, Xu, and Yaffe-Bellany "Worker Smashes 'Racist' Panel, Loses Job."

19. Menafee quoted in Michelle Liu, "Corey Menafee Joins Rename-Calhoun Cause," *New Haven Independent*, October 28, 2016.

20. Antony Dugdale, J. J. Fueser, and J. Celso de Castro Alves, "Calhoun College," *Yale, Slavery and Abolition*, 2001, http://www.yaleslavery.org/WhoYaleHonors/calhoun1.html.

21. Dugdale, Fueser, and Alves, "Calhoun College." Also see Craig Steven Wilder, *Ebony and Ivy: Race, Slavery, and the Troubled History of America's Universities* (New York: Bloomsbury Press, 2013), 63–64, 117–18, 120–22.

22. Zach Schwartz-Weinstein, "Broken Window Theory: Corey Menafee and the History of University Service Labor," *Weapon of Class Instruction Blog*, July 21, 2016, http://weaponofclassinstruction.blogspot.com/2016/07/broken-window-theory-corey-menafee-and.html.

23. "Investment Return of 3.4% Brings Yale Endowment Value to $25.4 Billion," *Yale News*, September 23, 2016. Number of faculty from "Yale by the Numbers," http://www.yale.edu/about-yale/yale-facts.

24. Ahmed, *Cultural Politics of Emotion*, 30.

25. Ahmed, *Cultural Politics of Emotion*, 30–31.

26. Ahmed, *Cultural Politics of Emotion*, 39.

27. Brighenti and Yaffe-Bellany, "Yale Gags Rehired Cafeteria Worker."

28. An example of the use of the norm of civility to suppress dissent is the

University of Illinois's use of the rhetoric of incivility to justify Steven
Salaita's termination. For an analysis of the colonial character of this
rhetoric, see Jakeet Singh, "Why Aren't We Talking about Racism and
Colonialism in the Salaita Affair?" *Electronic Intifada*, September 9, 2014.
29. Brighenti, Xu, and Yaffe-Bellany, "Worker Smashes 'Racist' Panel, Loses
Job."
30. Ahmed, *Cultural Politics of Emotion*, 65.
31. Ahmed, *Cultural Politics of Emotion*, 63–64.
32. According to Landauer's relational anarchist politics, "The state is a
relationship between human beings, a way by which people relate to one
another; and one destroys it by entering into other relationships, by be-
having differently to one another." Landauer, "Weak Statesmen, Weaker
People," excerpted in *Anarchism: A Documentary History of Libertarian
Ideas*, vol. 1, *From Anarchy to Anarchism (300CE–1939)*, ed. Robert Graham
(1910; Montreal: Black Rose Books, 2005), 165.
33. Bruno Latour, *Reassembling the Social: An Introduction to Actor-Network-
Theory* (Oxford: Oxford University Press, 2005), 254.
34. For example, the workers who occupied the Lip watch factory in Besançon,
France, in 1973 had learned through their involvement in the 1968 struggles
how to self-manage an occupied workplace through committees. Donald
Reid, *Opening the Gates: The Lip Affair, 1968–1981* (New York: Verso,
2018). For research on how participants in social movements engage in
studying practices, see Aziz Choudry, *Learning Activism: The Intellectual
Life of Contemporary Social Movements* (Toronto: University of Toronto
Press, 2015); and Chris Dixon, *Another Politics: Talking across Today's
Transformative Movements* (Berkeley: University of California Press, 2014).
35. Leanne Betasamosake Simpson, "Land as Pedagogy: Nishnaabeg Intelligence and Rebellious Transformation," *Decolonization: Indigeneity,
Education and Society* 3, no. 3 (2014): 1–25. I developed my understanding of these differences between Indigenous modes of studying and the
education-based mode of study through writing with Fern Thompsett in
our article Eli Meyerhoff and Fern Thompsett, "Decolonizing Study: Free
Universities in More-Than-Humanist Accompliceships with Indigenous
Movements," *Journal of Environmental Education* 48, no. 4 (2017): 234–47.
36. Different Indigenous groups have different modes of studying and differ-
ent interpretations of "land." For some examples of these differences, see
Simpson, "Land as Pedagogy"; Jennifer Adese, "Spirit Gifting: Ecological
Knowing in Métis Life Narratives," *Decolonization: Indigeneity, Education
& Society* 3, no. 3 (2014): 48–66; Eve Tuck, Marcia McKenzie, and Kate
McCoy, "Land Education: Indigenous, Post-colonial, and Decolonizing

Perspectives on Place and Environmental Education Research," *Environmental Education Research* 20, no. 1 (2014): 1–23; and Hilary Whitehouse, Felecia Lui, Juanita Sellwood, M. J. Barrett, and Philemon Chigeza, "Sea Country: Navigating Indigenous and Colonial Ontologies in Australian Environmental Education," *Environmental Education Research* 20, no. 1 (2014): 56–69.

37.   On the role of bacteria in co-producing "more-than-human" emotions, see Myra Hird, *The Origins of Sociable Life* (London: Palgrave, 2009). On "sympoetic relations," or "sympoiesis," Donna Haraway notes that "M. Beth Dempster suggested the term sympoiesis for 'collectively-producing systems that do not have self-defined spatial or temporal boundaries. Information and control are distributed among components. The systems are evolutionary and have the potential for surprising change.'" Haraway, *Staying with the Trouble: Making Kin in the Chthulucene* (Durham: Duke University Press, 2016), 61, quoting M. Beth Dempster, "A Self-Organizing Systems Perspective on Planning for Sustainability" (MA thesis, Environmental Studies, University of Waterloo, 1998).

38.   On the radical resurgence project, see Leanne Betasamosake Simpson, *As We Have Always Done: Indigenous Freedom through Radical Resistance* (Minneapolis: University of Minnesota Press, 2017).

39.   For eighty lists of demands, see http://www.thedemands.org/.

40.   Amy Goodman, "Black Student Revolt Ousts 2 Top Officials at University of Missouri," *Democracy Now*, November 10, 2015.

41.   Robin D. G. Kelley, "Black Study, Black Struggle," *Boston Review*, March 7, 2016, https://bostonreview.net/forum/robin-d-g-kelley-black-study-black-struggle.

42.   Kelley, "Black Study, Black Struggle"; Harney and Moten, *The Undercommons*.

43.   Kelley and the other forum participants shift between "study" and "education" in an undifferentiated way. Kelley seems to favor "study"—as seen in his essay's title and in his promotion of study groups—but he neither gives any reasons for doing so nor distinguishes it from "education." At times Kelley appeals to some more differentiated concepts of study, such as in his essay's title, "Black Study." Also, in reply to Randall L. Kennedy, professor at Harvard Law School, who implies that Kelley "sneers at intellectuality," Kelley stresses the importance of "critical study" and describes students who practice such study as "attempting to work horizontally, not just across the faculty/student divide, but the university/aggrieved community divide," and as "not afraid to read anything, to change their minds, to challenge their own assumptions." Rather than simply promot-

ing study in general, Kelley's concept of "critical study" implies the need to ask questions of who is engaging in study, for what purposes, and how they are doing it.

44. Fred Moten, Stefano Harney, and Marc Bousquet, "On Study: A *Polygraph* Roundtable Discussion with Marc Bousquet, Stefano Harney, and Fred Moten," *Polygraph* 21 (2009): 159–75.

45. On the university's "unequal temporal architecture," see Eli Meyerhoff and Elsa Noterman, "Revolutionary Scholarship by Any Speed Necessary: Slow or Fast but for the End of This World," *ACME: An International Journal for Critical Geographies* 18, no. 1 (2017): 217–45, https://www .acme-journal.org/index.php/acme/article/view/1429.

46. For this analysis of the two ways that Yale reproduces itself as a community through expressions of shame—having shame brought onto it and bringing it on itself—I draw on Ahmed's theory of two ways that "the nation is reproduced through expressions of shame," and I analogize the university community with the national community. Ahmed, *Cultural Politics of Emotion*, 108.

47. Ahmed, *Cultural Politics of Emotion*, 107.

48. On the ethical and political importance of unforgetting for efforts to dismantle settler colonialism and white supremacy, see Alexis Shotwell, *Against Purity: Living Ethically in Compromised Times* (Minneapolis: University of Minnesota Press, 2016), 23–54.

49. According to Yale's president, Peter Salovey, these forms of healing for the Yale community include an interactive history project on the legacy of Calhoun, a competition to select new art to be displayed in Calhoun College, and a committee surveying art on campus and recommending "ways that art can help us to engage with and understand our past." Salovey, letter reprinted in "Slavemaster Still Honored; 'Master' Bites the Dust," *New Haven Independent*, April 28, 2016.

50. The relation between shame and the Yale community here is similar to what Ahmed observes in the case of Australia's reconciliation with Indigenous peoples: "Declarations of shame can bring 'the nation' into existence as a felt community," as "a form of nation building in which what is shameful about the past is covered over by the statement of shame itself" (*Cultural Politics of Emotion*, 15, 101–2).

51. On the expansion of Yale's university-medical complex and struggles against it, see Jennifer Klein, "New Haven Rising," *Dissent Magazine*, Winter 2015, https://www.dissentmagazine.org/article/new-haven -rising.

52. Marx, *Capital*, vol. 1, 874–75.

53.   On the romance genre as a quest and a form of wish fulfillment that aims
at transformation of the everyday world, entailing a struggle between
forces of good and evil, "white and black magics," or "higher and lower
realms," see Northrop Frye, *Anatomy of Criticism* (Princeton: Princeton
University Press, 1957), 187–88, 193. In building off of Frye's work, Fredric
Jameson sees in romance that the organizational categories of good and
evil subsume all other attributes (light and dark, high and low). Evil is
linked with the category of Otherness: "The point, however, is not that
in such figures the Other is feared because he is evil; rather, he is evil
because he is Other, alien, different, strange, unclean, and unfamiliar."
Jameson, "Magical Narratives: Romance as Genre," *New Literary History*
7, no. 1 (Autumn 1975): 140. This ideology linked with the romance genre
serves the political functions of "drawing the boundaries of a given social
order and providing a powerful internal deterrent against deviancy or
subversion." In Jameson's historical analysis of the romance genre, what
had been its magical elements in medieval times becomes replaced with
the miracle of conversion and eventually, in more modern times, with
elements of psychology: an interiorization of the struggle between two
worlds (144–45).

54.   How one characterizes these affective conditions depends on the genres of
political narrative through which one is describing them. In her treatment
of political melodramas, Elisabeth Anker uses the term "unfreedom,"
while Lauren Berlant, in her analysis of political impasses, uses the term
"precarity." Anker, *Orgies of Feeling: Melodramatic Politics and the Pursuit of
Freedom* (Durham: Duke University Press, 2014); Berlant, *Cruel Optimism*
(Durham: Duke University Press, 2011).

55.   For more on this strike and related solidarity protests, see Amy Pason,
"We Are All Workers: A Class Analysis of University Labour Strikes,"
ephemera 8, no. 3 (2008): 331–39; and Isaac Kamola and Eli Meyerhoff,
"Creating Commons: Divided Governance, Participatory Management,
and Struggles against Enclosure in the University," *Polygraph* 21 (2009):
5–27.

56.   To read many of these interviews, see http://classwaru.org/interviews,
where I have posted twenty-one interviews in versions that I edited in
collaboration with my interviewees.

57.   Pierre Riché, *Education and Culture in the Barbarian West: From the Sixth
through the Eighth Century* (Columbia: University of South Carolina Press,
1978). The original sense of "university" was the totality of a group of
students who organized as a kind of union to study together, manage their
own affairs, and protect themselves from the price-gouging activities of

the townspeople and teachers. Alison Hearn, "Interdisciplinarity/Extra-disciplinarity: On the University and the Active Pursuit of Community," *History of Intellectual Culture* 3, no. 1 (2003): 1–13.

58. Ivan Illich, *Toward a History of Needs* (New York: Pantheon Books, 1977), 75.

1. "WE ARE THE CRISIS"

1. "WE ARE THE CRISIS: The Student Movement and the Coming Decade," November 22, 2009, http://wearethecrisis.blogspot.com/2009/11/we-are-crisis-student-movement-and.html.
2. Occupy California, "Chronology: Occupations and Struggles in California," https://occupyca.wordpress.com/timeline/.
3. "An Occupation Statement," November 19, 2009, https://occupyucla.wordpress.com/2009/11/19/an-occupation-statement/.
4. Amanda Armstrong and Paul Nadal, "Building Times: How Lines of Care Occupied Wheeler Hall," *Reclamations Journal* 1, no. 1 (2009), https://web.archive.org/web/20170613070307/http://reclamationsjournal.org/issue01_armstrong_nadal.html.
5. This observation of the "double barricade" is from another essay on the Wheeler Hall occupation: Jasper Bernes, "The Double Barricade and the Glass Floor," *Reclamations Journal* 2 (April 2010), https://web.archive.org/web/20170612044629/http://www.reclamationsjournal.org/issue02_jasper_bernes.html.
6. Armstrong and Nadal, "Building Times."
7. "WE ARE THE CRISIS."
8. For an account of liberal-capitalist modernity in universities, with attention to its current "neoliberal multiculturalist" phase, see Jodi Melamed, *Represent and Destroy: Rationalizing Violence in the New Racial Capitalism* (Minneapolis: University of Minnesota Press, 2011).
9. According to Berlant, "the impasse is a stretch of time in which one moves around with a sense that the world is at once intensely present and enigmatic, such that the activity of living demands both a wandering absorptive awareness and a hypervigilance that collects material that might help to clarify things, maintain one's sea legs, and coordinate the standard melodramatic crises with those processes that have not yet found their genre of event." Lauren Berlant, *Cruel Optimism* (Durham: Duke University Press, 2011), 4.
10. Janet Roitman, *Anti-Crisis* (Durham:. Duke University Press, 2013).

11. Abigail Boggs and Nick Mitchell, "Critical University Studies and the Crisis Consensus," *Feminist Studies* 44, no. 2 (2018): 432–63.

12. Robert Samuels, *Why Public Higher Education Should Be Free: How to Decrease Cost and Increase Quality at American Universities* (New Brunswick, N.J.: Rutgers University Press, 2013), vii.

13. Goldie Blumenstyk, *American Higher Education in Crisis? What Everyone Needs to Know* (New York: Oxford University Press, 2015).

14. Books on American higher education with "crisis" in their title, published since 1994, include Jeffrey Docking and Carman Curton, *Crisis in Higher Education: A Plan to Save Small Liberal Arts Colleges in America* (East Lansing: Michigan State University Press, 2015); Martin Finkelstein and Philip Altbach, eds., *The Academic Profession: The Professoriate in Crisis* (New York: Routledge, 2014); Michael Berube and Cary Nelson, *Higher Education under Fire: Politics, Economics, and the Crisis of the Humanities* (New York: Routledge, 1994); Christopher Lucas, *Crisis in the Academy: Rethinking American Higher Education* (New York: St. Martin's Press, 1996); Samuel Natale, Anthony F. Libertella, and Geoff Hayward, *Higher Education in Crisis: The Corporate Eclipse of the University* (Binghamton, N.Y.: Global Publications, 2001); William Smith, Philip Altbach, and Kofi Lomotey, *The Racial Crisis in American Higher Education: Continuing Challenges for the Twenty-First Century*, rev. ed. (Albany: SUNY Press, 2012); William C. Barba, *Higher Education in Crisis: New York in National Perspective* (New York: Routledge, 1995); Melanie M. Morey and John J. Piderit, *Catholic Higher Education: A Culture in Crisis* (New York: Oxford University Press, 2006); Henry Giroux and Susan Searls Giroux, *Take Back Higher Education: Race, Youth, and the Crisis of Democracy in the Post–Civil Rights Era* (New York: Palgrave Macmillan, 2004); Peter Smith, *The Quiet Crisis: How Higher Education Is Failing America* (New York: Wiley, 2004); Philip H. Francis, *Reconstructing Alma Mater: The Coming Crisis in Higher Education, a Blueprint for Reform* (New York: Algora, 2006); Noliwe Rooks, *White Money/Black Power: The Surprising History of African-American Studies and the Crisis of Race in Higher Education* (Boston: Beacon Press, 2006); and Wilfried Decoo, *Crisis on Campus: Confronting Academic Misconduct* (Cambridge: MIT Press, 2002).

15. Right-wing and left-wing versions of these crisis narratives have important differences but also overlaps. Both tend to combine jeremiads and melodramas. Right-wing melodramas about education tend to portray "big government" and teacher unions as the villains who prey upon parents, who are the victims in their roles as taxpayers. The victims can become heroes by rejecting the government's educational "welfare" and control-

ling their education locally. (I draw this theory of political melodrama from Elisabeth R. Anker, *Orgies of Feeling: Melodrama and the Politics of Freedom* [Durham: Duke University Press, 2014].) The right's education narratives also use another kind of genre: the jeremiad. This narrative is encapsulated in Donald Trump's slogan (borrowed from Ronald Reagan): "Make America great again." These are usually what Andrew Murphy calls a traditional type of jeremiad, i.e., lamenting the loss of a past practice, such as local-controlled schools or prayer in schools. (On the distinction between traditional and progressive jeremiads, see Murphy, *Prodigal Nation* [New York: Oxford University Press, 2009], 109–12.) The left shares the right's tendency to deploy narratives that combine melodramas with jeremiads. Unlike the right, the left tends to use what Murphy calls "progressive jeremiads," which appeal, not to a past practice, but to the promise of some past ideal as a basis for inspiring reform in the present (109). The threatened ideal that leftist narratives lament is often a variant of "equality of educational opportunity" or "public higher education for all" or "democracy's college," framed as a key part of the American dream and as an integral practice in American democracy. Yet many people find little credence in these ideals, having been disillusioned through seeing little evidence of their realization. If the jeremiad story resonates poorly with their experiences of unfreedom and precarity, they find little of use in it for guiding their lives. The left often combines such jeremiads with melodramas as well. For example, Martin Luther King Jr. used the promise of the Declaration of Independence as a backstory for the heroes of the civil rights movement in their struggles for school desegregation, among other goals. Both the left and the right can find their jeremiads in tension with their melodramas, as these genres of political storytelling have different modes of accountability and temporality (see Anker, *Orgies of Feeling*, 21–22). Yet they can also complement each other through using common characters and events in their story lines and building on each other's production of legitimacy and affective resonance for their audiences. On "left melodramas" more generally, see Anker, *Orgies of Feeling*, 203–24. On the use of the progressive jeremiad in the Black freedom movement, see David Howard-Pitney, *The African-American Jeremiad: Appeals for Justice in America*, 2nd ed. (Philadelphia: Temple University Press, 2005); see also George Shulman, *American Prophecy: Race and Redemption in American Political Culture* (Minneapolis: University of Minnesota Press, 2008).

16. Suzanne Mettler, *Degrees of Inequality: How the Politics of Higher Education Sabotaged the American Dream* (New York: Basic Books, 2014), 2–20.

17. Mettler, *Degrees of Inequality*, 5. Stanley Aronowitz's *Against Schooling* also

exemplifies this mix of genres. On the one hand, he uses a jeremiad about the decline of "the possibility of genuine education" and "the remnants of intellectual culture in the academy." (Aronowitz, *Against Schooling: For an Education That Matters* [Boulder: Paradigm, 2008], xiii–xix.) On the other hand, he portrays a melodrama with villains who are undermining those ideals—conservatives who push a "neoliberal cost-cutting doctrine," university administrators who defund teaching labor, and university departments who overproduce PhDs and MFAs for cheap labor—against the victims: teachers who become deskilled and exploited as adjunct labor, students who are expected to "lead a privatized existence" and face an increasing class divide, and parents who go into debt for their children's schooling. The heroes in Aronowitz's melodrama are critical educators, academic unions with independent organizations to prod them, and a common struggle of teachers across the division of higher and lower education.

Another variation on the theme is Michael S. Roth's *Beyond the University*, which gives a jeremiad about losing "access to a broad, self-critical and pragmatic education," a "deep American tradition of humanistic education." (Roth, *Beyond the University* [New Haven: Yale University Press, 2014], 2–9.) He combines this jeremiad with a melodrama that casts villains of economists, pundits, and politicians who attack liberal education for its potential elitism and irrelevance, injuring the victims—students and teachers—who cherish liberal education. Against these threats, the heroes are the teachers, administrators, and public figures who promote and defend the ideal of liberal, humanistic education, struggling in the tradition of such luminaries as Jefferson, Jane Addams, Emerson, Dewey, and Du Bois.

Another example, Ellen Schrecker's *The Lost Soul of Higher Education*, starts with a jeremiad about corporatization that "threatens the very mission of the academy as an institution devoted to the common good" and as the protector of "the American mind." (Schrecker, *The Lost Soul of Higher Education: Corporatization, the Assault on Academic Freedom, and the End of the American University* [New York: The New Press, 2010], 3–5.) She combines this with a melodrama with villains of two main threats to "the academic community": conservatives ramping up attacks on academic freedom after 9/11, and university administrators adopting corporate practices that increase their own power while casualizing the faculty. The victims in her melodrama are professors who have their academic freedom violated and who are being casualized, as well as students whose education suffers. The heroes are the professors who unite into professional bodies, especially the American Association of University Professors (AAUP), in order to overcome their divisions and defend academic freedom.

Larry G. Gerber's *The Rise and Decline of Faculty Governance* gives a narrative similar to Schrecker's, starting with a jeremiad about the deprofessionalization of the faculty, which undermines their justification to have academic freedom and to participate in faculty governance; he combines this with a melodrama that casts villains of people who apply the logic of the market to higher education, which injures the faculty victims by deprofessionalizing them, and conversely, the heroes are the faculty who resist these processes and advocate professionalization, especially through the collective body of the AAUP. (Gerber, *The Rise and Decline of Faculty Governance: Professionalization and the Modern American University* [Baltimore: Johns Hopkins University Press, 2014], 1–9.)

18. Christopher Newfield, *The Great Mistake: How We Wrecked Public Universities and How We Can Fix Them* (Baltimore: Johns Hopkins University Press, 2016), 16.
19. Newfield, *The Great Mistake,* 64.
20. Newfield, *The Great Mistake,* 17.
21. Newfield, *The Great Mistake,* 44, 34.
22. Newfield, *The Great Mistake,* 309–14.
23. Jeffrey Selingo, *College (Un)Bound: The Future of Higher Education and What It Means for Students* (New York: Houghton Mifflin Harcourt, 2013), xvii, 73.
24. Selingo, *College (Un)Bound,* xvii–xviii, 77.
25. Selingo, *College (Un)Bound,* xvii, 5.
26. On the Black freedom movement's impact on American higher education, see Ibram H. Rogers, *The Black Campus Movement: Black Students and the Racial Reconstruction of Higher Education, 1965–1972* (New York: Palgrave Macmillan, 2012).
27. Selingo, *College (Un)Bound,* xviii.
28. Other recent books on education that combine the genres of neoliberal consumerist impasse with a technocratic melodrama and progressive jeremiad include Michael B. Horn and Heather Staker, *Blended: Using Disruptive Innovation to Improve Schools* (San Francisco: Jossey-Bass, 2014); Clayton Christensen, Michael B. Horn, and Curtis W. Johnson, *Disrupting Class: How Disruptive Innovation Will Change the Way the World Learns* (New York: McGraw-Hill, 2010); and Clayton Christensen and Henry Eyring, *The Innovative University: Changing the DNA of Higher Education from the Inside Out* (San Francisco: Jossey-Bass, 2011).
29. "Meet Jonathan W.," You Can Go! *The College Board,* https://web.archive

.org/web/20170216180028/http://youcango.collegeboard.org/students/
jonathan-w?play=true.

30. "College Success Stories: 5 Students Like You Who Made It Through,"
Rasmussen College, http://www.rasmussen.edu/student-life/blogs/
college-life/college-success-stories-students-like-you-who-made-it/.

31. On the prevalence of the bounded, unified self and the individually autonomous self in liberal, capitalist societies, see Chad Lavin, *Eating Anxiety:
The Perils of Food Politics* (Minneapolis: University of Minnesota Press,
2013); and Claire Rasmussen, *The Autonomous Animal: Self-Governance
and Modern Subjectivity* (Minneapolis: University of Minnesota Press,
2011). For a critical genealogy of security as "liberalism's key concept"
and "the supreme concept of bourgeois society," see Mark Neocleous,
Critique of Security (Edinburgh: Edinburgh University Press, 2008), 7.

32. On how narratives of crisis frame a moral distinction between past and
future, see Roitman, *Anti-Crisis*.

33. W. E. B. Du Bois, *Darkwater: Voices from Within the Veil* (New York:
Harcourt, Brace, 1920), chapter 2, "The Souls of White Folk," https://
www.gutenberg.org/files/15210/15210-h/15210-h.htm.

34. Charles W. Mills, "White Ignorance," in *Black Rights/White Wrongs: The
Critique of Racial Liberalism* (New York: Oxford University Press, 2017),
49–71.

35. Linda Martín Alcoff, "Epistemologies of Ignorance: Three Types," in *Race
and Epistemologies of Ignorance*, ed. Shannon Sullivan and Nancy Tuana
(Albany: SUNY Press, 2007), 47–48.

36. Frank Margonis, "John Dewey, W. E. B. Du Bois, and Alain Locke:
A Case Study in White Ignorance and Intellectual Segregation," in *Race
and Epistemologies of Ignorance*, ed. Shannon Sullivan and Nancy Tuana
(Albany: SUNY Press, 2007), 174, 175–76.

37. John Dewey, *Democracy and Education* (New York: The Free Press, 1916).

38. "Why I Made This Site," http://academiaiskillingmyfriends.tumblr.com
/About.

39. Anonymous submission #15, *Academia Is Killing My Friends*, March 18,
2014, http://academiaiskillingmyfriends.tumblr.com/post/79951511895/15.

40. Anonymous submission #86, *Academia Is Killing My Friends*, June 26,
2015, http://academiaiskillingmyfriends.tumblr.com/post/1224913388
09/86.

41. For writings on relational selves, autonomy, and ethics, the work of feminist
scholars is essential. See, e.g., Catriona MacKenzie, "The Importance of
Relational Autonomy and Capabilities for an Ethics of Vulnerability," in
Vulnerability: New Essays in Ethics and Feminist Philosophy, ed. Catriona

Mackenzie, Wendy Rogers, and Susan Dodds (Oxford: Oxford University Press, 2014), 33–60; and Andrea Westlund, "Rethinking Relational Autonomy," *Hypatia* 24, no. 4 (2009): 26–49. Also see the chapters in Catriona Mackenzie and Natalie Stoljar, eds., *Relational Autonomy: Feminist Perspectives on Autonomy, Agency, and the Social Self* (Oxford: Oxford University Press, 2000).

42. On "temporal architectures" that structure interdependent, unequal relations between people's differential temporalities, see Sarah Sharma, *In the Meantime: Temporality and Cultural Politics* (Durham: Duke University Press, 2014). For an application of this theory to universities, see Eli Meyerhoff and Elsa Noterman, "Revolutionary Scholarship by Any Speed Necessary: Slow or Fast but for the End of This World," *ACME: An International Journal for Critical Geographies* 18, no. 1 (2017), 217–45, https://www.acme-journal.org/index.php/acme/article/view/1429.

43. "Why I Made This Site."

44. To read many of these interviews, see http://classwaru.org/interviews, where I have posted twenty-one of the interviews, in versions that I edited in collaboration with my interviewees. A problem with my approach was that I only interviewed people positioned as students and faculty, neglecting to interview any non-academic campus workers. Unfortunately, this perpetuated the tendency in university studies of marginalizing the perspectives of non-academic workers. For exceptions to this tendency, see Zach Schwartz-Weinstein, "Beneath the University: Service Workers and the University-Hospital City, 1964–1980" (PhD diss., New York University, 2015); Toni Gilpin, Gary Isaac, Dan Letwin, and Jack Mckivigan, *On Strike for Respect: The Clerical and Technical Workers' Strike at Yale University, 1984–85* (Champaign: University of Illinois Press, 1995); John Hoerr, *We Can't Eat Prestige: The Women Who Organized Harvard* (Philadelphia: Temple University Press, 1997); and Karen Brodkin Sacks, *Caring by the Hour: Women, Work, and Organizing at Duke Medical Center* (Champaign: University of Illinois Press, 1987).

45. Carolina Sarmiento, interview by Eli Meyerhoff, June 25, 2012. In the fall of 2014, Sarmiento became an assistant professor at the University of Wisconsin–Madison.

46. Sarmiento said that these community-engaged projects "build some bridges between the students and the community, but I think they are really temporary, and I always get the feeling that the students get so much more than the community actually did, and that we're asking a lot of the community members for a lot of their time, and it's really to the benefit of the students in the university" (Sarmiento, interview)

47. The figure of over 70 percent non-tenure-track faculty is from the American Association of University Professors' webpage, "Background Facts on Contingent Faculty," http://www.aaup.org/issues/contingency/background-facts (as of June 21, 2017).
48. Matthew Evsky (pseudonym), interview by Eli Meyerhoff, June 11, 2012. An edited version of the interview is available at http://classwaru.org/2013/04/30/a-brief-history-of-cuny-time/
49. George said: "When the student occupations popped off, I was in and around and involved in those, and knew folks that were more directly involved in supporting those. But also, I had an eye to, on the one hand, connecting directly to community struggles, overcoming this divide, and on the other hand, connecting struggles at top-tier universities like Berkeley downward to the state university level in California, and onward down to the community college level. The way that student organizing has been able to move vertically into community colleges is one of the more powerful things that it can do, because when you do that, you move beyond the very limiting elite demands to simply oppose cuts or fee hikes and to demand the privilege of being at a top-tier university for low cost. These are opposed to understanding the broader questions of access, broader questions of the ethnic cleansing of these elite universities, and the way in which struggles need to be understood in a much more broad fashion." George Ciccariello-Maher, interview by Eli Meyerhoff, June 6, 2012. An edited version of the interview is available at http://classwaru.org/2013/08/19/against-academic-alibis/.
50. This quote is from his public resignation letter, posted on Facebook at https://www.facebook.com/george.ciccariellomaher/posts/10155729883545325. For an interview with Ciccariello-Maher about this controversy in relation to tensions around academic freedom, free speech, and academics' abilities to engage in radical political activity, see George Ciccariello-Maher, "'White Genocide' and the Myth of White Victimhood," interview by Daniel Denvir, *Abolition: A Journal of Insurgent Politics*, February 25, 2017, https://abolitionjournal.org/white-genocide-and-the-myth-of-white-victimhood/.
51. Fred Moten in Moten and Stefano Harney, *The Undercommons: Fugitive Planning and Black Study* (New York: Minor Compositions, 2013), 105–6.
52. Mills, "White Ignorance," 59.
53. Paolo Freire, *Pedagogy of the Oppressed* (New York: Continuum, 1990), 58–59, 72–73.
54. Freire, *Pedagogy of the Oppressed*, 87.
55. Freire, *Pedagogy of the Oppressed*, 72, 101.

56. Gert Biesta, *The Beautiful Risk of Education* (Boulder: Paradigm, 2014).
57. Biesta, *The Beautiful Risk of Education*, 76.
58. Biesta, *The Beautiful Risk of Education*, 86.
59. Jan Masschelein and Maarten Simons, *In Defense of the School: A Public Issue* (Leuven: E-ducation, Culture and Society Publishers, 2013).
60. Masschelein and Simons, *In Defense of the School*, Kindle locations 2026–27.
61. Their definition of "the school" idealizes it as "a democratic intervention in the sense that it 'makes' free time for everyone, regardless of background or origin, and for these reasons it installs equality," and their definition of "study" idealizes it as "an open-ended event that can only occur if there is no end purpose to it and no established external functionality." Masschelein and Simons, *In Defense of the School*, Kindle locations 1376–85, 1205–9.
62. Masschelein and Simons, *In Defense of the School*, Kindle locations 1387–94. Related to their neglecting the coloniality underlying modernist ideals, in their discussion of the earlier history of schools they fail to critique how the underside of the Greek school was slavery. They note that the pedagogue was often a slave, but they do not treat this as a problem (1274). Conversely, they use the metaphor of a "freed slave" in reference to the ideal teacher's "amateur and public character," while ignoring the racial, colonial, gendered history of slavery (1784–92).
63. Lewis defines the "educational logic of learning" as "the putting to work of potentiality in the name of self-actualization and economic viability." He frames learning as "not some sort of universal and necessary aspect of the human condition but a specific, historically contextual set of concepts, practices, and institutional norms." Tyson E. Lewis, *On Study: Giorgio Agamben and Educational Potentiality* (New York: Routledge, 2013), 4–5.
64. Lewis, *On Study*, 12. Other examples are his definition of study as "to care for the indeterminate potentiality of potentiality itself," or as "ultimately to study the appearance of an impotentiality that refuses to be managed, optimized, commodified, controlled or captured, and ultimately fulfilled through a social orthopedic or economic or institutional imperative" (36, 15).
65. Madhu Suri Prakash and Gustavo Esteva, *Escaping Education: Living as Learning within Grassroots Cultures* (New York: Peter Lang, 1998), 19.
66. Prakash and Esteva, *Escaping Education*, 18, 49.
67. The constellation of concepts they promote includes "lived pluralness," "refusenik cultures," "grassroots postmodernity," "cultural autonomy," "decolonization," "localization," and "commons," among many others. They oppose these concepts to education in association with a constellation

of normatively negative concepts, including "development," "progress," "law of scarcity," and "non-subsistence economy," among others.

68. Consider, e.g., the "alter-globalization" movement, and colonial and capitalist forms of commons that have destroyed Indigenous commons. On "conflicting commons," see Allan Greer, "Commons and Enclosure in the Colonization of North America," *American Historical Review* 117, no. 2, (2012): 365–86.

69. Sara Ahmed, "Resignation Is a Feminist Issue," *Feminist Killjoys Blog*, August 27, 2016, https://feministkilljoys.com/2016/08/27/resignation -is-a-feminist-issue/.

2. DISPOSING OF THREATS

1. Howard Winant, *The World Is a Ghetto: Race and Democracy since World War II* (New York: Basic Books, 2001), 145.

2. Gunnar Myrdal, *An American Dilemma: The Negro Problem and Modern Democracy* (New York: Harper and Brothers, 1944).

3. Jodi Melamed, *Represent and Destroy: Rationalizing Violence in the New Racial Capitalism* (Minneapolis: University of Minnesota Press, 2011), 6–7.

4. On these movements' anti-racist, anti-colonial world-making projects, see Penny Von Eschen, *Race against Empire: Black Americans and Anticolonialism, 1937–1957* (Ithaca: Cornell University Press, 1997); Nikhil Singh, *Black Is a Country: Race and the Unfinished Struggle for Democracy* (Cambridge: Harvard University Press, 2004); Brenda Gayle Plummer, *In Search of Power: African American in the Era of Decolonization, 1956–1974* (Cambridge: Cambridge University Press, 2012); John Munro, *The Anticolonial Front: The African American Freedom Struggle and Global Decolonisation, 1945–1960* (Cambridge: Cambridge University Press, 2017); Nicholas Grant, *Winning Our Freedoms Together: African Americans and Apartheid, 1945–1960* (Chapel Hill: University of North Carolina Press, 2017); Keisha N. Blain, *Set the World on Fire: Black Nationalist Women and the Global Struggle for Freedom* (Philadelphia: University of Pennsylvania Press, 2018); and Adom Getachew, *Worldmaking after Empire: The Rise and Fall of Self-Determination* (Princeton: Princeton University Press, 2019). On the history of movements criticizing "internal colonialism" as an American theory of race, see Ramón A. Gutiérrez, "Internal Colonialism: An American Theory of Race," *Du Bois Review* 1, no. 2 (2004): 281–95.

5. On racial liberalism's postwar reliance on modernization theory, see Karen Ferguson, *Top Down: The Ford Foundation, Black Power, and the Reinvention of Racial Liberalism* (Philadelphia: University of Pennsylvania Press, 2013), 32–45; and Melamed, *Represent and Destroy*, 18–22.

6. On "modernity/coloniality" see Walter Mignolo, *The Darker Side of Western Modernity: Global Futures, Decolonial Options* (Durham: Duke University Press, 2011).

7. Donna Murch, *Living for the City: Migration, Education, and the Rise of the Black Panther Party in Oakland, California* (Chapel Hill: University of North Carolina Press, 2010), 11.

8. Further research is needed on other transformations in the education system in response to these threats to liberal capitalism, such as the vast expansion of community colleges, especially in the mid-1960s with the American Association of Junior Colleges pushing vocationalization, foundation funding support from the Ford Foundation and the Kellogg Foundation, policy support from the National Education Association, and the federal government's 1963 Vocational Education Act. Steven Brint and Jerome Karabel, *The Diverted Dream: Community Colleges and the Promise of Educational Opportunity in America, 1900–1985* (New York: Oxford University Press, 1989), 84–102.

9. My research for this chapter draws on the archives of the Ford Foundation and the National Education Association. The former are at the Rockefeller Archive Center, in Sleepy Hollow, New York, and the latter are at the George Washington University Archives in Washington, D.C.

10. Daniel Schreiber, Project: School Dropouts, Final Report, December 1965, p. 12, microform reel 0255, PA 61-208, "National Education Association of the United States (06100208), 1961 June 01–1964 May 31," Finding Aid 732E, Grants, Ford Foundation Records, Rockefeller Archive Center [hereafter FFR, RAC].

11. Graph created using Google Books Ngram Viewer (https://books.google .com/ngrams) for the phrases "school dropout" and "juvenile delinquent" between 1930 and 2000.

12. Sherman Dorn, *Creating the Dropout: An Institutional and Social History of School Failure* (Westport, Conn.: Praeger, 1996), 3.

13. Dorn's own presentation of data from census public-use samples shows that, during or soon after 1950, more than 50 percent of all U.S. citizens between 20 and 24 years of age had high school diplomas (*Creating the Dropout*, 15).

14. James Conant, *Slums and Suburbs: A Commentary on Schools in Metropolitan Areas* (New York: McGraw-Hill, 1961), 2.

15. Grant Application for Investigation of School Leavers in Uganda, approved February 3, 1961, microform reel 0771, PA 61-92, "Makerere University (06100092), 1961 February 08–1964 February 07," Finding Aid 732E, Grants, FFR, RAC.

16. Ferguson, *Top Down*, 41–48.

17. Vijay Prashad, *The Darker Nations: A People's History of the Third World* (New York: The New Press, 2007); and Getachew, *Worldmaking after Empire*.

18. On the *bracero* program see Timothy J. Henderson, "Bracero Blacklists: Mexican Migration and the Unraveling of the Good Neighbor Policy," *Latin Americanist* 55, no. 4 (2011): 199–217.

19. On the "autonomy of migration" and "imperceptible politics" see Dimitris Papadopoulos, Niamh Stephenson, and Vassilis Tsianos, *Escape Routes: Control and Subversion in the 21st Century* (Ann Arbor: Pluto Press, 2008). On "hidden and public transcripts" of resistance, see James C. Scott, *Domination and the Arts of Resistance: Hidden Transcripts* (New Haven: Yale University Press, 1990). For more on the "autonomy of migration" approach see Sandro Mezzadra and Brett Neilson, *Border as Method, or, the Multiplication of Labor* (Durham: Duke University Press, 2013); and Natasha King, *No Borders: The Politics of Immigration Control and Resistance* (London: Zed Books, 2016).

20. Clyde Woods, *Development Arrested: The Blues and Plantation Power in the Mississippi Delta* (Brooklyn: Verso, 1998), 29.

21. Woods, *Development Arrested*, 35.

22. Woods, *Development Arrested*, 36.

23. Woods, *Development Arrested*, 127.

24. Woods, *Development Arrested*, 128–30.

25. Woods, *Development Arrested*, 143.

26. Woods, *Development Arrested*, 145.

27. Woods, *Development Arrested*, 146.

28. William Barlow, *Looking Up at Down: The Emergence of Blues Culture* (Philadelphia: Temple University Press, 1989), 310, quoted in Woods, *Development Arrested*, 146–47.

29. Woods, *Development Arrested*, 147.

30. Richard Wright, "I Bite the Hand That Feeds Me," *Atlantic Monthly*, June 1940, 826–28; cf. Dan McCall, *The Example of Richard Wright* (New York: Harcourt Brace Jovanovich, 1969), 79, quoted in Woods, *Development Arrested*, 147.

31. Woods, *Development Arrested*, 148.

32. Woods, *Development Arrested*, 148.

33. Woods, *Development Arrested*, 149.

34. Anne M. Knupfer, *The Chicago Black Renaissance and Women's Activism* (Chicago: University of Illinois Press, 2006), 76–81.

35. On Dyett's central role in training many thousands of musicians in the

Chicago jazz community, see Arthur C. Cromwell, "Jazz Mecca: An Eth-
nographic Study of Chicago's South Side Jazz Community" (PhD diss.,
Ohio University, 1998), 135–45; John F. Behling, "Music Practices as Social
Relations: Chicago Music Communities and the Everyday Significance
of Playing Jazz" (PhD diss., University of Michigan, 2010), 76–77; and
Thomas A. Newsome, "It's after the End of the World! Don't You Know
That Yet? Black Creative Musicians in Chicago (1946–1976)" (PhD diss.,
University of North Carolina at Chapel Hill, 2001), 78–80, 88, 175–76.

36. Michael Hines, "The Blackboard and the Color Line: Madeline Morgan and the Alternative Black Curriculum in Chicago's Public Schools,
1941–1945" (PhD diss., Loyola University Chicago, 2017), 66–67.

37. Hines, "The Blackboard and the Color Line," 157.

38. Ian Rocksborough-Smith, "Contentious Cosmopolitans: Black Public
History and Civil Rights in Cold War Chicago, 1942–1972" (PhD diss.,
University of Toronto, 2014), 27.

39. James Smethurst, *The Black Arts Movement: Literary Nationalism in the
1960s and 1970s* (Chapel Hill: University of North Carolina Press, 2005),
193, quoted in Rocksborough-Smith, "Contentious Cosmopolitans," 39.

40. Knupfer, *The Chicago Black Renaissance,* 75–81.

41. Damien Sojoyner, *First Strike: Educational Enclosures in Black Los Angeles*
(Minneapolis: University of Minnesota Press, 2016), Kindle location 302.

42. Sojoyner, *First Strike,* 305–7.

43. Naomi Murakawa, *The First Civil Right: How Liberals Built Prison America*
(New York: Oxford University Press, 2014), 11; her embedded quote is
from Von Eschen, *Race against Empire,* 157.

44. Murakawa, *The First Civil Right,* 11.

45. Melamed, *Represent and Destroy.*

46. The NEA ran simultaneous projects on juvenile delinquents and academi-
cally talented students in the mid- to late 1950s. Also, for an example in
the Ford Foundation's Gray Areas/Great Cities Program, a proposal from
William Rafsky, development coordinator for Philadelphia, described
the project in Philadelphia as "really directed to two objectives: discovery and development of *talent*—identification of incipient *delinquency*
and prevention" (emphasis added). Great Cities Project, minutes from
Milwaukee meeting, April 22, 1960, p. 9, microform reel P-1022, D-132,
"Schools and Urban 'Gray Areas' (Ford Foundation Initiated, Education
and Public Affairs Programs), 1960," Finding Aid 733, Projects, FFR,
RAC.

47. Notes from meeting on Gray Areas/Great Cities Program, May 16, 1960,
microform reel P-1022, D-132, "Schools and Urban 'Gray Areas' (Ford

Foundation Initiated, Education and Public Affairs Programs), 1960," Finding Aid 733, Projects, FFR, RAC.

48. G. K. Hodenfield, "Adults Cash in on 'Delinquency,'" *New York Journal-American*, May 12, 1959. Hodenfield is drawing this point from his reading of the NEA report *Delinquent Behavior: Culture and the Individual*, box 2725, folder 4, Project Juvenile Delinquency, RG0197 National Education Association Archives, Special Collections Research Center, George Washington University Libraries, Washington, D.C. [hereafter SCRC, GWUL]. In its description of the Juvenile Delinquency project, the NEA also describes the delinquent as an "institutional scapegoat": "The irritating young delinquent appears to syphon off much of the adult frustration and aggression that is incident to the complexities of our society; he serves admirably as a handy hate target—a classic case of the institutional scapegoat." Project Juvenile Delinquency, Introduction, box 2722, folder 2, ca. 1958–1959, RG0197 National Education Association Archives, SCRC, GWUL.

49. Sylvia L. M. Martinez and John L. Rury, "From 'Culturally Deprived' to 'At Risk': The Politics of Popular Expression and Educational Inequality in the United States, 1960–1985," *Teachers College Record* 114, no. 6, (June 2012): 3.

50. In his project proposal for the Great Cities School Improvement Project, Willis used the language of "culturally deprived children" along with a focus on reducing "drop-outs." Ben Willis, "Project Proposal #1, for the Great Cities School Improvement Project," December 28, 1959, microform reel 0213, PA 60-220, "Board of Education of the City of Chicago (06000220), 1960 May 18–1961 May 17," Finding Aid 732A, Grants, FFR, RAC.

51. Alice O'Connor, "Community Action, Urban Reform, and the Fight against Poverty: The Ford Foundation's Gray Areas Program," *Journal of Urban History* 22, no. 5 (July 1996): 607.

52. Paul Ylvisaker, interview by Charles T. Morrissey, October 27, 1973, p. 58, Ford Foundation Oral History Project, Bernard Berelson Files, box 265, folder 2457, Finding Aid 432, Population Council Records (Record Group 2, Accession 2, Series 1 to 4), Rockefeller Archive Center.

53. Discussion paper, The Gray Areas Program, August 14, 1964, p. 1, microform reel P-1022, D-132, "Schools and Urban 'Gray Areas' (Ford Foundation Initiated, Education and Public Affairs Programs), 1960," Finding Aid 733, Projects, FFR, RAC. Emphasis added.

54. Minutes of staff meeting, Great Cities–Grey Area Project, Prepared by Henry Saltzman, October 3, 1960, p. 4, microform reel P-1022, D-132, "Schools and Urban 'Gray Areas' (Ford Foundation Initiated, Education

and Public Affairs Programs), 1960," Finding Aid 733, Projects, FFR, RAC. Emphasis added.

55. Daniel Schreiber, "The Dropout and the Delinquent: Promising Practices Gleaned from a Year of Study," *Phi Delta Kappan*, February 1963, 220–21, box 2718, folder 1, RG0197 National Education Association Archives, SCRC, GWUL.

56. For example, from the *NEA Newsletter*: "[The Higher Horizons] program, which involves intensive efforts to discover hidden academic talents among *culturally deprived groups* and to raise the educational and vocational sights of children from these groups, is generally conceded to have achieved substantial results" (emphasis added). "NEA Announces Intensive Program to Salvage High-School Drop-Outs," *NEA Newsletter*, July 11, 1961, box 2718, folder 1, RG0197 National Education Association Archives, SCRC, GWUL.

57. On "actor-network-theory," see Bruno Latour, *Reassembling the Social: An Introduction to Actor-Network-Theory* (New York: Oxford University Press, 2004).

58. On the role that "venture philanthropies" such as the Broad and Gates Foundations play today as a "shadow state" in influencing state education policy, see Pauline Lipman, "Capitalizing on Crisis: Venture Philanthropy's Colonial Project to Remake Urban Education," *Critical Studies in Education* 56, no. 2 (2015): 241–58.

59. Schreiber, Project: School Dropouts, Final Report, 8.

60. John F. Kennedy quoted in Daniel Schreiber, Second Annual Interim Report, December 30, 1963, p. 1, microform reel 0255, PA 61-208, "National Education Association of the United States (06100208), 1961 June 01-1964 May 31," Finding Aid 732E, Grants, FFR, RAC.

61. Schreiber, Second Annual Interim Report, 4.

62. Schreiber, Second Annual Interim Report, 4.

63. Ben Willis, Project Proposal #1, for the Great Cities School Improvement Project, December 28, 1959, microform reel 0213, PA 60-220, "Board of Education of the City of Chicago (06000220), 1960 May 18–1961 May 17," Finding Aid 732A, Grants, FFR, RAC; Ben Willis, "Experimental Work and Study Program for Potential and Actual School Drop-outs," Project Proposal to Ford Foundation, May 12, 1961, microform reel 0049, PA 61-207, "Board of Education of the City of Chicago (06100207), 1961 June 01–1962 May 31," Finding Aid 732A, Grants, FFR, RAC.

64. Willis, "Experimental Work and Study Program for Potential and Actual School Drop-outs."

65. Willis, "Experimental Work and Study Program for Potential and Actual School Drop-outs."

66. Willis used the language of aiming to make potential and actual dropouts into "productive and responsible citizens" in a follow-up proposal, "Double C Project (Census and Counseling)," Chicago Public Schools, August 22, 1962, microform reel 0049, PA 61-207, "Board of Education of the City of Chicago (06100207), 1961 June 01–1962 May 31," Finding Aid 732A, Grants, FFA, RAC.

67. Jerry Long, Interim Report on "Experimental Work and Study Program for Potential and Actual School Drop-outs," September 1, 1961, microform reel 0049, PA 61-207, "Board of Education of the City of Chicago (06100207), 1961 June 01–1962 May 31," Finding Aid 732A, Grants, FFA, RAC.

68. "School Boycott, Chicago, 1963," Chicago History Museum website, http://facingfreedom.org/public-protest/school-boycott.

69. For an example of this narrative, see Bob Hunter, "Public School 'Drop Outs' Blamed on Segregation," *Chicago Daily Defender*, October 10, 1961, 16. Another example is from a North Carolina African American newspaper: "I don't like the word [dropouts]. It gives a wrong picture of what actually happens to these kids. I'd rather call them 'pushouts,' because they leave school not because of any great defect in themselves, but because the educational system doesn't make the effort needed to motivate them and teach them." Whitney M. Young Jr., "To Be Equal," *Carolina Times*, July 8, 1967, 1.

70. I draw the concept of "excessive desires" from theorists in the "autonomy of migration" tendency, particularly Papadopoulos, Stephenson, and Tsianos, *Escape Routes*.

71. Silvia Federici and Arlen Austin, eds., *Wages for Housework: The New York Committee 1972–1977: History, Theory, Documents* (New York: Autonomedia, 2017); The Wages for Students Students, "Wages for Students" (self-published pamphlet, 1975), http://zerowork.org/WagesForStudents.html.

72. Kevin Hetherington, "Secondhandedness: Consumption, Disposal, and Absent Presence," *Environment and Planning D: Society and Space* 22, no. 1 (2004): 163.

73. Hetherington, "Secondhandedness," 164; Michael Thompson, *Rubbish Theory* (Oxford: Oxford University Press, 1979).

74. Proposal to the Fund for Public Affairs, Ford Foundation, "A Consultation and Clearinghouse Service on School Programs with Reference to Potential School Dropouts and Unemployed Youth," March 3, 1961, microform reel 0255, PA 61-208, "National Education Association of

the United States (06100208), 1961 June 01–1964 May 31," Finding Aid 732E, Grants, FFR, RAC. For more on the links between the dropout and automation narratives, see the NEA's Project on the Educational Implications of Automation in the early 1960s (NEA Archives). Also see Daniel Schreiber's article "The Low Ability Group and the World of Automation," November 1964, Project on School Dropouts, box 2716, folder 3, RG0197 National Education Association Archives, SCRC, GWUL.

75. I draw the concept of "emotional economies" from Sara Ahmed, *The Cultural Politics of Emotion*, 2nd ed. (Edinburgh: Edinburgh University Press, 2014). I also draw on Paula Ioanide's use of the concept: "Emotional economies that are attached to race and sexuality are an important site of inquiry because they have the unique ability to foreclose people's cognitive receptivity. . . . Any time our emotional structures experience danger, fear, or anxiety—affects that are all too common in discussions of systemic oppression—our capacity to integrate knowledge and participate in communicative acts also tends to diminish." Ioanide, *The Emotional Politics of Racism: How Feelings Trump Facts in an Era of Colorblindness* (Palo Alto: Stanford University Press, 2015), 2.

76. Ahmed describes emotions as productive of the impression of surfaces of individuals and collectives through "intensifications of feeling" (*Cultural Politics of Emotion*, 24).

77. I draw here on Ahmed's theory of two ways in which "the nation is reproduced through expressions of shame" (*Cultural Politics of Emotion*, 108).

78. On the difference between stereotyping and ontological subject construction, particularly with criminalization, Lisa Cacho argues: "To transparently recognize a black man or a black woman as a 'looter' is not equivalent to misrecognizing a hurricane victim as a criminal. Seeing a looter rather than a recognizing a victim does not emerge from an inability to conceive of certain people as entitled to personhood. This way of seeing emerges from the refusal to see them as such. Cultural studies scholar Sara Ahmed's work on 'stranger fetishism' helps to clarify why transparent recognition is not just seeing a stereotype, not merely an act of misrecognition. . . . Akin to 'the stranger,' so-called 'unlawful' people (looters, gang members, illegal aliens, suspected terrorists) and so-imagined 'lawless' places (totalitarian regimes, inner cities, barrios) are ontologized. These grossly overrepresented, all-too-recognizable figures with lives of their own—the looter, the gang member, the illegal alien, the suspected terrorist—have real world referents. We can transparently recognize criminals (with their disreputable traits and deceitful nature) only if we refuse to recognize the material histories, social relations, and structural

conditions that criminalize populations of color and the impoverished places where they live." Cacho, *Social Death: Racialized Rightlessness and the Criminalization of the Unprotected* (New York: New York University Press, 2012), 9. On "stranger fetishism," see Sara Ahmed, *Strange Encounters: Embodied Others in Post-Coloniality* (London: Routledge, 2000), 2–6.

79. Nancy Fraser and Linda Gordon, "A Genealogy of *Dependency*: Tracing a Keyword of the U.S. Welfare State," *Signs* 19 (Winter 1994): 309–36.

80. Donna Haraway, *Staying with the Trouble: Making Kin in the Chthulucene* (Durham: Duke University Press, 2016).

81. Leanne Simpson, "Land as Pedagogy: Nishnaabeg Intelligence and Rebellious Transformation," *Decolonization: Indigeneity, Education and Society* 3, no. 3, (2014): 7. Also see Leanne Simpson, *As We Have Always Done: Indigenous Freedom through Radical Resistance* (Minneapolis: University of Minnesota Press, 2017).

82. On "more-than-humanist" politics, see Bruce Braun and Sarah Whatmore. *Political Matter: Technoscience, Democracy, and Public Life* (Minneapolis: University of Minnesota Press, 2010). On the central roles of bacteria in the performance of emotions, cognition, and identity, see Myra Hird, *The Origins of Sociable Life: Evolution after Science Studies* (New York: Palgrave, 2009).

83. Latour, *Reassembling the Social.*

84. On "excessive desires," see Papadopoulos, Stephenson, and Tsianos, *Escape Routes.*

85. For promotions of the "pushout" framing as a way to draw attention to structural racism in schools, see Monique W. Morris, *Pushout: The Criminalization of Black Girls in Schools* (New York: The New Press, 2016); and Eve Tuck, *Urban Youth and School Pushout: Gateways, Get-aways, and the GED* (New York: Routledge, 2012).

86. For more on how the education-based mode of study is part of primitive accumulation, see chapters 3 and 4. For a theory of primitive accumulation as creating new relations of separation between producers and means of production, see Massimo De Angelis, *The Beginning of History: Value Struggles and Global Capital* (London: Pluto Press, 2007).

87. Schools internalized segregation with racialized tracking, wherein "gifted and talented" tracks of courses tend to be dominated with white students and the "remedial and compensatory" tracks are dominated with Black, Latinx, and Indigenous students. See Jeannie Oakes, *Keeping Track: How Schools Structure Inequality*, 2nd ed. (New Haven: Yale University Press, 2005).

88. For this argument about the depoliticizing effects of the vertical education imaginary, I am inspired by Timothy Mitchell's theory of how development discourses portray the nation-state as a self-contained unit and thereby depoliticize the construction of, and flows across, its boundaries. Mitchell, *Rule of Experts: Egypt, Techno-Politics, Modernity* (Berkeley: University of California Press, 2002).

89. Gutiérrez, "Internal Colonialism."

90. O'Connor, "Community Action," 615.

91. On the rise of the "economically disadvantaged" narrative in the 1970s and the "at risk" narrative in the 1980s, influenced by the publication of *A Nation at Risk* in 1983, see Martinez and Rury, "From 'Culturally Deprived' to 'At Risk,'" 24.

92. On the "non-profit industrial complex" see INCITE! Women of Color against Violence, *The Revolution Will Not Be Funded: Beyond the Non-Profit Industrial Complex* (Boston: South End Press, 2007).

93. "Our History," http://www.americaspromise.org/our-history.

94. Robin D. G. Kelley argues that the phrase "culture wars" describes the "ongoing battle over representations of the black urban condition, as well as the importance of the cultural terrain as a site of struggle." Kelley, *Yo' Mama's Disfunktional! Fighting the Culture Wars in Urban America* (Boston: Beacon Press, 1997), 8, quoted in Sojoyner, *First Strike* (Kindle locations 1379–80).

95. Melamed, *Represent and Destroy*, 137–64.

96. "History of the Police Foundation," *Police Foundation,* https://www.policefoundation.org/about/history/. For a critique of community policing, see Stuart Schrader, "Against the Romance of Community Policing," *A World without Police,* September 7, 2016, http://aworldwithoutpolice.org/2016/09/07/against-the-romance-of-community-policing/.

97. George Caffentzis, "University Struggles at the End of the Edu-Deal," *Mute,* April 15, 2010, http://www.metamute.org/editorial/articles/university-struggles-end-edu-deal.

98. On how an epistemology of ignorance around racism is supported by certain emotional economies, see Ioanide, *Emotional Politics of Racism*.

3. DEGREES OF ASCENT

1. See, e.g., Gerald Gutek, *A History of the Western Educational Experience*, 2nd ed. (Prospect Heights, Ill.: Waveland Press, 1995); John D. Pulliam and James J. Van Patten, *The History and Social Foundations of American Education*, 10th ed. (New York: Pearson, 2012); and Wayne J. Urban and

234 NOTES TO CHAPTER 3

Jennings L Wagoner Jr., *American Education: A History*, 5th ed. (New York: Routledge, 2013).

2. Silvia Federici, *Caliban and the Witch: Women, the Body, and Primitive Accumulation* (New York: Autonomedia, 2004), 63. On primitive accumulation as creating new relations of separation between producers and means of production, see Massimo De Angelis, *The Beginning of History: Value Struggles and Global Capital* (London: Pluto Press, 2007).

3. This account of the Black Plague's enabling the subversion of hierarchies is summarized from Federici, *Caliban and the Witch*, 40–44.

4. Federici, *Caliban and the Witch*, 57n29.

5. Federici, *Caliban and the Witch*, 37–38.

6. Federici, *Caliban and the Witch*, 47–49.

7. Federici, *Caliban and the Witch*, 25–26.

8. Federici, *Caliban and the Witch*, 92. Cf. John Riddle, *Eve's Herbs: A History of Contraception in the West* (Cambridge: Harvard University Press, 1999).

9. Jan Luiten van Zanden, "The Paradox of the Marks: The Exploitation of Commons in the Eastern Netherlands, 1250–1850," *Agricultural History Review* 47, no. 2 (1999): 128.

10. Van Zanden, "The Paradox of the Marks," 129.

11. Federici, *Caliban and the Witch*, 29–31.

12. Federici, *Caliban and the Witch*, 30–31.

13. At least eleven beguinages had between 100 and 400 beguines, one in Ghent numbered 610–730 beguines in the late thirteenth century, one in Liège numbered about 1,000 members, and one in Mechelen was a community of about 1,500–1,900 beguines in the late fifteenth and early sixteenth centuries. Walter Simons, *Cities of Ladies: Beguine Communities in the Medieval Low Countries, 1200–1565* (Philadelphia: University of Pennsylvania Press, 2001), 54–55.

14. Simons, *Cities of Ladies*, 116.

15. Simons, *Cities of Ladies*, 10–12.

16. Simons, *Cities of Ladies*, 36.

17. Simons, *Cities of Ladies*, 83–84.

18. Simons, *Cities of Ladies*, 84, quoting *Vita Beatricis*, in *The Life of Beatrice of Nazareth*, trans. Roger DeGanck (Kalamazoo, Mich.: Cistercian Publications, 1991), 24, 26.

19. Simons, *Cities of Ladies*, 15; R. I. Moore, "Heresy, Repression and Social Change in the Age of Gregorian Reform," in *Medieval Christendom and Its Discontents: Exclusion, Persecution, and Rebellion, 1000–1500*, ed. Scott J. Waugh and Peter D. Diehl (Cambridge: Cambridge University Press, 1996), 19–46.

20. Simons, *Cities of Ladies*, 69.
21. Simons, *Cities of Ladies*, 65.
22. Simons, *Cities of Ladies*, 14, 114.
23. Joanne M. Robinson, *Nobility and Annihilation in Marguerite Porete's "Mirror of Simple Souls"* (Albany: SUNY Press, 2001), 30.
24. Simons, *Cities of Ladies*, 22.
25. Simons, *Cities of Ladies*, 48, 52.
26. Simons, *Cities of Ladies*, 115.
27. Simons, *Cities of Ladies*, 132–34.
28. This area of Lower Germany in the Middle Ages was also known as Flanders, its most populous region, and it would become known as the Low Lands or Low Countries from the 1530s. John Van Engen, *Sisters and Brothers of the Common Life: The Devotio Moderna and the World of the Later Middle Ages* (Philadelphia: University of Pennsylvania Press, 2008), 48.
29. On popular protest against feudal hierarchies, see Samuel Cohn Jr., *Popular Protest in Late Medieval Europe: Italy, France, and Flanders* (New York: Manchester University Press, 2004); and Samuel Cohn Jr., *Lust for Liberty: The Politics of Social Revolt in Medieval Europe, 1200–1425* (Cambridge: Harvard University Press, 2006).
30. B. J. P. van Bavel. *Manors and Markets: Economy and Society in the Low Countries, 500–1600* (Oxford: Oxford University Press, 2010), 292.
31. Van Engen, *Sisters and Brothers*, 14–15.
32. Van Engen, *Sisters and Brothers*, 23–27. The Free Spirits were converts who led a spiritual life that took a radical turn inward.
33. Van Engen, *Sisters and Brothers*, 37.
34. Van Engen, *Sisters and Brothers*, 42–43.
35. Van Engen, *Sisters and Brothers*, 28.
36. Pepijn Brandon, "Marxism and the 'Dutch Miracle': The Dutch Republic and the Transition-Debate," *Historical Materialism* 19, no. 3 (2011): 119–20.
37. Van Engen, *Sisters and Brothers*, 53, 61.
38. Van Engen, *Sisters and Brothers*, 72, 75, 82.
39. Van Engen, *Sisters and Brothers*, 81–83.
40. Van Engen, *Sisters and Brothers*, 60, 124–25.
41. On the three-tiered class struggle in Lower Germany, see Brandon, "Marxism and the 'Dutch Miracle,'" 124.
42. Van Engen, *Sisters and Brothers*, 77–79.
43. Van Engen, *Sisters and Brothers*, 131.
44. Van Engen, *Sisters and Brothers*, 126, 135.
45. Van Engen, *Sisters and Brothers*, 86–107.

46. Van Engen, *Sisters and Brothers*, 135, 142.
47. Van Engen, *Sisters and Brothers*, 139.
48. Van Engen, *Sisters and Brothers*, 144.
49. Julia S. Henkel, "School Organizational Patterns of the Brethren of the Common Life," in *Essays on the Northern Renaissance*, ed. Kenneth Strand (Ann Arbor: Ann Arbor Publishers, 1968), 43.
50. Van Engen, *Sisters and Brothers*, 144.
51. Henkel, "School Organizational Patterns," 38.
52. De Angelis, *Beginning of History*.
53. From the perspective of twenty-first-century capitalism, the process of these individualized producers increasing their capacities could be framed as increasing human capital. For example, a recent article by economic historians analyzes the impact of the Sisters and Brothers of the Common Life on the early capitalist economic development of the Netherlands: "The [Sisters and Brothers] stimulated human capital accumulation by educating Dutch citizens without inducing animosity from the dominant Roman Catholic Church or other political rulers. Human capital had an impact on the structure of economic development in the period immediately after 1400." İbrahim Semih Akçomak, Herman Dinand Webbink, and Bas ter Weel, "Why Did the Netherlands Develop So Early? The Legacy of the Brethren of the Common Life," *Discussion Paper Series, Forschungsinstitut zur Zukunft der Arbeit*, no. 7167 (2013): 824.
54. William Harrison Woodward, *Desiderius Erasmus concerning the Aim and Method of Education* (1904; New York: Columbia University Press, 1964), 3–5.
55. Henkel, "School Organizational Patterns," 46–47.
56. Henkel, "School Organizational Patterns," 44, 45. On Puritan education in America, see Douglas McKnight, *Schooling, the Puritan Imperative, and the Molding of an American National Identity: Education's "Errand into the Wilderness"* (Mahwah, N.J.: Lawrence Erlbaum, 2003).
57. Karl Marx, *Capital*, vol. 1, chapter 26.
58. On how explanatory abstractions have the effect of short-circuiting descriptive inquiry, see Bruno Latour, *Reassembling the Social: An Introduction to Actor-Network-Theory* (New York: Oxford University Press, 2004).
59. Karl Marx, *Capital*, vol. 3, chapter 48, https://www.marxists.org. Quoted in Douglas Kellner, "Marxian Perspectives on Educational Philosophy: From Classical Marxism to Critical Pedagogy" (2006), https://pages.gseis.ucla.edu/faculty/kellner/essays/marxianperspectivesoneducation.pdf.
60. On the use of melodrama in political narratives, see Elisabeth R. Anker,

Orgies of Feeling: Melodrama and the Politics of Freedom (Durham: Duke University Press, 2014).

61. See Locke's chapter "On Property" in *Two Treatises concerning Government* (1690). On the "tragedy of the commons" see William Forster Lloyd, *Two Lectures on the Checks to Population* (1833); and Garrett Hardin, "The Tragedy of the Commons," *Science* 162, no. 3859 (1968): 1243–48. On private property as key for development, see Hernando de Soto, *The Mystery of Capital: Why Capitalism Triumphs in the West and Fails Everywhere Else* (New York: Basic Books, 2000).

62. Federici, *Caliban and the Witch*, 47–49.

63. Jason Read, "Primitive Accumulation: The Aleatory Foundation of Capitalism," *Rethinking Marxism* 14, no. 2 (2002): 39. Forms of enclosure predate the forms that it takes in primitive accumulation from the fifteenth century on, as the processes that create the preconditions of the capitalist mode of production—preconditions both in the sense of a prelude to its rise and during its prevalence, for its expansion and intensification (De Angelis, *Beginning of History*). According to Jesse Goldstein: "When the Statute of Merton authorized the enclosure of manorial waste lands in 1235, it required that the lord doing the enclosing leave sufficient commons to provide for his tenants' subsistence, insuring that commoners would not be completely separated from their means of production and reproduction. Most historians, Marx included, agree that it was not until the fifteenth century that enclosure took its infamous form as a mechanism of dispossession and agrarian change." Goldstein, "*Terra Economica*: Waste and the Production of Enclosed Nature," *Antipode* 45, no. 2 (2013): 360.

64. One Marxist historian who combines jeremiad and melodrama is Peter Linebaugh, who argues, "Commons is antithetical to capital," and "Enclosure indicates private property and capital." He unconditionally promotes the activity of "commoning," with its foundation in the slogan "All for one and one for all," and elaborates how it occurs in eighteen "common places," including food, health, housing, and security. (Linebaugh, *Stop, Thief! Commons, Enclosures, and Resistance* [Oakland, Calif.: PM Press, 2014], 13–14, 16–20, 142.) Other autonomist Marxist writers on the commons, as well as critical geographers and other writers on the "new enclosures," appeal to principles of commons and commoning as normative guidance for contemporary movements. I include my own previous writing as having this problem of combining a jeremiad and melodrama around commons and enclosure. (Isaac Kamola and Eli Meyerhoff, "Creating Commons: Divided Governance, Participatory Management, and Struggles against Enclosure in the University," *Polygraph* 21 [2009]:

5–27.) For other examples of this problem see De Angelis, *Beginning of History*; articles in Donald Nonini, ed., *The Global Idea of the Commons* (New York: Berghahn Books, 2007); Patrick Bond, "Emissions Trading, New Enclosures and Eco-Social Contestation," *Antipode* 44, no. 3 (2012): 684–701; and Stuart Hodkinson "The New Urban Enclosures," *City* 16, no. 5 (2012): 500–518.

65. On conflicting types of commons, see Allan Greer, "Commons and Enclosure in the Colonization of North America," *American Historical Review* 117, no. 2 (2012): 365–86; also see George Caffentzis and Silvia Federici, "Commons against and beyond Capitalism," *Community Development Journal* 49, no. 1 (January 2014): 92–105.

66. Greer, "Commons and Enclosure," 369.

67. Greer gives many examples of these Indigenous commons: "Around the great cities of Mesoamerica lay villages and hamlets with intensively cultivated fields, some of the latter belonging to particular households, others owned by temples, local chiefs, or urban nobles and worked by the community. Plots were carefully measured, marked, and recorded; tenure displayed some characteristics associated with enclosed areas of England and some characteristics of what Locke would call legal, particular commons. Thus this can be viewed as a zone of enclosure and 'inner commons.' Beyond the villages and cornfields lay a different kind of commons: the forest or mountains or desert terrain where local people went for firewood, wild herbs and berries, game, and other resources" ("Commons and Enclosure," 369–70).

68. Greer, "Commons and Enclosure," 372.

69. For example, in Mexico: "Colonization created conditions favorable to the ambitions of ruthless ranchers who were determined to expand their enterprises at the Indians' expense. Attacked by successive waves of epidemic disease, native numbers fell dramatically over the course of the sixteenth century. To make matters worse, great herds of feral cattle and horses spread northward in advance of human conquerors, undermining the fragile ecology, and thus Indian subsistence, in northern New Spain. There was massive dislocation for the survivors, battered by the economic demands of tribute and forced, in some cases, to relocate in concentrated settlements called *congregaciones*, the better to administer and Christianize them" (Greer, "Commons and Enclosure," 378).

70. Greer, "Commons and Enclosure," 379.

71. Caffentzis and Federici, "Commons against and beyond Capitalism," 97. Also, on "the tragedy of the capitalist commons," see De Angelis, *Beginning of History*.

72. Caffentzis and Federici, "Commons against and beyond Capitalism," 97–98.
73. Caffentzis and Federici, "Commons against and beyond Capitalism," 98.
74. See, e.g., De Angelis, *Beginning of History;* and Linebaugh, *Stop, Thief!*
75. See Goldstein, "*Terra Economica.*"
76. Van Zanden, "The Paradox of the Marks," 131.
77. Simons, *Cities of Ladies*, 111–17.
78. On modernist/colonial dichotomies, see Walter Mignolo, *The Darker Side of Western Modernity: Global Futures, Decolonial Options* (Durham: Duke University Press, 2011).
79. I draw the language of "associating" and "creating connections" from Latour, *Reassembling the Social.*
80. On zero-point epistemology see Mignolo, *Darker Side of Western Modernity.*
81. I draw this distinction between explanations and descriptions from Latour, *Reassembling the Social*, 137.
82. On place-and-body political epistemology in opposition to the zero-point epistemology, see Mignolo, *Darker Side of Western Modernity.*
83. Glen Coulthard, *Red Skin, White Masks: Rejecting the Colonial Politics of Recognition* (Minneapolis: University of Minnesota Press, 2014), 13. This grounded ethical framework guides Indigenous peoples' struggles as "not only *for* land, but also deeply *informed* by what land as a mode of reciprocal *relationship* (which is itself informed by place-based practices and associated forms of knowledge) ought to teach us about living our lives in relation to one another and our surroundings in a respectful, nondominating and nonexploitative way" (60).
84. Coulthard says: "In the Weledeh dialect of Dogrib (which is my community's language), for example, 'land' (or *dè*) is translated in relational terms as that which encompasses not only the land (understood here as material), but also people and animals, rocks and trees, lakes and rivers, and so on. Seen in this light we are as much a part of the land as any other element. Furthermore, within this system of relations human beings are not the only constituent believed to embody spirit or agency. Ethically, this meant that humans held certain obligations to the land, animals, plants, and lakes in much the same way that we hold obligations to other people. And if these obligations were met, then the land, animals, plants, and lakes would reciprocate and meet their obligations to humans, thus ensuring the survival and well-being of all over time" (*Red Skin, White Masks*, 61).
85. Coulthard, *Red Skin, White Masks*, 12.
86. Coulthard, *Red Skin, White Masks*, 61.

87. On "more-than-humanist" political theory, see Bruce Braun and Sarah Whatmore, *Political Matter: Technoscience, Democracy, and Public Life* (Minneapolis: University of Minnesota Press, 2010).

88. On bacterial self-organization, see Myra Hird, *The Origins of Sociable Life* (London: Palgrave, 2009).

89. "Perhaps there is no town in Holland which has suffered so considerably from epidemics of all kinds as Zwolle. In 1398, the year before Thomas [à Kempis] came there, the plague, called the black sickness (*peste noire*) devastated the poor city for the space of many months, carrying off victims at the rate of eighty a day, and not only from the town itself, but from the outlying villages, a rate of mortality which was enormous in proportion to the number of the inhabitants. The summer of 1422 was almost as fatal to the population as that of 1398, the number of deaths being so increased that they could not find grave-diggers to bury the dead." Samuel Kettlewell, *Thomas à Kempis and the Brothers of the Common Life*, 2nd ed., abridged (London: Kegan Paul, Trench, 1885), 177–78.

90. Groote died of the plague in 1384, and an outbreak in 1398 killed Zerbolt. Van Engen, *Sisters and Brothers*, 47, 117.

91. Zerbolt associates the lower spiritual realms with darkness and the higher spiritual realms with light. For example: "Consider then the chaos of hell, a place most dread beneath the earth and very deep; all dark it is, a well that is without bottom and all afire." "The third ascent, then, is this, to rise to a spiritual affection . . . Augustine, in the seventh chapter of the *Confessions*, saith: '. . . And I saw, as it were with the eye of my soul, the unchangeable light of the Lord shining upon that same eye and upon my mind. . . . He that knoweth the Truth, knoweth also this light.'" "If now thou being to ascend from thy lusts, and yet this present worthless world delight thee, do thou read the third seal that hath been opened, which is *This world of sense*. In Christ's death this was proved to be a place of darkness wherein blindness reigneth, because it knew not the true light." Gerard Zerbolt, *The Spiritual Ascent: A Devotional Treatise by Gerard of Zutphen* (London: Burns & Oates, 1908), 39, 59, 89.

92. On the politics of purity see Alexis Shotwell, *Against Purity: Living Ethically in Compromised Times* (Minneapolis: University of Minnesota Press, 2016).

93. Federici argues that "in pre-capitalist Europe women's subordination to men had been tempered by the fact that they had access to the commons and other communal assets, while in the new capitalist regime *women themselves became the commons*, as their work was defined as a natural resource, laying outside the sphere of market relations" (*Caliban and the Witch*, 97).

94. Drawing on Frank Wilderson's concept of "humanism's existential commons," Anita Juárez and Clayton Pierce argue that "whiteness is predicated on the ontological condition of social death imposed upon enslaved Black people—and maintained by a racial caste system in the post-Reconstruction period—as well as the genocidal relationship to Indigenous peoples endemic to settler states." Juárez and Pierce, "Educational Enclosure and the Existential Commons: Settler Colonialism, Racial Capitalism, and the Problem of the Human," in *Educational Commons in Theory and Practice: Global Pedagogy and Politics*, ed. Alexander J. Means, Derek R. Ford, Graham B. Slater (New York: Palgrave Macmillan, 2017), 147.

4. EDUCATIONAL COUNTERREVOLUTIONS

1. Ivan Illich, *Toward a History of Needs* (New York: Pantheon Books, 1977), 75.
2. On an economy of credit and debt as a "mode of accounting," see Miranda Joseph, *Debt to Society: Accounting for Life under Capitalism* (Minneapolis: University of Minnesota Press, 2014).
3. Entry for "education," *Oxford English Dictionary*.
4. Thomas Elyot, *The Boke Named the Governour* (1531).
5. Other new words that Elyot introduced include *execrate, involve, superstitiously, exactly, articulate, emulation, aggravate, activity, beneficence, clemency, equability, encyclopedia, frugality, implacability, imprudence, liberty of speech, loyalty, magistrate, mediocrity,* and *sincerity*. These words have all become fixtures of the English language. Elyot also innovates some words that are now obsolete or archaic or rare, which Major lists as: "adminiculate, adumbration (in the sense of shading in painting), annect, applicate, decerpt, falcate, humect, illecebrous, ostent, provect (all from the *Governour*), and a variety of medical terms." John Major, *Sir Thomas Elyot and Renaissance Humanism* (Lincoln: University of Nebraska Press, 1964), 17–18.
6. Major, *Sir Thomas Elyot*, 20.
7. Benedict Anderson, *Imagined Communities: Reflections on the Origin and Spread of Nationalism*, rev. ed. (New York: Verso, 2006), 39.
8. Simon, *Education and Society*, 130.
9. George H. Williams, *The Radical Reformation* (Kirksville, Mo.: Truman State University Press, 2000).
10. Michael Baylor, ed., *The Radical Reformation* (Cambridge: Cambridge University Press, 1991), 74n1.
11. Simon, *Education and Society*, 131.

12. Simon, *Education and Society,* 131.
13. Albert Hyma, *The Brethren of the Common Life* (Eugene, Ore.: Wipf and Stock, 2004), 168–69.
14. Simon, *Education and Society,* 135.
15. Luther quoted in Simon, *Education and Society*, 133. Emphasis added.
16. Anthony Fletcher and Diarmaid MacCulloch, *Tudor Rebellions*, 5th ed. (Harlow: Pearson Education, 2008), 26.
17. Fletcher and MacCulloch, *Tudor Rebellions*, 24.
18. Simon, *Education and Society,* 136.
19. Simon, *Education and Society,* 139.
20. Entry for "education," *Oxford English Dictionary*.
21. Simon, *Education and Society,* 143.
22. Julia S. Henkel, "School Organizational Patterns of the Brethren of the Common Life," in *Essays on the Northern Renaissance*, ed. Kenneth Strand (Ann Arbor: Ann Arbor Publishers, 1968), 47.
23. Lord Herbert of Cherbury, paraphrasing Wolsey, in his *The Life and Raigne of King Henry the Eighth* (1649), 157–58, quoted in Simon, *Education and Society,* 145.
24. David Knowles, *The Religious Orders in England,* vol. 3, *The Tudor Age* (Cambridge: Cambridge University Press, 1959), 197.
25. Richard Rex, "The Crisis of Obedience: God's Word and Henry's Reformation," *Historical Journal* 39, no. 4 (December 1996): 869, quoted in Christopher Moreland, "Resisting the Reformations: The Lincolnshire Rebellion, The Pilgrimage of Grace, and the Prayer Book Rebellion" (master's thesis, University of North Carolina, Wilmington, 2010), 17, http://dl.uncw.edu/etd/2010-2/morelandc/christophermoreland.pdf.
26. Madeleine Hope and Ruth Dodds, *The Pilgrimage of Grace and the Exeter Conspiracy* (London: Frank Cass and Co., 1915), 69, quoted in Moreland, "Resisting the Reformations," 12.
27. Fletcher and McCulloch, *Tudor Rebellions*, 19; Moreland, "Resisting the Reformations," 18–19.
28. On Cromwell's circular letters see G. R. Elton, *Policy and Police: The Enforcement of the Reformation in the Age of Thomas Cromwell* (Cambridge: Cambridge University Press, 1973), 230–43.
29. Fletcher and McCulloch, *Tudor Rebellions*, 9.
30. On the laws of treason, trials for treason, and the informal policing system, see Elton, *Policy and Police*, chapters 6, 7, and 8.
31. Karl Marx discusses this criminalizing of vagabondage under Henry VIII as part of primitive accumulation in *Capital,* vol. 1, chapter 28.

32. On these rebellions see Michael Bush, *The Pilgrimage of Grace: A Study of the Rebel Armies of October 1536* (Manchester: Manchester University Press, 1996); R. W. Hoyle, *The Pilgrimage of Grace and the Politics of the 1530s* (Oxford: Oxford University Press, 2001); Ethan Shagan, *Popular Politics and the English Reformation* (Cambridge: Cambridge University Press, 2003); and Moreland, "Resisting the Reformations."

33. Tracey A. Sowerby, *Renaissance and Reform in Tudor England: The Careers of Sir Richard Morison c. 1513–1556* (Oxford: Oxford University Press, 2010), 1, 14.

34. Sowerby notes that Morison, in his *Lamentation*, used this body politic imagery, arguing that "the English church was due protection from its head (the king) and support from its body (Henry's subjects)." Morison also deployed this imagery in his *Exhortation*. Sowerby, *Renaissance and Reform,* 90, 101.

35. Richard Morison, *A Remedy for Sedition* (1536), in David Berkowitz, *Humanist Scholarship and Public Order* (Washington, D.C.: The Folger Shakespeare Library, 1983), 86, 110.

36. On the point of how "the state" does not become widely used until the 1590s, see Fletcher and McCulloch, *Tudor Rebellions*, 10.

37. Timothy Mitchell, "Society, Economy, and the State Effect," in *State/Culture: State-Formation after the Cultural Turn* (Ithaca: Cornell University Press, 1999), 76–97.

38. Fletcher and McCulloch, *Tudor Rebellions*, 9.

39. Kim F. Hall, *Things of Darkness: Economies of Race and Gender in Early Modern England* (Ithaca: Cornell University Press, 1995), 4.

40. Silvia Federici, *Caliban and the Witch: Women, the Body, and Primitive Accumulation* (New York: Autonomedia, 2004).

41. Shagan, *Popular Politics and the English Reformation,* 80.

42. T. F. Mayer, *Thomas Starkey: A Dialogue between Pole and Lupset* (London: Offices of the Royal Historical Society, 1989), ix.

43. Paul Slack, *The English Poor Law, 1531–1782* (Cambridge: Cambridge University Press, 1990), 7.

44. Morison, *A Remedy for Sedition,* 128.

45. Elton, *Policy and Police,* 265.

46. Elton, *Policy and Police,* 274.

47. Elton, *Policy and Police,* 277.

48. Elton, *Policy and Police,* 339.

49. Elton, *Policy and Police,* 382.

50. Elton, *Policy and Police,* 304.

51. Elton, *Policy and Police*, 350.

52. Morison, *A Remedy for Sedition*, 129.

53. Morison, *A Remedy for Sedition*, 115–16.

54. Morison, *A Remedy for Sedition*, 128.

55. Ann McGruer, *Educating the "Unconstant Rabble": Arguments for Educational Advancement and Reform during the English Civil War and Interregnum* (Newcastle upon Tyne: Cambridge Scholars Publishing, 2010), 28.

56. McGruer, *Educating the "Unconstant Rabble,'* 47, 54, 81.

57. Johann Amos Comenius, *A reformation of schooles designed in two excellent treatises* . . . (London, 1642), 24, quoted in McGruer, *Educating the "Unconstant Rabble,"* 53.

58. McGruer, *Educating the "Unconstant Rabble,"* 68.

59. McGruer, *Educating the "Unconstant Rabble,"* 100.

60. McGruer, *Educating the "Unconstant Rabble,"* 170.

61. McGruer, *Educating the "Unconstant Rabble,"* 121.

62. McGruer, *Educating the "Unconstant Rabble,"* 153.

63. McGruer, *Educating the "Unconstant Rabble,"* 135, 166, 179.

64. McGruer, *Educating the "Unconstant Rabble,"* 154.

65. McGruer, *Educating the "Unconstant Rabble,"* 183.

66. McGruer, *Educating the "Unconstant Rabble,"* 192–93.

67. Federici, *Caliban and the Witch*, 22.

68. Lawrence Stone, "Literacy and Education in England, 1640–1900," *Past & Present*, no. 42 (1969): 81.

69. Ann Hughes, *The Causes of the English Civil War* (London: Macmillan, 1991), 127.

70. For an analysis of Hobbes's theorizing of fear, see Corey Robin, *Fear: The History of a Political Idea* (Oxford: Oxford University Press, 2006). My approach to comparing Locke and Hobbes is partly inspired by Robin's comparisons of Hobbes with later, more liberal theorists who, in contrast with Hobbes, obfuscate the relations of fear and domination in modernist, state-based political orders.

71. Peter King, "Thomas Hobbes's Children," in *The Philosopher's Child* (Rochester: University of Rochester Press, 1998), 81.

72. King, "Thomas Hobbes's Children," 68–82.

73. Lawrence Stone, "The Educational Revolution in England, 1560–1640," *Past & Present*, no. 28 (1964): 74.

74. Stone, "The Educational Revolution in England," 78.

75. A leader of the Diggers, Winstanley, promoted a universal program of education, which was "generally representative of the reform-minded concepts of other enlightened English sectaries of the mid-17th century."

Richard Greaves, "Gerrard Winstanley and Educational Reform in Puritan England," *British Journal of Educational Studies* 17, no. 2 (1969): 174.

76. Thomas Hobbes, *Leviathan*, ed. Edwin Curley (Indianapolis: Hackett, 1668), Review and Conclusion, 16.

77. Hobbes, *Leviathan*, II, xxx: 14.

78. Hobbes, *Leviathan*, II, xxx: 6–13.

79. Teresa M. Bejan, "Teaching the *Leviathan*: Thomas Hobbes on Education," *Oxford Review of Education* 36, no. 5 (2010): 615; Hobbes, *Leviathan*, I, vi: 57.

80. Thomas Hobbes, *The Elements of Law Natural and Politic* (1640), 10: 8.

81. Bejan, "Teaching the *Leviathan*," 616–17.

82. Hobbes, *The Elements of Law*, 13: 2.

83. Bejan, "Teaching the *Leviathan*," 619; Hobbes, *Leviathan*, IV, xlvi: 32.

84. "From 1669 to 1675, the Proprietors of the infant colony of Carolina (among them his patron Anthony Ashley Cooper, later the first Earl of Shaftesbury) employed Locke as their secretary. From October 1673 to December 1674, he was secretary and then also concurrently treasurer to the English Council for Trade and Foreign Plantations. Two decades later, near the end of his life, he was secretary to its successor, the Board of Trade, from 1696 to 1700." David Armitage, "John Locke, Carolina, and the Two Treatises of Government," *Political Theory* 32, no. 5 (2004): 603.

85. Locke invested "alongside his patron [Ashley] in the Royal African Company (£400 in 1674 and £200 more in 1675) and in the Bahamas trade (£100 in 1675) which he liquidated at profit (in 1676)." James Farr, "Locke, Natural Law, and New World Slavery," *Political Theory* 36, no. 4 (2008): 497.

86. Michel Foucault, "Technologies of the Self," in *Technologies of the Self: A Seminar with Michel Foucault*, ed. Luther H. Martin, Huck Gutman, and Patrick H. Hutton (London: Tavistock, 1988), 16–49.

87. Chad Lavin, *Eating Anxiety: The Perils of Food Politics* (Minneapolis: University of Minnesota Press, 2013), 37.

88. Lavin, *Eating Anxiety*, 35–36; John Locke, *Two Treatises of Government*, ed. Peter Laslett (Cambridge: Cambridge University Press, 1690), 2.27, 287–88.

89. Lavin, *Eating Anxiety*, 34; John Locke, *An Essay concerning Human Understanding*, ed. Roger Woolhouse (New York: Penguin Books, 1689), 2.27.19.

90. John Locke, *Some Thoughts concerning Education* (The Federalist Papers Project, 1693), 168, 59, 145.

91. Walter Mignolo, *The Darker Side of Western Modernity: Global Futures, Decolonial Options* (Durham: Duke University Press, 2011).
92. For histories of the co-constitutive developments of capitalism with colonialism and slavery, see Eric Williams, *Capitalism and Slavery* (Chapel Hill: University of North Carolina Press, 1944); and Robin Blackburn, *The American Crucible: Slavery, Emancipation and Human Rights* (New York: Verso, 2011). On the historical co-constitution of universities with these modes of world-making, see Craig Stephen Wilder, *Ebony and Ivy: Race, Slavery, and the Troubled History of America's Universities* (New York: Bloomsbury Press, 2013).
93. Federici, *Caliban and the Witch*, 64.
94. Locke notes his focus on education for boys: "I have said He here, because the principal aim of my discourse is, how a young gentleman should be brought up from his infancy, which in all things will not so perfectly suit the education of daughters" (*Some Thoughts concerning Education*, 6). A few exceptions are Locke's brief discussion of women and girls in relation to making clothes for their sons and shaping "the bodies of their children in their wombs," and shaping their own bodies to meet beauty norms, or as the "objects" of men's desires ("wine or women") (11, 12, 36).
95. Locke, *Some Thoughts concerning Education*, 9.
96. "A prudent and kind mother, of my acquaintance, was on such an occasion, forced to whip her little daughter, at her first coming home from nurse, eight times successively, the same morning, before she could master her stubbornness, and obtain a compliance in a very easy and indifferent matter" (Locke, *Some Thoughts concerning Education*, 78).
97. Locke, *Some Thoughts concerning Education*, 60.
98. ". . . that effeminacy of spirit, which is to be prevented or cured, as nothing, that I know, so much increases in children as crying" (Locke, *Some Thoughts concerning Education*, 113).
99. Locke, *Some Thoughts concerning Education*, 6.
100. John Locke, "An Essay on the Poor Law," in *Locke: Political Essays*, ed. Mark Goldie (Cambridge: Cambridge University Press, 1997), 184.
101. Locke, "An Essay on the Poor Law," 185–88.
102. Locke prescribes that "working schools be set up in each parish, to which the children of all such as demand relief of the parish, above 3 and under 14 years of age . . . shall be obliged to come" ("An Essay on the Poor Law," 190). This will free up the children's mother to work, and the children will learn dispositions to be "inured to work," "sober and industrious," as well as to force them to come to church every Sunday, "whereby they may be brought into some sense of religion" as well as "morality" (190,

192). The working schools are to take both boys and girls, while "if thought convenient, taught and kept to work separately." Locke was not alone in promoting such "working schools" in the mid- to late seventeenth century; "similar schemes to Locke's were mooted in Firmin's *Some Proposals for the Employing of the Poor* (1678), Sir Matthew Hale's *Discourse Touching Provision for the Poor* (1683), and John Beller's *Proposals for Raising a College of Industry* (1695)" (Mark Goldie in Locke, "An Essay on the Poor Law," 183).

103. Locke, *Some Thoughts concerning Education*, 59.

104. John Locke, "Study," in *Locke: Political Essays*, 367.

105. Locke, "An Essay on the Poor Law," 145.

106. Locke claims that "several nations of the Americans" have "a fruitful soil . . . yet, for want of improving it by labour, have not one hundreth part of the Conveniencies we enjoy" (*Two Treatises of Government*, 2.41).

107. "Every Freeman of Carolina shall have absolute power and Authority over his Negro slaves of what opinion or Religion soever." John Locke, "The Fundamental Constitution of Carolina," in *Locke: Political Essays*, 110, 180.

108. Although Locke seems to shy away from discussion of the body in his *Essay concerning Human Understanding* (1689), in *Some Thoughts concerning Education* (1693) he tries to deal with the body in order to use it as a tool for shaping the malleable self, via education. For this point, I draw from Claire Rasmussen, *The Autonomous Animal: Self-Governance and the Modern Subject* (Minneapolis: University of Minnesota Press, 2011), 30. Locke speaks often of the need for teaching children to control their bodily desires; for example, "children should be us'd to submit their desires, and go without their longings, even from their very cradles" (*Some Thoughts concerning Education*, 38).

109. Megan Boler theorizes the "collective, collaborative construction" of affects, emotions, and "structures of feeling" in and through education. Boler, *Feeling Power: Emotions and Education* (New York: Routledge, 1999).

110. On an "emotional economy" with circulating objects of emotion, see Sara Ahmed, *The Cultural Politics of Emotion*, 2nd ed. (Edinburgh: Edinburgh University Press, 2014).

111. "Esteem and disgrace are, of all others, the most powerful incentives to the mind, when one is brought to relish them. If you can get into children a love of credit, and an apprehension of shame and disgrace, you have put into them the true principle, which will constantly work, and incline them to the right" (Locke, *Some Thoughts concerning Education*, 56). Children are to be taught that the things they desire are "to be enjoyed by those

only, who are in a state of *reputation*," so as to "make them in love with the pleasure of *being well thought on*" (58, emphasis added).

112. Joseph, *Debt to Society*, x.

113. This point draws on Ahmed, *Cultural Politics of Emotion*, 10.

114. Locke, *Some Thoughts concerning Education*, 56.

115. Robert Sumser sees Locke's theory of education as having "laid the foundations of modern pedagogy and the capacity of experts to devise systems of education and schooling whose purpose was, in part at least, to form personality structures." Sumser, "John Locke and the Unbearable Lightness of Modern Education," *Educational Philosophy and Theory* 26 (1994): 4.

116. In contrast with the "tender, wax-like, sensitive" mind, "the environment impresses, moulds, imprints, instills, mends, and begets" (Sumser, "John Locke," 4).

117. As "costiveness," i.e., constipation, can signal a rebellion of the body against the mind—i.e., an inability of the mind to control the passage of "Nature" through the body's boundaries—Locke gives advice on how to instill proper habits for having regular bowel movements, "to have Nature very obedient," and "to obey and execute the orders of the mind" (*Some Thoughts concerning Education*, 26, 31). On the "digestive self," see Lavin, *Eating Anxiety*.

118. Locke, *Some Thoughts concerning Education*, 35.

119. The imaginary of the self as having clear, demarcated boundaries of "inside" and "outside" is important throughout Locke's descriptions of the education process. For example: "he that is a good, a virtuous, and able man, must be made so *within* . . . what he is to receive from education, what is to sway and influence his life, must be something *put into him* betimes, *habits woven into* the very principles of his nature; and not a counterfeit carriage, and dissembled *outside*, put on by fear" (*Some Thoughts concerning Education*, 42, emphases added).

120. Locke, *Some Thoughts concerning Education*, 41–42.

121. Locke, *Some Thoughts concerning Education*, 111–12. Against indulging children's crying, which "softens" their self-boundaries, Locke argues "they should be hardened against all sufferings, especially of the body, and have a tenderness only for shame and for reputation" (111).

122. Locke, *Some Thoughts concerning Education*, 124, 141.

123. The elder brother is to be empowered as a leader and teacher of "his younger brothers and sisters," both for guiding them and as a "spur" for his own learning (Locke, *Some Thoughts concerning Education*, 74, 119).

124. Locke, *Some Thoughts concerning Education*, 59.

125. Locke, *Some Thoughts concerning Education*, 68.
126. Locke reifies the class and gender hierarchies while prescribing "civility" as a way to legitimate it: he calls for educators to "accustom [children] to civility in their language and towards their inferiors, and the meaner sorts of people, particularly servants" (*Some Thoughts concerning Education*, 117). He simultaneously uses "fortune" to depoliticize this class hierarchy: "fortune has laid [domestics] below the level of others, at their master's feet."
127. On this historical connection between student rebellions and the emergence of grades at Yale, see Charles Tocci, "An Immanent Machine: Reconsidering Grades, Historical and Present," *Educational Philosophy and Theory* 42, no. 7 (2010): 769–70. Also see M. L. Smallwood, *An Historical Study of Examinations and Grading Systems in Early American Universities* (Cambridge: Harvard University Press, 1935).

5. EXPERIMENTAL COLLEGE

1. From conversations with an organizer of the protests, David Boehnke. For more on the Campaign to Defend Need-Blind Admissions at Macalester, see http://tinyurl.com/DNBAM.
2. Gary Berg, *Low-Income Students and the Perpetuation of Inequality: Higher Education in America* (Burlington, Vt.: Ashgate Press, 2010).
3. For Dames on Frames' zines, see http://microcosmpublishing.com/catalog/zines/2448/. For Unsettling Minnesota, see http://unsettling minnesota.org/. For the Map Shanty, see https://tinyurl.com/mapshanty.
4. We loosely draw this view of needs as the becoming-necessary of contingent encounters between forces, including desires, from Gilles Deleuze, *Nietzsche and Philosophy* (New York: Columbia University Press, 2006).
5. Rather than present a false appearance of comprehensiveness with our narratives, we acknowledge our *selectivity* in choosing these particular narratives for the political purposes of composing guidance that could be useful for such projects.
6. On "a/effective relationships," or the importance of attending to affective, everyday relationships for effective organizing, see Stevphen Shukaitis, *Imaginal Machines: Compositions of Autonomy and Self-Organization in the Revolutions of Everyday Life* (New York: Autonomedia, 2009), http://www.minorcompositions.info/ImaginalMachinesWeb.pdf. See also Nick Montgomery and Carla Bergman, *Joyful Militancy: Building Thriving Resistance in Toxic Times* (Oakland: AK Press, 2017).
7. On the zero-point epistemology see Walter Mignolo, *The Darker Side*

of Western Modernity: Global Futures, Decolonial Options (Durham: Duke University Press, 2011).

8. A note on pronoun usage: we take up EXCO as the object of our study, yet our selves and our past experiences are deeply entangled in its history and present, and at different times (Eli began working with EXCO in 2007, Erin in 2009). Throughout the text, we attempt to mark when "we" refers to Eli and Erin (the authors) or when "we/us" refers to our identification with and participation in EXCO as organizers. However, we used the third person in almost all of the narratives. Although we want to avoid the distance and feigned objectivity that this perspective implies, we used it in order to provide greater clarity for our readers.

9. Paulo Freire, *Pedagogy of the Oppressed* (New York: Continuum, 1970); Myles Horton and Paulo Freire, *We Make the Road by Walking: Conversations on Education and Social Change* (Philadelphia: Temple University Press, 1990).

10. Augusto Boal, *Theater of the Oppressed* (London: Pluto Press, 1979).

11. Gustavo Esteva, Madhu Suri Prakash, and Dana L. Stuchul, "From a Pedagogy for Liberation to Liberation from Pedagogy," in *Everywhere All the Time: A New Deschooling Reader*, ed. Matt Hern (Oakland, Calif.: AK Press, 2008), 97.

12. An example of such an approach is Paul Chatterton's integrating popular education approaches into his undergraduate course "Autonomous Geographies." See Chatterton, "Using Geography to Teach Freedom and Defiance: Lessons in Social Change from 'Autonomous Geographies,'" *Journal of Geography in Higher Education* 32, no. 3 (2008): 419–40. For other examples see Jim Crowther, Vernin Galloway, and Ian Martin, eds., *Popular Education: Engaging the Academy—International Perspectives* (Leicester: NIACE, 2005).

13. This account of the EC at San Francisco State is a summary of research that will be presented in a forthcoming article: Eli Meyerhoff, "'This Quiet Revolution': Alternative Modes of Study with the Experimental College at San Francisco State," *Cultural Politics*.

14. Jane Lichtman, *Bring Your Own Bag: A Report on Free Universities* (Washington, D.C.: American Association of Higher Education, 1973). The experimental colleges continuing today include those at Oberlin College, Tufts University, the University of Washington, and the University of California, Davis. See http://oberlinexco.org, http://www.excollege.tufts.edu/, https://depts.washington.edu/asuwxpcl/, and http://ecollege.ucdavis.edu/.

15. Ron Miller, *Free Schools, Free People: Education and Democracy after the 1960s* (Albany: State University of New York Press, 2002), ix.

16. Miller, *Free Schools, Free People*, 2.

17. Jonathan Kozol, *Free Schools* (Boston: Houghton Mifflin, 1972); John Holt, *How Children Fail* (New York: Delta, 1964); Miller, *Free Schools, Free People*, 56–72. Kozol has continued to engage in such struggles around public schools up to the present day; see, e.g., his *The Shame of the Nation: The Restoration of Apartheid Schooling in America* (New York: Crown, 2005).

18. Miller, *Free Schools, Free People*, 130.

19. Kozol, *Free Schools*, 8–10.

20. Kathleen McConnell, "Inventing Pluralistic Education: Compulsory Schooling as a Technique of Democratic Deliberation" (PhD diss., Indiana University, 2008), 100.

21. Kozol, *Free Schools*, 44.

22. For example, Kozol treated university researchers as merely instrumental to "run interference for the much less influential and much less prestigious Free School people in obtaining government or foundation funds" (*Free Schools*, 98).

23. Judith Suissa, *Anarchism and Education: A Philosophical Perspective* (New York: Routledge, 2006), 110.

24. On the Escuela Moderna and the Ferrer School, see Mark Bray and Robert H. Haworth, eds., *Anarchist Education and the Modern School: A Francisco Ferrer Reader* (Oakland, Calif.: PM Press, 2018); Emma Goldman, "Francisco Ferrer and the Modern School," in *Anarchism and Other Essays*, 2nd rev. ed. (New York: Mother Earth Publishing Association, 1911), 151–72; Paul Avrich, *The Modern School Movement* (Princeton: Princeton University Press, 1980); and Suissa, *Anarchism and Education*.

25. For links to currently active free skools see http://en.wikipedia.org/wiki/ Anarchistic_free_school. For information on the Toronto Anarchist Free School, see Allan Antliff, "Breaking Free: Anarchist Pedagogy," in *Utopian Pedagogy: Radical Experiments against Neoliberal Globalization*, ed. Mark Coté, Richard J. F. Day, and Greig de Peuter (Toronto: University of Toronto Press, 2007), 248–65; and Erik Stewart, "Toronto Anarchist Free University," presentation at Beneath the University, the Commons conference, Minneapolis, Minnesota (2010), http://beneaththeu.org/ Beneath_the_University/Saturday_AM.html. For interviews with organizers of several current free skools (Baltimore Free Skool, East Bay Free Skool, Santa Cruz Free Skool, and Seattle Free Skool), see abaker,

"Community Skillsharing Breaks from the Bubble: A Look at Free Skool Networking," Slingshot, no. 104 (2010), https://slingshotcollective.org/65a6259af13429eb16c89b3059bc14eb/. The Occupy movement of 2011 to 2013 has inspired a more recent resurgence of free skools and free universities (e.g., the New York Free University and the Brooklyn Freedom School, among others).

26.   For accounts of these free universities, see, on the Really Open University, Elsa Noterman and Andre Pusey, "Inside, Outside, and on the Edge of the Academy: Experiments in Radical Pedagogies," in *Anarchist Pedagogies: Collective Actions, Theories, and Critical Reflections on Education,* ed. Robert H. Haworth (Oakland, Calif.: PM Press, 2012), 175–99; on Meine Akadamie, Anja Kanngieser, "It's Our Academy: Transforming Education through Self-Organized Autonomous Universities," originally presented as part of the RMIT Student Union event, *Institutions, Capitalism, and Dissent: A Rogue Education Conference* (2007); and on the Free Metropolitan University of Rome, Claudia Bernardi, interview by Eli Meyerhoff, "Contaminating the University, Creating Autonomous Knowledge: Occupied Social and Cultural Centers in Italy," *ClassWarU,* September 24, 2012, available at http://classwaru.org/2012/09/24/contaminating-the-university-creating-autonomous-knowledge-occupied-social-and-cultural-centers-in-italy/. Eli has also interviewed participants in the Free University of New York and the Really Open University.

27.   Madhu Suri Prakash and Gustavo Esteva, *Escaping Education: Living as Learning within Grassroots Cultures* (New York: Peter Lang, 1998), 91–92.

28.   Ivan Illich, *Deschooling Society* (New York: Harper and Row, 1970), iv–v.

29.   Illich summarized in Prakash and Esteva, *Escaping Education*, 97.

30.   Ivan Illich, foreword, in *Everywhere All the Time: A New Deschooling Reader,* ed. Matt Hern (Oakland, Calif.: AK Press 2008), v.

31.   Illich, foreword, vi.

32.   Ibram H. Rogers, *The Black Campus Movement: Black Students and the Racial Reconstruction of Higher Education, 1965–1972* (New York: Palgrave Macmillan, 2012).

33.   Miriam Larson, interview by Eli, June 23, 2014.

34.   Callie Recknagel, interview by Eli, June 5, 2014.

35.   Arnoldas, interview by Eli, June 9, 2014.

36.   Lucia Pawlowski, interview by Erin, June 1, 2014.

37.   U of M chapter notes, February 8, 2008.

38.   Notes from visioning session, June 22, 2008.

39.   This account of the beginnings of Academia Comunitaria is based mostly

on former EXCO organizer David Boehnke's writing about the project in 2010.

40. Notes from visioning session, May 14, 2009.

41. For our call for engagement with this "complex mess" we are influenced by actor-network-theory, such as in John Law's *After Method,* which promotes diving into messiness in social science research, and Bruno Latour's *Reassembling the Social,* which offers guidance against taking short-cuts around the challenges of describing the messy controversies encountered in attempts to compose the world. Law, *After Method: Mess in Social Science Research* (New York: Routledge, 2004); Latour, *Reassembling the Social: An Introduction to Actor-Network-Theory* (Oxford: Oxford University Press, 2005).

42. For an ideal of continual circuits of study, teaching, and knowledge, forestalling "preparation for governance," we draw on Fred Moten, Stefano Harney, and Marc Bousquet, "On Study: A *Polygraph* Roundtable Discussion with Marc Bousquet, Stefano Harney, and Fred Moten," *Polygraph* 21 (2009): 159–75; and Fred Moten and Stefano Harney, *The Undercommons: Fugitive Planning and Black Study* (New York: Minor Compositions, 2013).

43. On subverting normative life trajectories, see Dimitris Papadopoulos, Niamh Stephenson, and Vassilis Tsianos, *Escape Routes: Control and Subversion in the 21st Century* (Ann Arbor: Pluto Press, 2008). On how modernist liberalism's institutions, including education, construct such autonomous, responsible, sovereign selves, see Claire Rasmussen, *The Autonomous Animal: Self-Governance and the Modern Subject* (Minneapolis: University of Minnesota Press, 2011).

44. We draw inspiration here from Timothy J. Lensmire's theory of the "ambivalent racial self" in "Ambivalent White Racial Identities: Fear and an Elusive Innocence," *Race Ethnicity and Education* 13, no. 2 (2010): 159–72. On the liberal anxieties produced from subscribing to fantasies of the bounded, unified self, see Chad Lavin, *Eating Anxiety: The Perils of Food Politics* (Minneapolis: University of Minnesota Press, 2013).

45. On primitive accumulation and the education-based mode of study, see chapters 3 and 4.

46. For our reflections and analysis of our research on this EXCO course, see Erin Dyke and Eli Meyerhoff, "An Experiment in 'Radical' Pedagogy and Study: On the Subtle Infiltrations of 'Normal' Education," *Journal of Curriculum Theorizing* 29, no. 2 (2013): 267–80.

47. On the concept of "playful work," see Cindi Katz, "Accumulation, Excess, Childhood: Toward a Countertopography of Risk and Waste," *Documents D'Anàlisi Geogràfica* 57, no. 1 (2011): 47–60.

48. Jodi Melamed, *Represent and Destroy: Rationalizing Violence in the New Racial Capitalism* (Minneapolis: University of Minnesota Press, 2011).
49. We focus on the U of M chapter here because we have much better capacities for interpreting the notes from their meetings, as we were both present at most of these meetings and were ourselves often the note-takers. For the sake of space we are forgoing a close reading of the Macalester chapter's and Academia chapter's meeting discussions during this year. Yet we are taking into account the perspectives of organizers from those two chapters through interviews with some of them.
50. U of M chapter meeting notes, May 26, 2010.
51. U of M chapter meeting notes, June 30, 2010. The list of potential class projects expanded later to include "Joining existing organizing . . . Supporting existing organizing . . . Opening up research and organizing on key issues . . . Student workers and the university, Undergraduate solidarity with graduate student organizing, Organizing for a National Day of Action in Defense of Education on October 7th, Military research and the university, Corporatization of the university: Rise of an Administrative Class, Relationships between Cedar Riverside and U of M, Making U of M resources accessible, Un/equal access at the U of M, Immigration issues at the U, Educational segregation in the Twin Cities, High Schools and U of M Student Demographics, U of M Donors, History of X struggles at the U, History of departments created through struggles, General College Lessons and Application, Gender, Labor, and Affect at the U, Corporate vs Open Source: the University's Software, University research: patents and corporate control, Responding to staff firings, developing a flying picket squad, Student unionizing, Cross-sector organizing: understanding different positionalities, Student apathy, why?, Branding: the University of spectacle, Corporate accountability struggles at the U: Coke, Arrowmark, TCF Bank, The U and the Prison-Industrial Complex, The Schools-to-Prisons Pipeline, The casualization of academia: potentials for contingent faculty organizing, Mental health at the U of M, Connecting Immigrant Rights Struggles and Education Struggles . . . among many others!" (email blurb about the project, July 16, 2010)
52. We explained the source of the idea in an email overview of the project: "This would be similar to what can already happen in the University with 'service learning,' independent studies, and internships, but EXCO would facilitate the building of more direct relationships between the students, movements, and communities for organizing and valuing their collaborative projects on their own terms, rather than mediated through the disciplinary metrics that the University mandates. We have adopted this

strategy of 'inflating the credit' from conversations with Claudia Bernardi and Paolo Do, based on their work within the Eccedi Sottrai Crea (ESC) Atelier, a social center and militant research collective in Rome, Italy, which creates a radical interface between their University—La Sapienza—and the wider metropolis. Through occupying an administrative building, they forced the administration to grant University credit for the projects of self-education and self-organizing that they facilitate through connecting sympathetic professors with movements, such as around precarious labor and migrant struggles. They are following the Italian autonomist Marxist tradition of struggling to 'inflate the wage' to value all laboring activity, including that in the home, not only that within the traditional workplace" (email, Eli to the U of M chapter, July 16, 2010).

53. U of M chapter meeting notes, July 14 and 21, 2010.

54. Email regarding "Re-imagining EXCO at the U" reflection dinner, August 25, 2010.

55. U of M chapter meeting notes, July 21, 2010.

56. U of M chapter meeting notes, August 30, 2010. For examples of disorientation guides that were particularly inspirational for EXCO organizers, see those of the Counter-Cartographies Collective: http://www.counter cartographies.org/category/disorientation-guides/.

57. These included struggles to save the General College, the AFSCME strikes, the IWW Jimmy John's Workers Union, the founding of the Black Student Union through occupying a campus administrative building, and contemporary struggles around space for students of color on campus.

58. The "Whose University?" crew rekindled the campus conversation around institutional racism through creating a documentary and putting on a major event that included more than six hundred undergraduate and high school students who were bused in for the event. After 2011, a new group called "Whose Diversity?" continued and built off of the movement of "Whose University?" See https://whosediversity.weebly.com.

59. U of M chapter meeting notes, May 26, 2010.

60. U of M chapter meeting notes, October 18, 2010.

61. The counter-spelling of "skool" signified their affiliation with the wider network of anarchistic "free skools." For a list of recent North American free skools, see https://web.archive.org/web/20130723111649/http://freeskoolsproject.wikispaces.com/.

62. Jason Rodney, interview by the authors, June 12, 2014.

63. Notes from organizer retreat, November 14, 2010.

64. Notes from organizer retreat, November 14, 2010.

65. Notes from U of M chapter meeting, December 14, 2010.

66. Proposal for "Transforming EXCO's Structure," March 18, 2010.

67. Mignolo, *The Darker Side of Western Modernity.*

68. Timothy Mitchell, "Society, Economy, and the State Effect," in *State/ Culture: State-Formation after the Cultural Turn* (Ithaca: Cornell University Press, 1999), 76–97.

69. Structure proposal, March 18, 2010, and meeting notes from U of M chapter, December 14, 2010.

70. On the distinction between allies and accomplices, see Indigenous Action, "Accomplices Not Allies: Abolishing the Ally Industrial Complex" (2014), http://www.indigenousaction.org/accomplices-not-allies-abolishing-the -ally-industrial-complex/.

71. On group formations of the "self" through subscriptions to individual- izing, subjectivizing "plug-ins," see Latour, *Reassembling the Social.* On how emotional economies construct the "surfaces" of bodies, see Sara Ahmed, *The Cultural Politics of Emotion*, 2nd ed. (Edinburgh: Edinburgh University Press, 2014).

72. David Graeber, *The Utopia of Rules: On Technology, Stupidity, and the Secret Joys of Bureaucracy* (New York: Melville House, 2016).

73. Notes from U of M chapter meeting, October 18, 2010. On how a romanti- cizing of community is supplementary to capitalism, see Miranda Joseph, *Against the Romance of Community* (Minneapolis: University of Minnesota Press, 2002).

74. For a thorough critique of such romanticizing of community in a different context, see Joseph, *Against the Romance of Community.*

75. Notes from citywide meeting, December 5, 2010.

76. From emails in preparation for upcoming citywide meeting, December 2, 2010.

77. This paragraph draws from an article that Eli wrote with Fern Thompsett. For more on possible relationships of accompliceship between free univer- sities and Indigenous study projects, see Eli Meyerhoff and Fern Thomp- sett, "Decolonizing Study: Free Universities in More-Than-Humanist Accompliceships with Indigenous Movements," *Journal of Environmental Education* 48, no. 4 (2017): 234–47.

78. For more on Unsettling Minnesota, including their sourcebook and "points of unity," see https://unsettlingminnesota.org.

79. Eric Angell, interview by Eli and Rita Hardie, June 4, 2010.

80. An example of these affective relations between humans, the land, and non-human actors is seen in a story by the Dakota writer Ohiyesa (Charles Eastman) about "An Indian Sugar Camp": "the women began to test the trees—moving leisurely among them, axe in hand, and striking a single

quick blow, to see if the sap would appear. The trees, like people, have their individual characters; some were ready to yield up their life-blood, while others were more reluctant." Charles Eastman, *Indian Boyhood* (New York: McClure, Phillips, 1902), 32.

CONCLUSION

1. Erica Meiners, *Right to Be Hostile: Schools, Prisons, and the Making of Public Enemies* (New York: Routledge, 2007); William H. Watkins, *The White Architects of Black Education: Ideology and Power in America, 1865–1954* (New York: Teachers College Press, 2001); Damien M. Sojoyner, *First Strike: Educational Enclosures in Black Los Angeles* (Minneapolis: University of Minnesota Press, 2016); Nancy Lesko, *Act Your Age: A Cultural Construction of Adolescence* (New York: Routledge Falmer, 2000); Jeannie Oakes, "Tracking, Inequality, and the Rhetoric of Reform: Why Schools Don't Change," *Journal of Education* 168, no. 1 (1986): 60–80.

2. I am beginning such a research project with historian Zach Schwartz-Weinstein. The rest of this section of the chapter is based on our initial conversations for this project.

3. Craig Steven Wilder, *Ebony and Ivy: Race, Slavery, and the Troubled History of America's Universities* (New York: Bloomsbury, 2013); Alfred Brophy, *University, Court, and Slave: Pro-Slavery Thought in Southern Colleges and Courts and the Coming of Civil War* (Oxford: Oxford University Press, 2016); Marisa J. Fuentes and Deborah Gray White, eds., *Scarlet and Black: Slavery and Dispossession in Rutgers History* (New Brunswick, N.J.: Rutgers University Press, 2016). For a list of some of the many universities that have undertaken historical studies of their own entwinement with slavery, see http://slavery.virginia.edu/universities-studying-slavery/.

4. On the importance of enslaved people's intellectual agency in their organizing of marronage, see Neil Roberts, *Freedom as Marronage* (Chicago: University of Chicago Press, 2015).

5. Sharon Stein, "A Colonial History of the Higher Education Present: Rethinking Land-Grant Institutions through Processes of Accumulation and Relations of Conquest," *Critical Studies in Education*, December 2017. Sandy Grande, *Red Pedagogy: Native American Social and Political Thought,* 10th anniversary ed. (Lanham, Md.: Rowman and Littlefield, 2015); Roxanne Dunbar-Ortiz, *An Indigenous Peoples' History of the United States* (Boston: Beacon Press, 2015).

6. Clyde Barrow, *Universities and the Capitalist State: Corporate Liberalism and the Reconstruction of American Higher Education, 1894–1928* (Madison:

University of Wisconsin Press, 1990). See also Christopher Newfield, *Ivy and Industry: Business and the Making of the American University, 1880–1980* (Durham: Duke University Press, 2003); and Isaac Kamola and Eli Meyerhoff, "Creating Commons: Divided Governance, Participatory Management, and Struggles against Enclosure in the University," *Polygraph* 21 (2009): 5–27.

7. Barrow, *Universities and the Capitalist State*, 219.
8. On divided governance, see Newfield, *Ivy and Industry*.
9. Roderick Ferguson, *The Reorder of Things: The University and Its Pedagogies of Minority Difference* (Minneapolis: University of Minnesota Press, 2012); Roderick Ferguson, *We Demand: The University and Student Protests* (Berkeley: University of California Press, 2017); Nick Mitchell, "The Fantasy and Fate of Ethnic Studies in an Age of Uprisings: An Interview with Nick Mitchell," *Undercommoning*, July 13, 2016, http://undercommoning.org/nick-mitchell-interview/.
10. I have written about this relationship between the Experimental College, Black studies, and the Third World Liberation Movement at San Francisco State. Eli Meyerhoff, "'This Quiet Revolution': Alternative Modes of Study with the Experimental College at San Francisco State," *Cultural Politics* (forthcoming).
11. Davarian Baldwin, "The '800-Pound Gargoyle': The Long History of Higher Education and Urban Development on Chicago's South Side," *American Quarterly* 67, no. 1 (2015): 81–103; Sharon Haar, *The City as Campus: Urbanism and Higher Education in Chicago* (Minneapolis: University of Minnesota Press, 2011); LaDale C. Winling, *Building the Ivory Tower: Universities and Metropolitan Development in the Twentieth Century* (Philadelphia: University of Pennsylvania Press, 2018).
12. In calling for an abolition university I invoke the ideal of an abolition democracy developed by abolitionist scholar-activists such as W. E. B. Du Bois, Angela Davis, and Joel Olson. Du Bois, *Black Reconstruction in America, 1860–1880* (Harcourt Brace, 1935); Davis, *Abolition Democracy: Beyond Empire, Prisons, and Torture* (New York: Seven Stories Press, 2005); and Olson, *The Abolition of White Democracy* (Minneapolis: University of Minnesota Press, 2004). I am co-organizing a conference around the theme of an abolition university called "Whose Crisis? Whose University? Abolitionist Study in and beyond Global Higher Education," on October 11–12, 2019. For information and material from the conference, see https://abolition.university.
13. This final section is a revised version of a statement I published on the *Abolition* journal's blog: "Prisons and Universities Are Two Sides of the

Same Coin: Eli Meyerhoff on Abolition," *Abolition: A Journal of Insurgent Politics*, July 24, 2015, https://abolitionjournal.org/eli-meyerhoff -abolitionist-study-against-and-beyond-higher-education/.

14. Erica Meiners, "Ending the School-to-Prison Pipeline/Building Abolitionist Futures," *Urban Review* 43 (2011): 547–65; Meiners, *Right to Be Hostile*, 31–32. Also see Sojoyner, *First Strike*; and Camille Acey, "This Is an Illogical Statement: Dangerous Trends in Anti-prison Activism," *Social Justice Journal* 27, no. 3 (2000): 206–11.

15. For example, Meiners describes teacher education programs as part of the PIC through their production of discourses that support zero-tolerance discipline practices and racialized surveillance with special education tracking (*Right to Be Hostile*). Also, they train teachers in ways that reproduce the racialized, gendered, heteronormative character of the teaching profession, i.e., with a disproportionate number of white women becoming teachers. Another example is Judah Schept, Tyler Wall, and Avi Brisman's article on how criminology programs are complicit with the PIC through training school resource officers who police schools, as well as in producing narratives that legitimate such school policing and the racist criminalization of children. Schept, Wall, and Brisman, "Building, Staffing and Insulating: An Architecture of Criminological Complicity in the School-to-Prison Pipeline," *Social Justice* 41, no. 4 (2014): 96–115.

Index

abolitionist movements, 31, 175, 205–6
abolition university, 31, 204, 206
abuse: in academia, 1, 45, 50, 53, 199
Academia Comunitaria (EXCO chapter), 180–81, 183–84, 187, 189, 195, 197
Academia Is Killing My Friends (blog), 50–52
academic freedom, 30, 201, 202–3, 219n17
actor-networks, 84–85
actor-network-theory, 96
adjunct faculty. *See* contingent faculty
administrators: as experts, 94; as villains, 41
affective economy, 4, 19–20, 132–33; and EXCO, 191; in Locke's work, 155–56, 158–62; and Yale University, 11–12
African people, 71, 146, 158
Ahmed, Sara, 1–2, 7, 10, 62, 210n16
alternative modes of study, 5, 15, 91, 101, 200, 202, 206; blues epistemology, 74–78; at EXCO, 165, 173; history of, 168–75, 200; Indigenous, 16, 196, 211n35. *See*

also Black radical study; popular education
American Association of University Professors (AAUP), 202–3
American dilemma, 66, 89
American dream, 40, 90, 217
America's Promise Alliance, 103
anarchist education, 171; contemporary, 172; free universities, 172; historical examples, 171; reemergence, 172; South Side Free Skool, 188, 195
anticapitalism, 109, 123, 127; in EXCO, 172, 197; narratives, 124–25
anticolonial movements, 65
appropriation of university resources, 203; by EXCO, 25

bacteria: as non-human actors, 96, 99, 131; plague-causing, 131, 132
Barton, Elizabeth (Nun of Kent), 146, 147
beguines, 112–15, 234n13; commons in beguinages, 127; contrasted with nuns, 114; criminalization of, 115, 116; critique of rich by, 117; defined, 112; education of girls, 113; form of community, 113–14;

ignorance, educated. *See*
epistemology of educated
ignorance
Illich, Ivan, 60, 172
impasse, 6, 26; defined, 38, 215n9
incarceration, 68, 93, 99, 100,
101; and education-based mode
of study, 206; juvenile, 99; in
primitive accumulation, 129;
racialized mass, 103, 104; school-
to-prison pipeline, 205
Indigenous people, 96; on campus,
18–19; common property, 126;
genocide of, 202, 241n94;
institutional trajectories of,
100; in Locke's work, 158;
modes of study, 16, 196, 211n35;
Nishnaabeg, 16, 96; relationship
building among, 197; relationships
to land, 130–31, 196, 239n83,
239n84; resistance by, 202; and
settler colonialism, 16, 25, 123,
130; views of self, 96; under white
supremacist norms, 132–33
individualism, 29, 46, 79, 93–96,
102, 121, 129; in educational
trajectory, 42, 53; and production,
98, 100, 109, 119, 122, 136, 137,
155
inequality, 91; educational, 18,
40, 88, 95; global, 24; in higher
education, 163; racial, 50, 89, 103,
170

jails. *See* incarceration
jeremiad, 217n15, 218n17; defined,
40; in educational narratives, 40;
in left-wing narratives, 216n15
Johnson administration, 85, 103
juvenile delinquents, 79, 228n48;

associated with dropouts, 94; use
of term, 69, 71

Kelley, Robin D. G., 17, 18, 212n43
Kennedy administration, 85
Kozol, Jonathan, 170

labor, 133; cooperative, 111;
gendered division of, 111, 116, 118;
hierarchical division on campuses,
201; in Locke's work, 155; paid vs.
unpaid, 91; unskilled, 92
Latinx people: in EXCO, 180, 189;
institutional trajectories of, 100;
in Southeast Minneapolis, 195;
undocumented, 183
Lewis, Tyson, 59–60
liberal capitalism: crisis
management, 102; framing of
students and workers, 102;
and hip-hop culture, 103;
life trajectories, 98, 182; and
modernity, 99
life trajectories, 26; ascending, 28,
40, 100, 105, 119, 137, 204–5; of
dropouts, 98; education's role in,
39; individualist, 42, 53; liberal
capitalist, 98, 182; in Locke's
work, 137; migrants' imagined,
90; possibilities for imagining,
99; romantic, 40; vertical, 28, 40,
100, 105, 119
Locke, John, 29, 124, 136–37, 137,
151, 154–62; affective economy,
158–62; biographical information,
154; colonialism, 156; comparison
with Hobbes, 154, 155, 158,
161; and gender, 156, 246n94;
influence on modern pedagogy,
248n115; and Others, 29, 137,

schools, 80, 81, 88; in Dewey's work, 49; and free schools, 170; in neighborhoods, 99; by school district, 95; in schools, 99, 100; white violence to maintain, 78. *See also* desegregation

self, 96, 158–59; in EXCO, 193; feminist scholarship on, 220n41; in Hobbes' work, 155; Indigenous views of, 96; in Locke's work, 155, 158–59, 161, 248n119; more-than-humanist views of, 96–97

Selingo, Jeffrey, 41–43

settler colonialism, 101, 130, 185, 197, 199, 202; and Indigenous people, 16, 25, 123, 126; mode of world-making, 77, 101; and primitive accumulation, 133; and universities, 28. *See also* colonialism

sexism, 194; in higher education, 1–2, 3–4, 51; institutional, 7. *See also* women: repression of

shame, 19–20, 51; and affective economy, 15, 137, 159, 161, 191; in Locke's work, 157–58, 159, 161

sharecropping, 75

Simons, Maarten, 59, 60

Simpson, Leanne Betasamosake, 96

Sisters and Brothers of the Common Life, 109, 128–29, 135, 137; and Black Plague, 131–32; and capitalism, 236n53; class divisions within, 120, 121; first communities of, 117; gendered division of labor in, 118, 120–21; hierarchies within, 119–20; schools run by, 118; structure of communities, 117; verticalist tendencies of, 115; women in, 118

slavery, 3, 75, 140, 146, 154, 202, 223n62; and Yale University, 3, 7, 9, 12, 19–20. *See also* enslaved people

snapping, 1, 2, 4, 24, 199

society, 145

South Side Community Arts Center (Chicago), 77

spiritual ascent, 119, 121–22, 128–29, 132

Starkey, Thomas, 145, 146

state: during English Civil War, 149; Hobbes on, 152; as means of primitive accumulation, 157; pushing students out of school, 98; as relationship, 13, 211n32; as term, 144, 145, 243n36; undermining class solidarity, 108, 111; as zero-point subject-position, 128

stereotyping: of Black men, 12; of Black youth, 79; and criminalization, 231n78; in dropout narratives, 95; and juvenile delinquency, 79, 80

strikes: San Francisco State University (1968–1969), 168; University of Minnesota, 164, 177; University of Minnesota AFSCME, 24, 25

student debt, 23, 35, 36, 37, 41, 45, 104

student occupations: ESC Atelier, 255n52; New School (2008), 35; NYU (2009), 35; University of California (2009–2010), 31–36. *See also* strikes

students: attitudes toward education, 52; examples of, 43–46; as heroes, 41; liberal-capitalist

framing of, 102; reappropriating resources to EXCO, 173; as victims, 41
study, 13; modes of (*see* modes of study); relations of, 13–14
suicide, 4, 24, 26, 50

talentization of whiteness, 95
teachers: in affective economy, 95; Black, 77, 81; and decolonization, 25; in early schools, 119, 121–22, 141, 153; at EXCO, 179; as experts, 14, 94; roles in educational narratives, 58
technocracy, 166
tenured faculty, 18, 19–20, 54, 55
tenure system, 30, 201, 202–3
tracking, 49, 87, 95, 99–101, 200, 232n87
trajectories of education, 43
treason, 147

undercommons, 6, 18; defined, 17
unemployment, 99
unions: and AAUP, 202–3; faculty, 55; at University of Minnesota, 164
universities: early American, 201; historically Black, 8; land-grant, 202; and prisons, 205
University of California, 55; administration's crisis narratives, 35–36; student narratives, 54; student occupations (2009–2010), 31–36
University of Minnesota, 164; AFSCME strike, 24, 25, 177; and EXCO, 176–78, 185–88, 254n49
unschooling, 172
urban areas: crisis narratives

about, 66, 72, 89, 92; under feudalism, 110–12; governance of, 66; grant programs for, 80–81; responsibility for problems of, 68, 90; universities and, 204

value scales, 90–91; defined, 95; in dropout narrative, 94; in education-based mode of study, 101
vertical imaginary, 82–83, 100; of education, 15, 68, 93, 95, 101, 129, 140, 160; spiritual (*see* spiritual ascent)
verticalist mode of study, 108–9, 128; emergence of, 115; non-human actors in, 131–32; and patriarchy, 133; as precondition for capitalism, 123–25
verticalist narratives, 51

Waite House (Minneapolis), 180. *See also* Academia Comunitaria
War on Poverty, 103
waste, 26, 127; in colonialism, 128; disposal in carceral state, 104; in dropout narrative, 94; dropouts as, 93; migrants' cultures associated with, 84; narratives of, 93; in Reformation thought, 145. *See also* rubbish
white ignorance, 49
white people: "talentization" of, 95
white students, 93; specific students, 45, 46
white supremacy, 50; and educated ignorance, 49; and education-based mode of study, 171; norms of, 132–33; in universities, 173; at Yale University, 11

Eli Meyerhoff is a visiting scholar at Duke University's John Hope Franklin Humanities Institute and program coordinator of the Social Movements Lab. He earned a PhD in political science from the University of Minnesota.